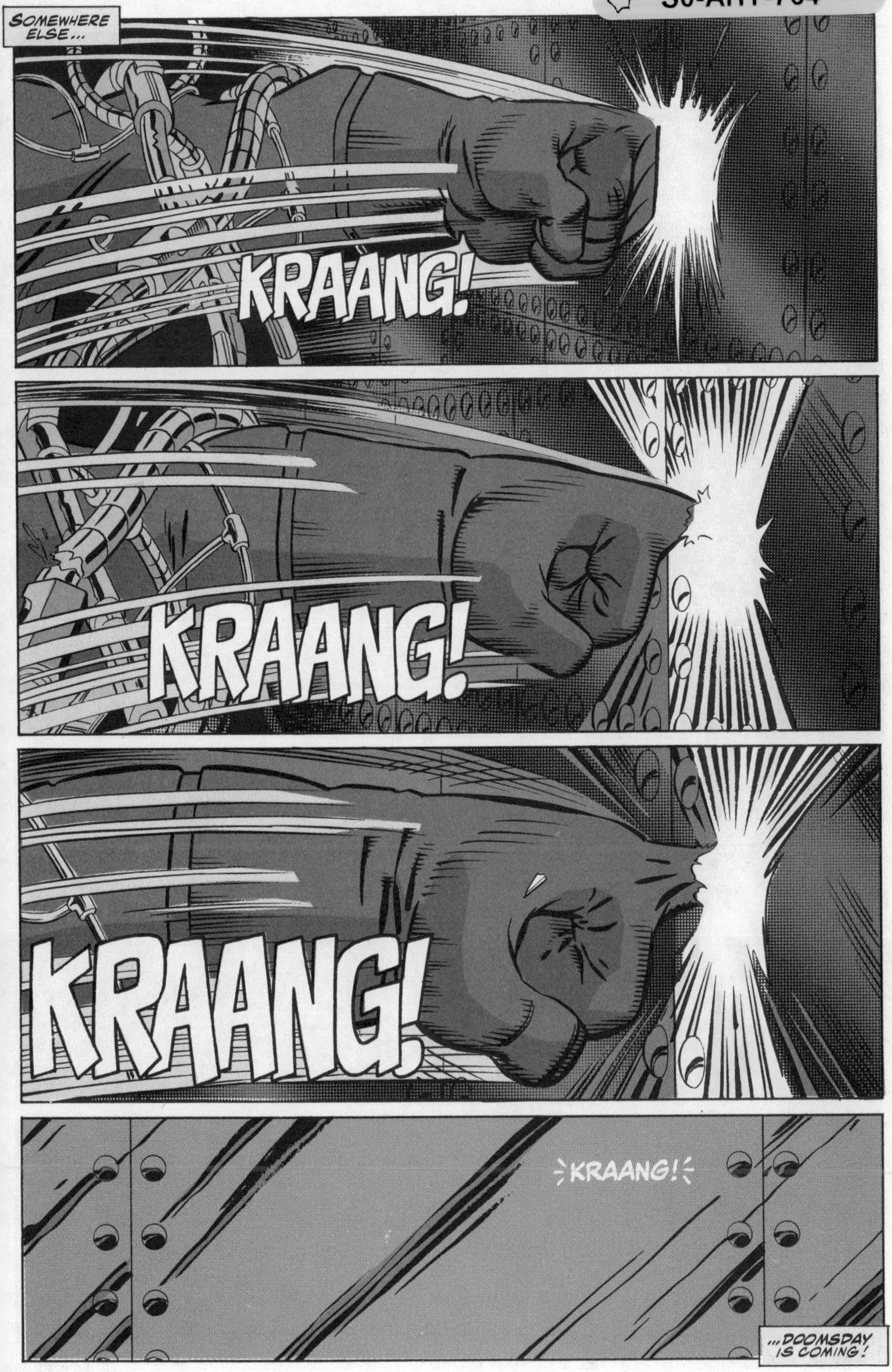
SOMEWHERE ELSE...
KRAANG!
KRAANG!
KRAANG!
KRAANG!
...DOOMSDAY IS COMING!

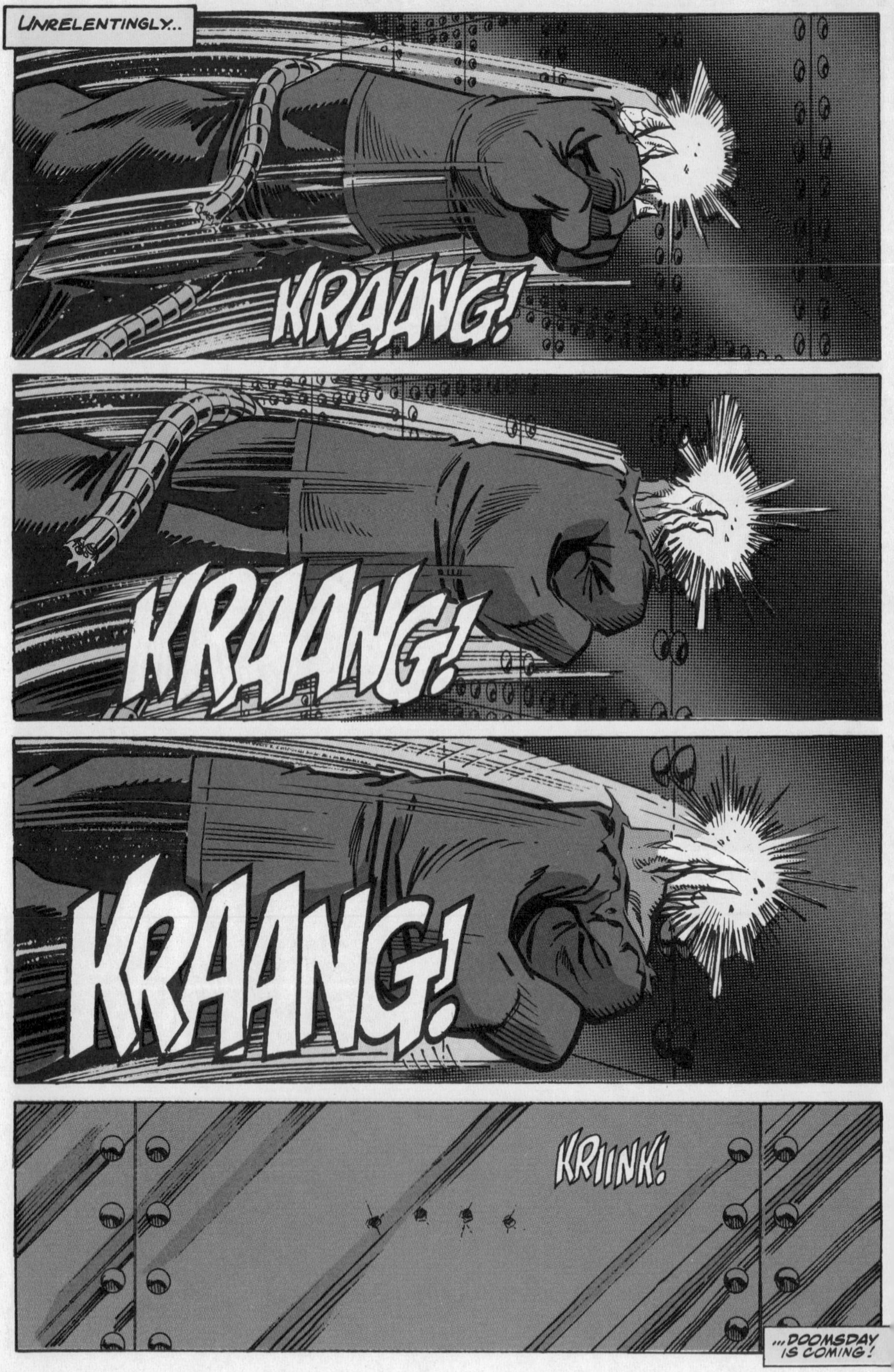
UNRELENTINGLY...
KRAANG!
KRAANG!
KRAANG!
KRIINK!
...DOOMSDAY IS COMING!

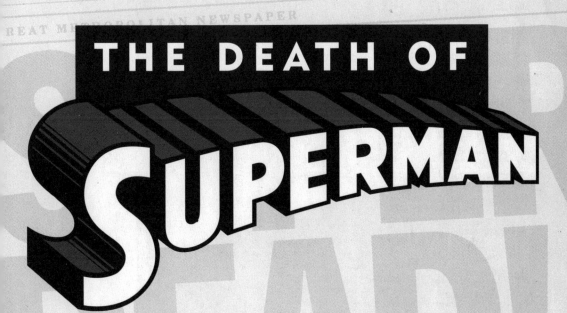

THE DEATH OF SUPERMAN

DAN JURGENS
JERRY ORDWAY
LOUISE SIMONSON
ROGER STERN

WRITERS

JON BOGDANOVE
TOM GRUMMETT
JACKSON GUICE
DAN JURGENS

PENCILLERS

BRETT BREEDING
RICK BURCHETT
DOUG HAZLEWOOD
DENNIS JANKE
DENIS RODIER

INKERS

JOHN COSTANZA
ALBERT DeGUZMAN
BILL OAKLEY
WILLIE SCHUBERT

LETTERERS

GENE D'ANGELO
GLENN WHITMORE

COLORISTS

SUPERMAN created by
JERRY SIEGEL and JOE SHUSTER

Dan DiDio
VP-Executive Editor

Mike Carlin, Brian Augustyn
Editors-original series

Jennifer Frank, Ruben Diaz
Assistant Editors-original series

Bob Kahan
Editor-collected edition

Robbin Brosterman
Senior Art Director

Paul Levitz
President & Publisher

Georg Brewer
VP-Design & DC Direct Creative

Richard Bruning
Senior VP-Creative Director

Patrick Caldon
Senior VP-Finance & Operations

Chris Caramalis
VP-Finance

Terri Cunningham
VP-Managing Editor

Stephanie Fierman
Senior VP-Sales & Marketing

Alison Gill
VP-Manufacturing

Rich Johnson
VP-Book Trade Sales

Hank Kanalz
VP-General Manager, WildStorm

Lillian Laserson
Senior VP & General Counsel

Jim Lee
Editorial Director-WildStorm

Paula Lowitt
Senior VP-Business & Legal Affairs

David McKillips
VP-Advertising & Custom Publishing

John Nee
VP-Business Development

Gregory Noveck
Senior VP-Creative Affairs

Cheryl Rubin
Senior VP-Brand Management

Jeff Trojan
VP-Business Development, DC Direct

Bob Wayne
VP-Sales

DC Comics
1700 Broadway, New York, NY 10019
A Warner Bros. Entertainment Company
Printed in Canada
Fourteenth Printing
ISBN: 1-56389-097-6
ISBN 13: 978-1-56389-097-0
Cover art by Dan Jurgens and Brett Breeding
Cover color by Glenn Whitmore
Publication design by Brian Pearce

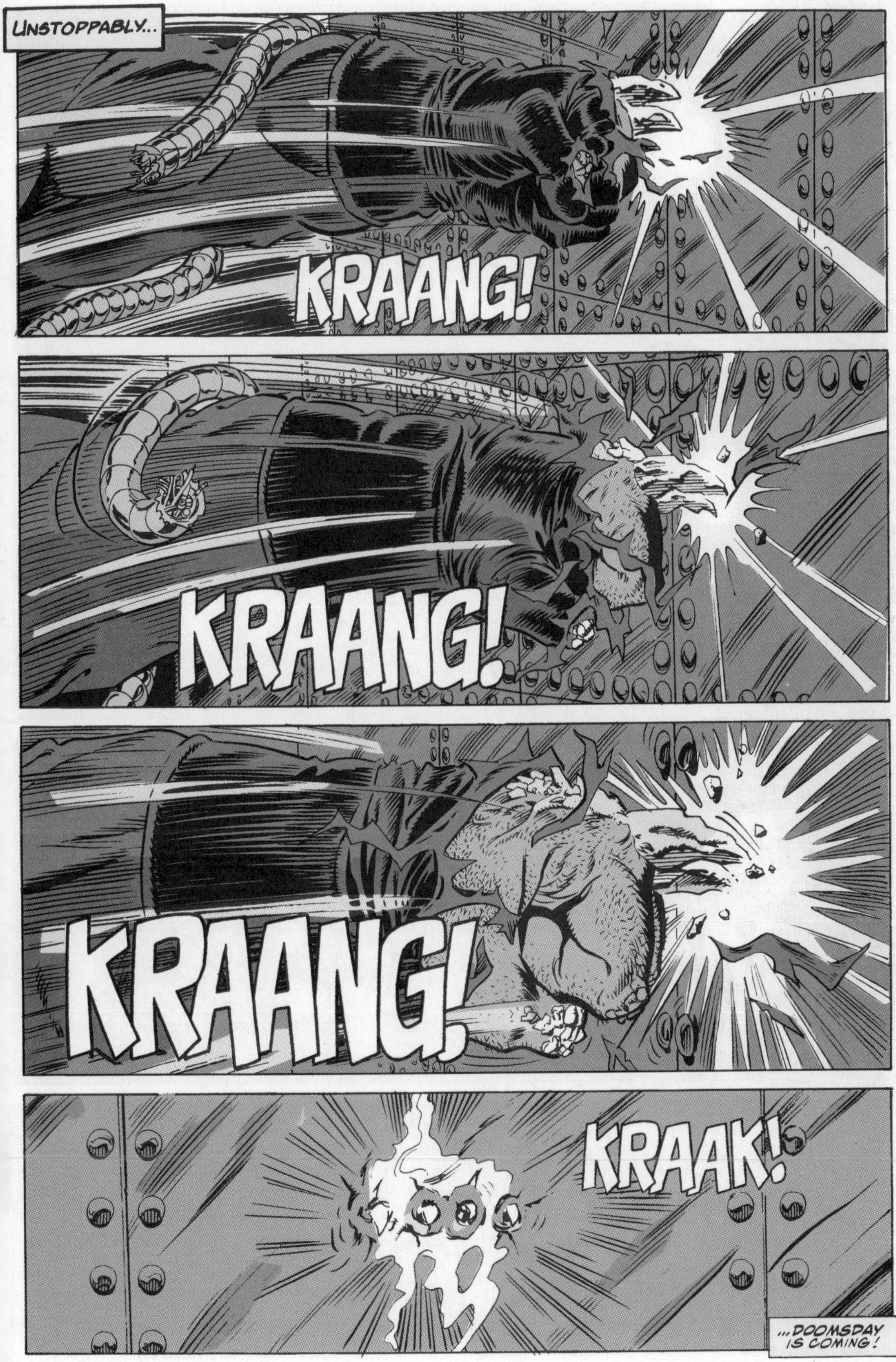
UNSTOPPABLY...
KRAANG!
KRAANG!
KRAANG!
KRAAK!
...DOOMSDAY IS COMING!

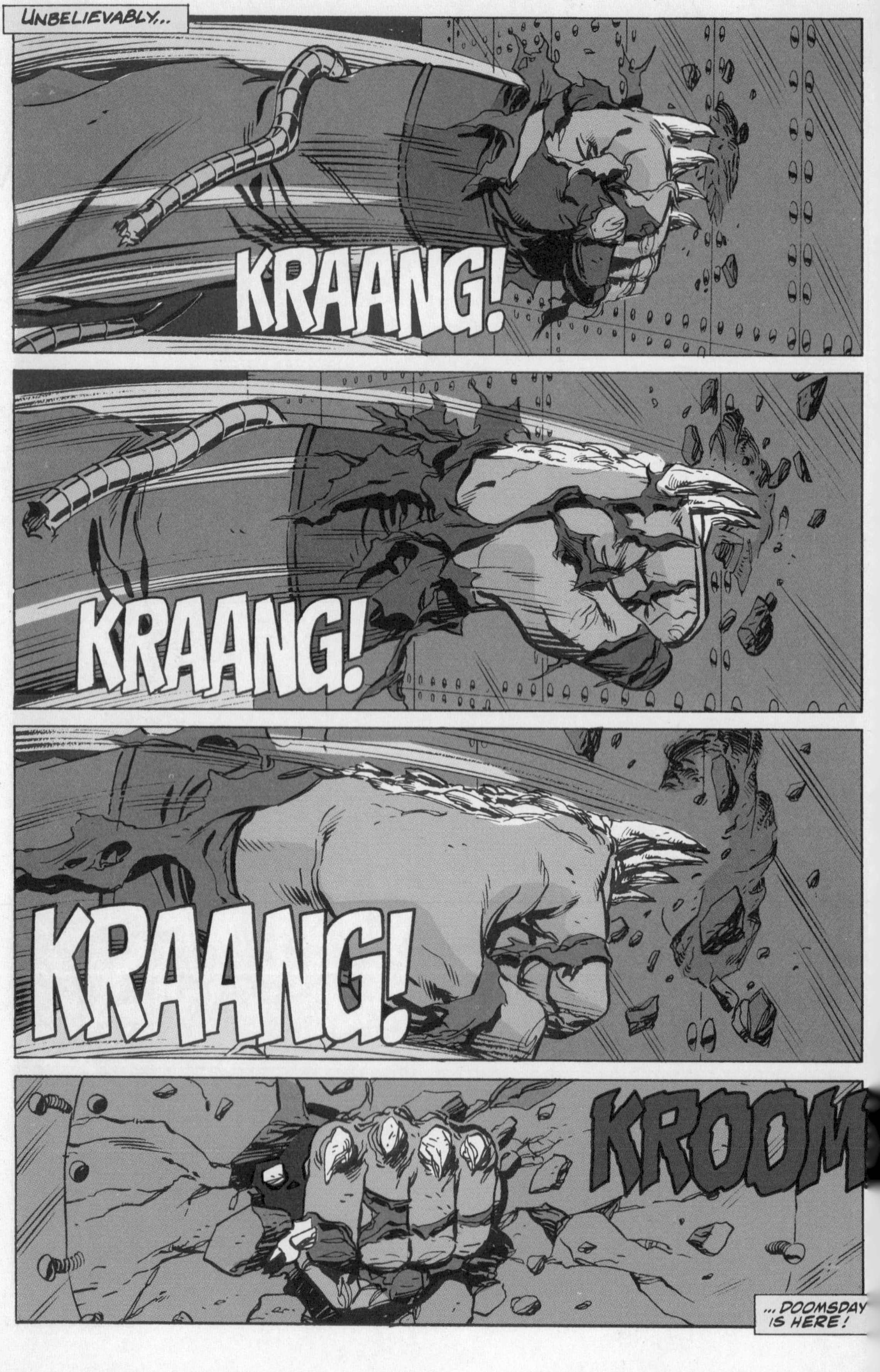

UNBELIEVABLY...
KRAANG!
KRAANG!
KRAANG!
KROOM
...DOOMSDAY IS HERE!

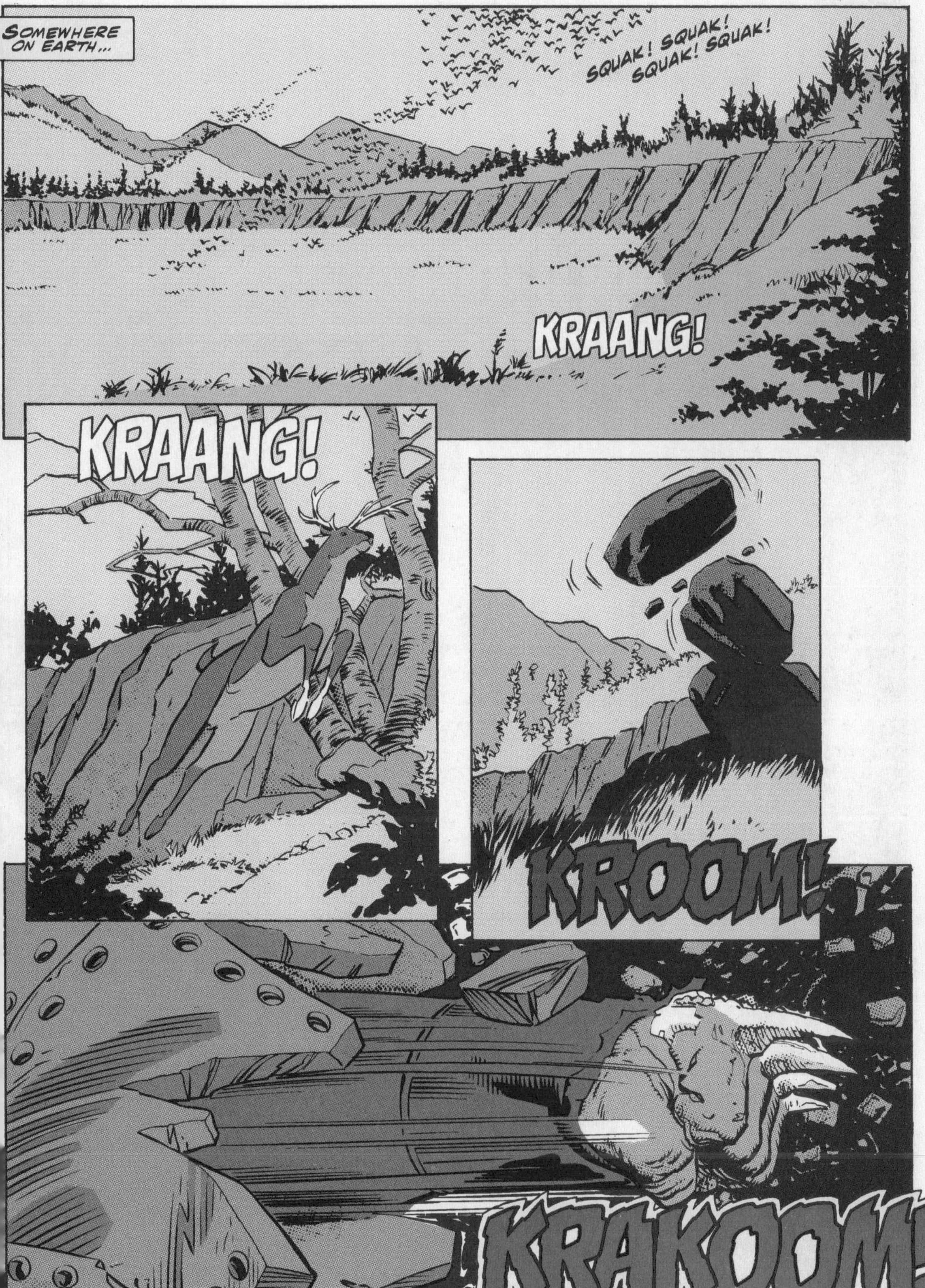
SOMEWHERE ON EARTH...
SQUAK! SQUAK! SQUAK! SQUAK!
KRAANG!
KRAANG!
KROOM!
KRAKOOM!

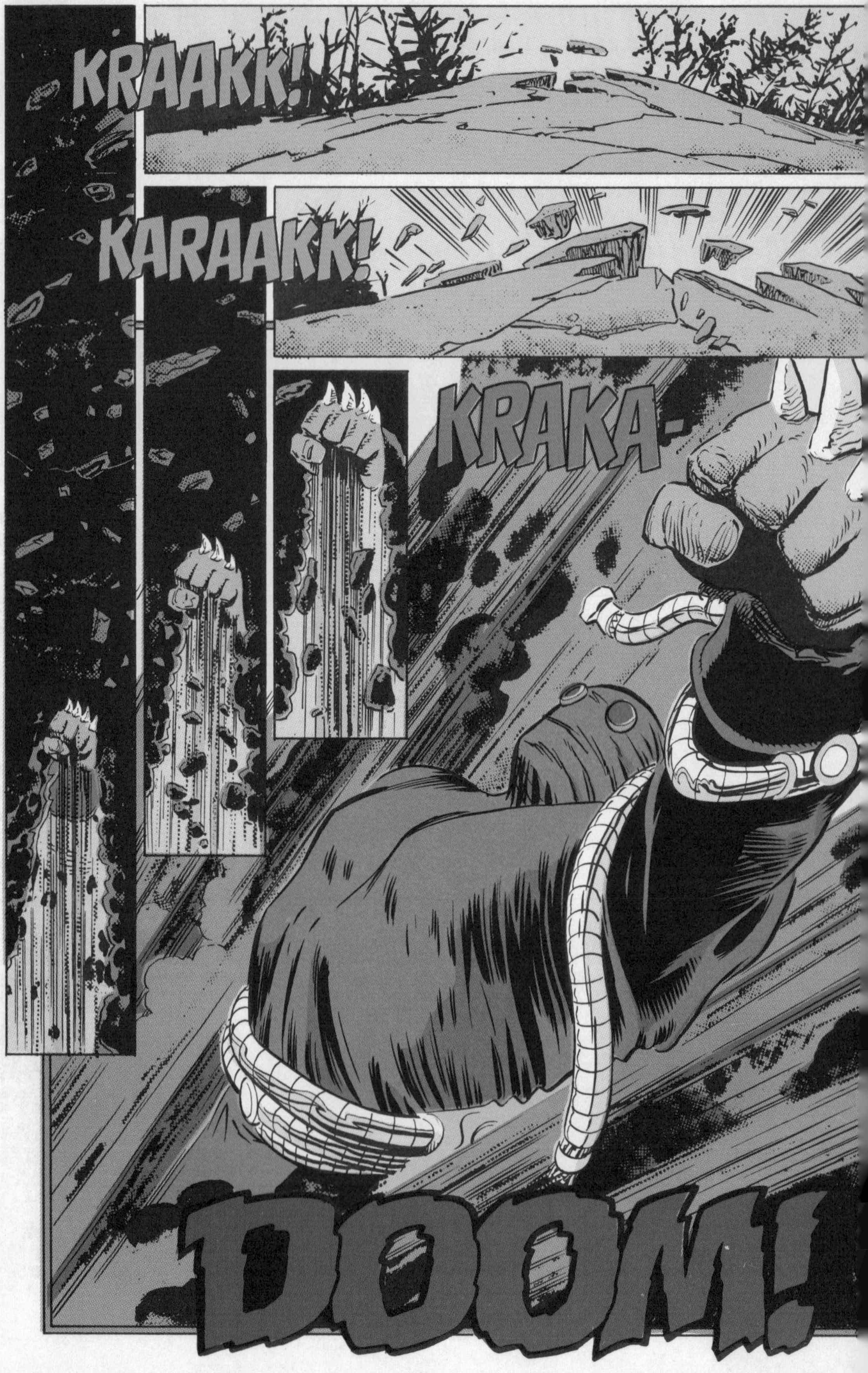
KRAAKK!
KARAAKK!
KRAKA-
DOOM!

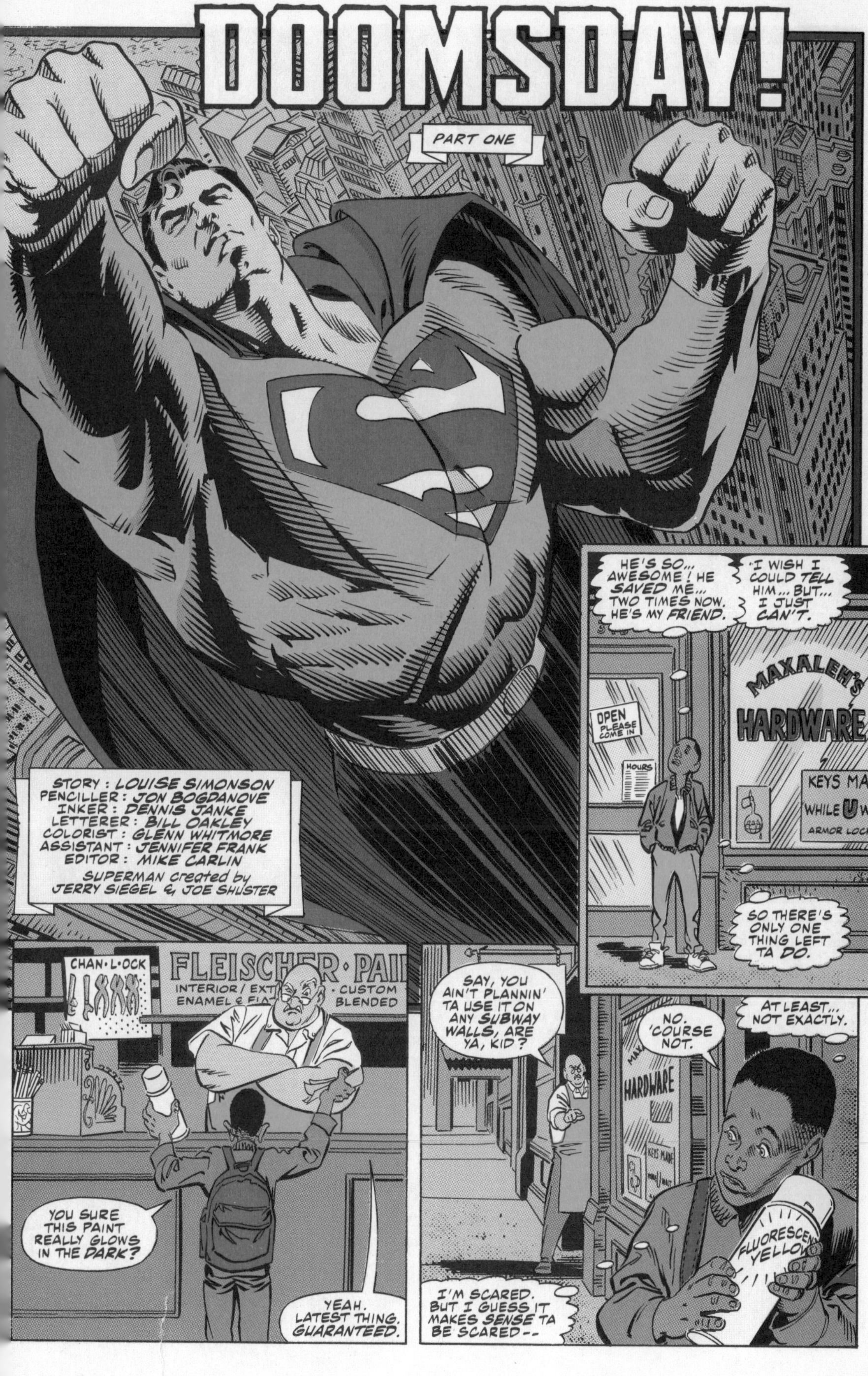
DOOMSDAY!
PART ONE
STORY : LOUISE SIMONSON
PENCILLER : JON BOGDANOVE
INKER : DENNIS JANKE
LETTERER : BILL OAKLEY
COLORIST : GLENN WHITMORE
ASSISTANT : JENNIFER FRANK
EDITOR : MIKE CARLIN
SUPERMAN created by JERRY SIEGEL & JOE SHUSTER
HE'S SO... AWESOME! HE SAVED ME... TWO TIMES NOW. HE'S MY FRIEND.
I WISH I COULD TELL HIM... BUT... I JUST CAN'T.
OPEN PLEASE COME IN
HOURS
MAXALEH'S HARDWARE
KEYS MA
WHILE U W
ARMOR LOCK
SO THERE'S ONLY ONE THING LEFT TA DO.
CHAN·L·OCK
FLEISCHER · PAI
INTERIOR / EXT
CUSTOM BLENDED
ENAMEL & FLA
YOU SURE THIS PAINT REALLY GLOWS IN THE DARK?
YEAH. LATEST THING. GUARANTEED.
SAY, YOU AIN'T PLANNIN' TA USE IT ON ANY SUBWAY WALLS, ARE YA, KID?
NO. 'COURSE NOT.
AT LEAST... NOT EXACTLY.
HARDWARE
FLUORESCEN YELLOW
I'M SCARED. BUT I GUESS IT MAKES SENSE TA BE SCARED--

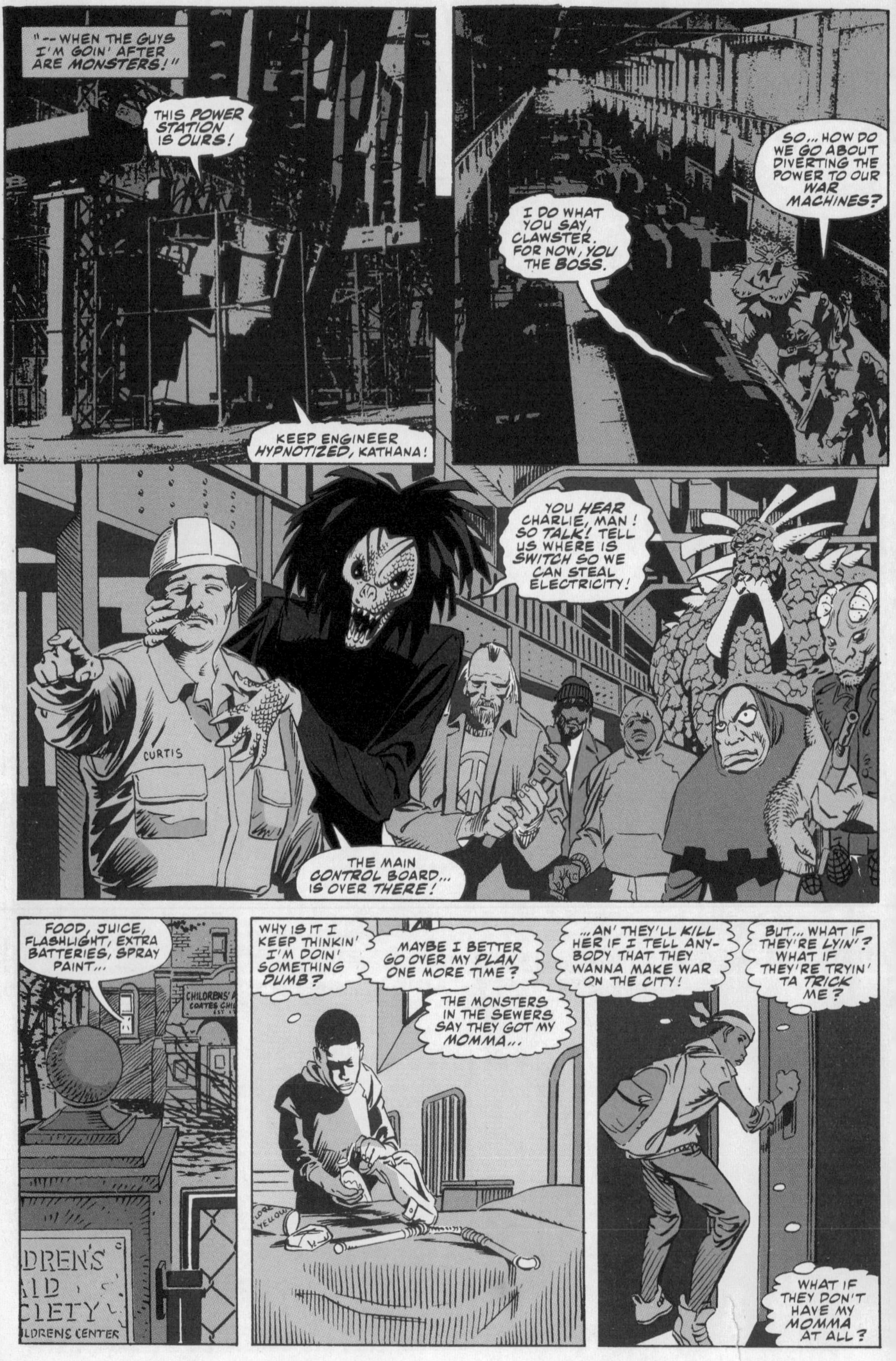
"--WHEN THE GUYS I'M GOIN' AFTER ARE MONSTERS!"
THIS POWER STATION IS OURS!
KEEP ENGINEER HYPNOTIZED, KATHANA!
SO... HOW DO WE GO ABOUT DIVERTING THE POWER TO OUR WAR MACHINES?
I DO WHAT YOU SAY, CLAWSTER. FOR NOW, YOU THE BOSS.
CURTIS
YOU HEAR CHARLIE, MAN! SO TALK! TELL US WHERE IS SWITCH SO WE CAN STEAL ELECTRICITY!
THE MAIN CONTROL BOARD... IS OVER THERE!
FOOD, JUICE, FLASHLIGHT, EXTRA BATTERIES, SPRAY PAINT...
WHY IS IT I KEEP THINKIN' I'M DOIN' SOMETHING DUMB?
MAYBE I BETTER GO OVER MY PLAN ONE MORE TIME?
THE MONSTERS IN THE SEWERS SAY THEY GOT MY MOMMA...
...AN' THEY'LL KILL HER IF I TELL ANYBODY THAT THEY WANNA MAKE WAR ON THE CITY!
BUT... WHAT IF THEY'RE LYIN'? WHAT IF THEY'RE TRYIN' TA TRICK ME?
WHAT IF THEY DON'T HAVE MY MOMMA AT ALL?

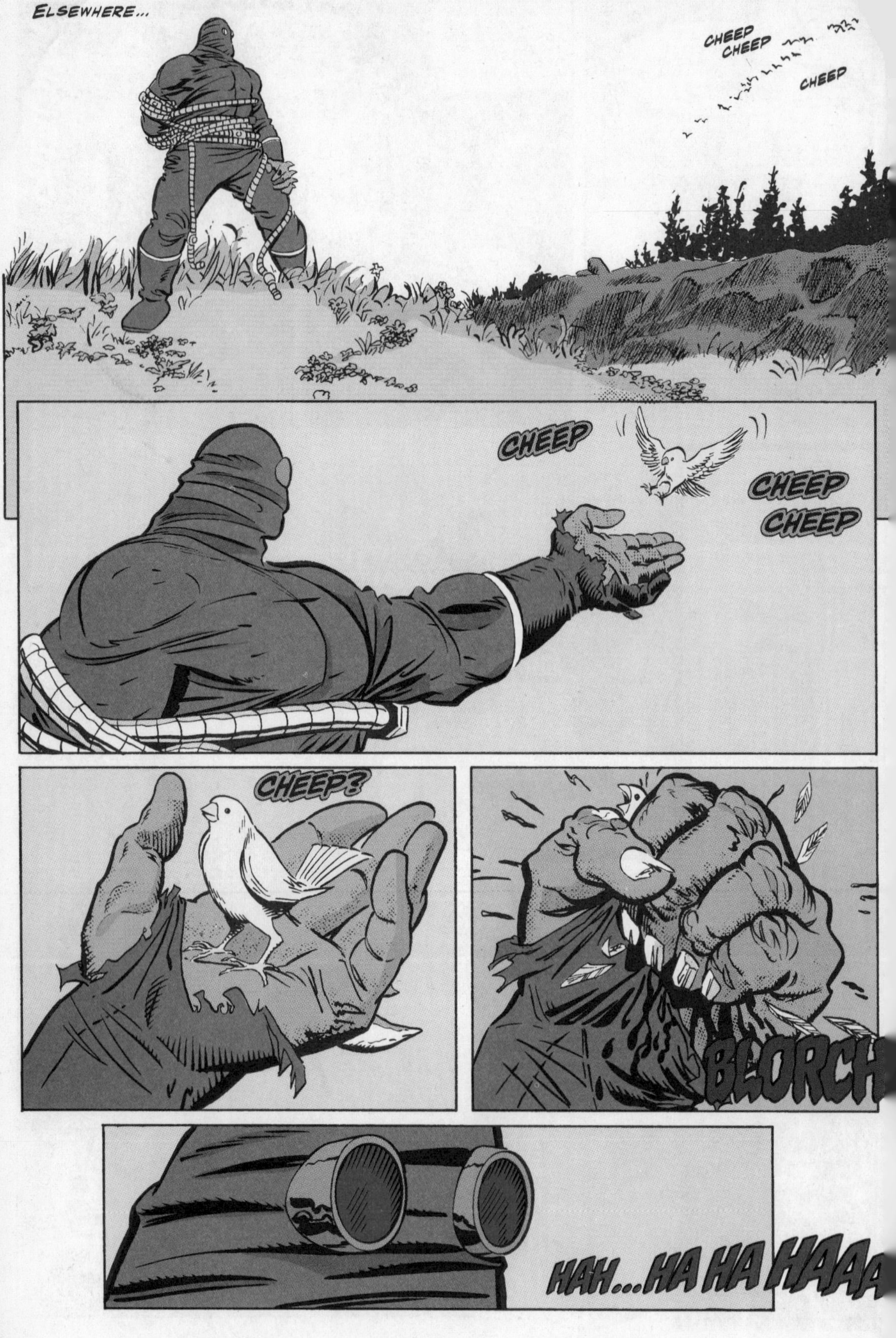
ELSEWHERE...
CHEEP
CHEEP
CHEEP
CHEEP
CHEEP
CHEEP
CHEEP?
BLORCH
HAH...HA HA HAAA

SCANNED THE CITY, BUT DIDN'T SEE ANY UNDER-WORLDERS ON THE SURFACE.

MUST BE LYING LOW FOR NOW. MAYBE IT'S TIME --

"--I GOT BACK TO WORK!"

HI, CLARK. LOIS LEFT YOU A COMPUTER MESSAGE.

VERY HIGH TECH OF HER. THANKS, FRAN.

TAK-TAP-TAK-TAP!

READ: MESSAGES

WHAT NOW?

ALL THE COMPUTERS DON'T WORK?

LIGHTS, EITHER!

DON'T TELL ME... WE'RE HAVING ANOTHER BLACKOUT?!

WE DO IT!

YEAAAA!

WE STEAL METROPOLIS'S ELECTRICITY!

NOW CITY IS HELPLESS... AND UNDERWORLD CAN KICK BUTT!

13

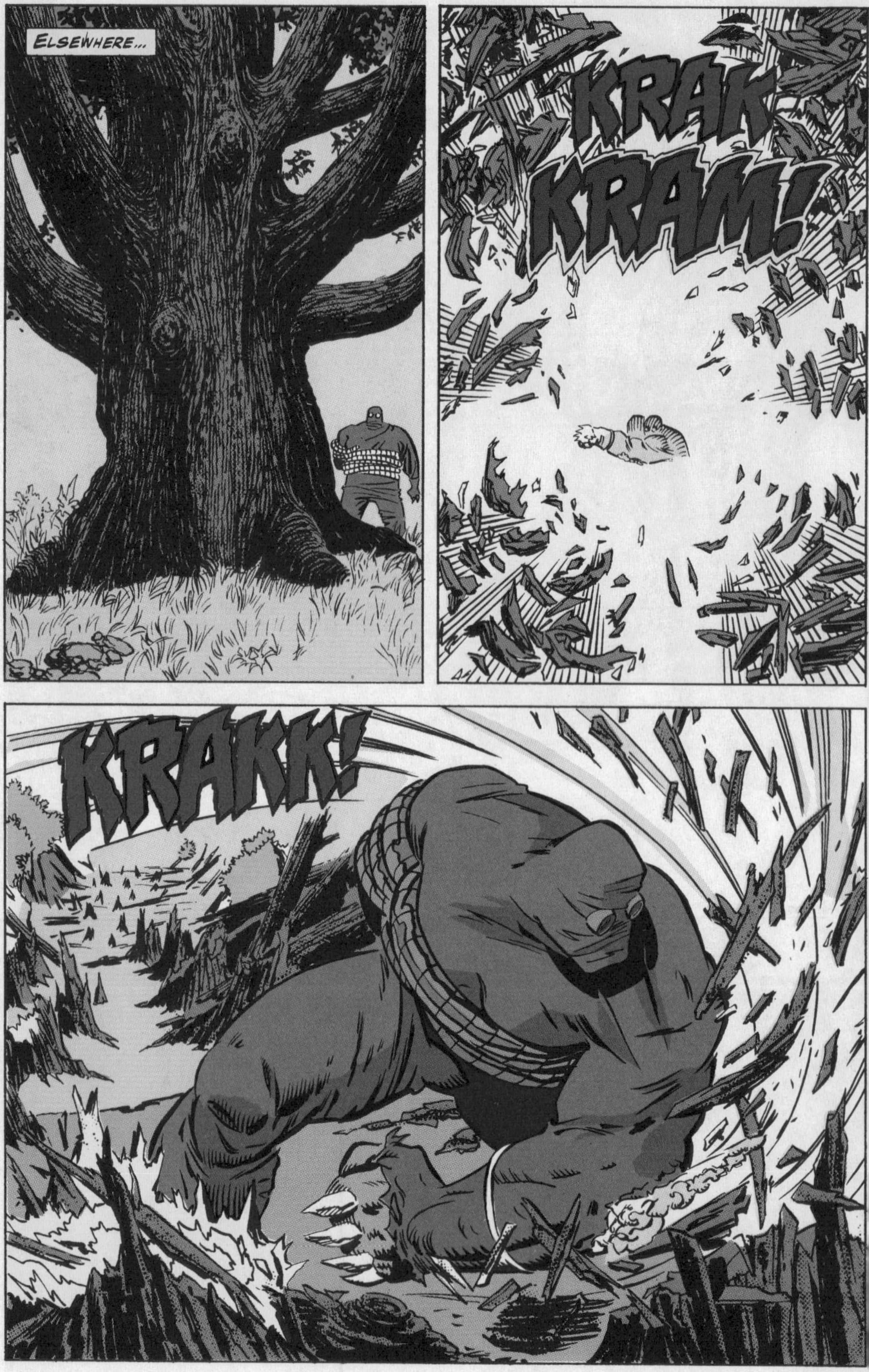
ELSEWHERE...
KRAK
KRAM!
KRAKK!

THE MONSTERS DON'T HAVE MY MOMMA.

THIS PROBABLY MEANS I'M NEVER GONNA FIND HER...

BUT THEY REALLY DO HAVE THAT REPORTER LADY.

THEY'RE GONNA KILL HER. AN' ATTACK THE CITY.

THAT'S REAL. I CAN STOP THAT. AN' THAT MEANS TELLIN' SUPERMAN--FAST!

IT'S AWFUL DARK UP HERE! WHERE ARE THE STREET LIGHTS?

I BET THE MONSTERS DID IT.

I READ HOW THEY USE A BAT SYMBOL TO CALL BATMAN. ONLY IT'S IN THE SKY...

FFSSSTT

...AN' THIS ONE'S ON THE GROUND.

FPSSSSSTT

IT'S ALL MY FAULT! IF I TOLD SUPERMAN, 'STEAD OF BELIEVIN' MONSTERS' LIES...

...HE WOULDA ALREADY STOPPED 'EM!

I JUST HOPE MY IDEA WORKS!

SUPERMAN! SUPERMAN! PLEASE PLEASE SEE THE SIGNAL!

KEITH?

SUPERMAN, IT'S YOU! I KNEW YOU'D COME!

THERE'S THIS REPORTER LADY IN THE TUNNELS! MONSTERS HAVE HER--

17

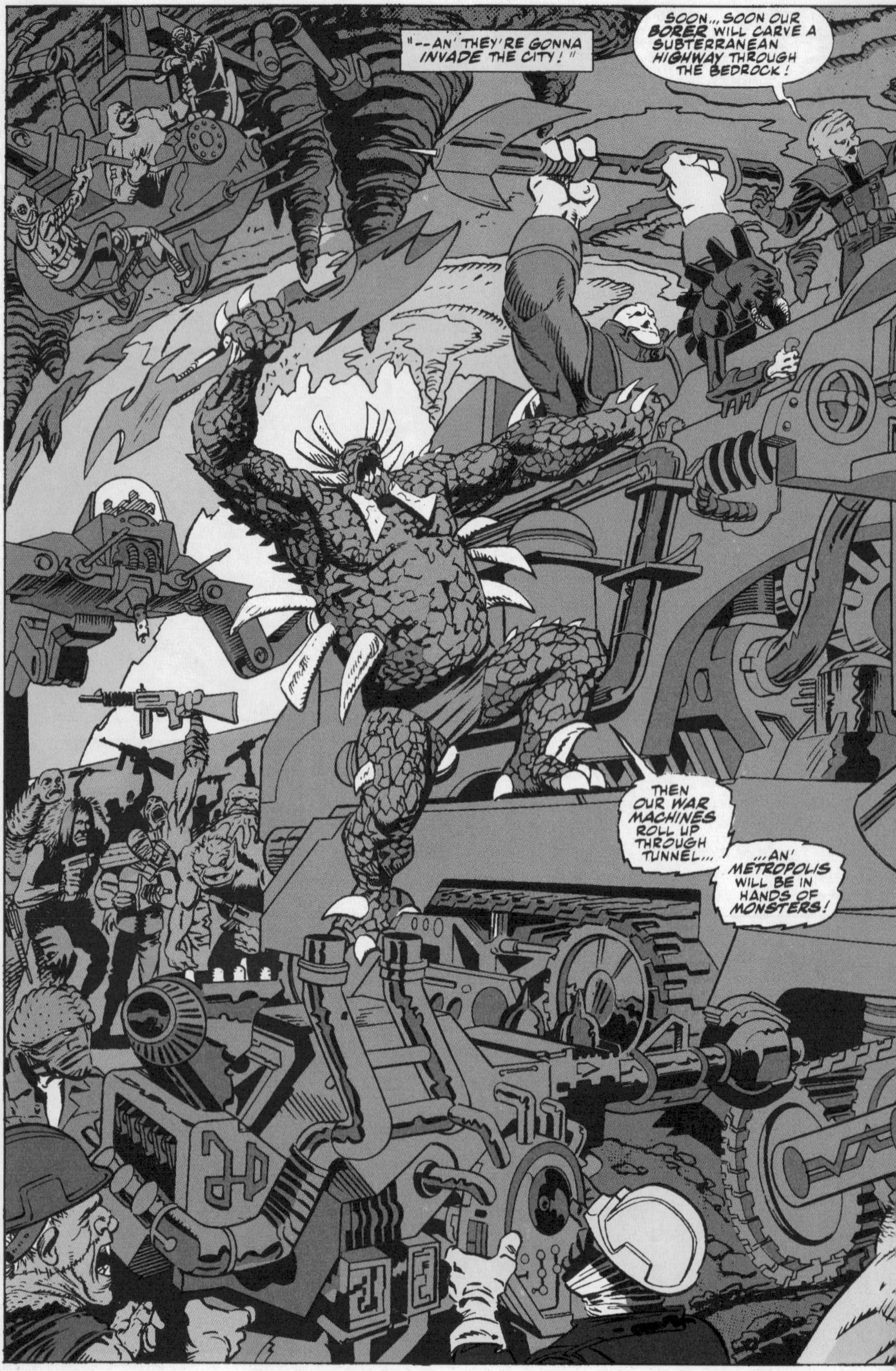

"--AN' THEY'RE GONNA INVADE THE CITY!"
SOON... SOON OUR BORER WILL CARVE A SUBTERRANEAN HIGHWAY THROUGH THE BEDROCK!
THEN OUR WAR MACHINES ROLL UP THROUGH TUNNEL...
...AN' METROPOLIS WILL BE IN HANDS OF MONSTERS!

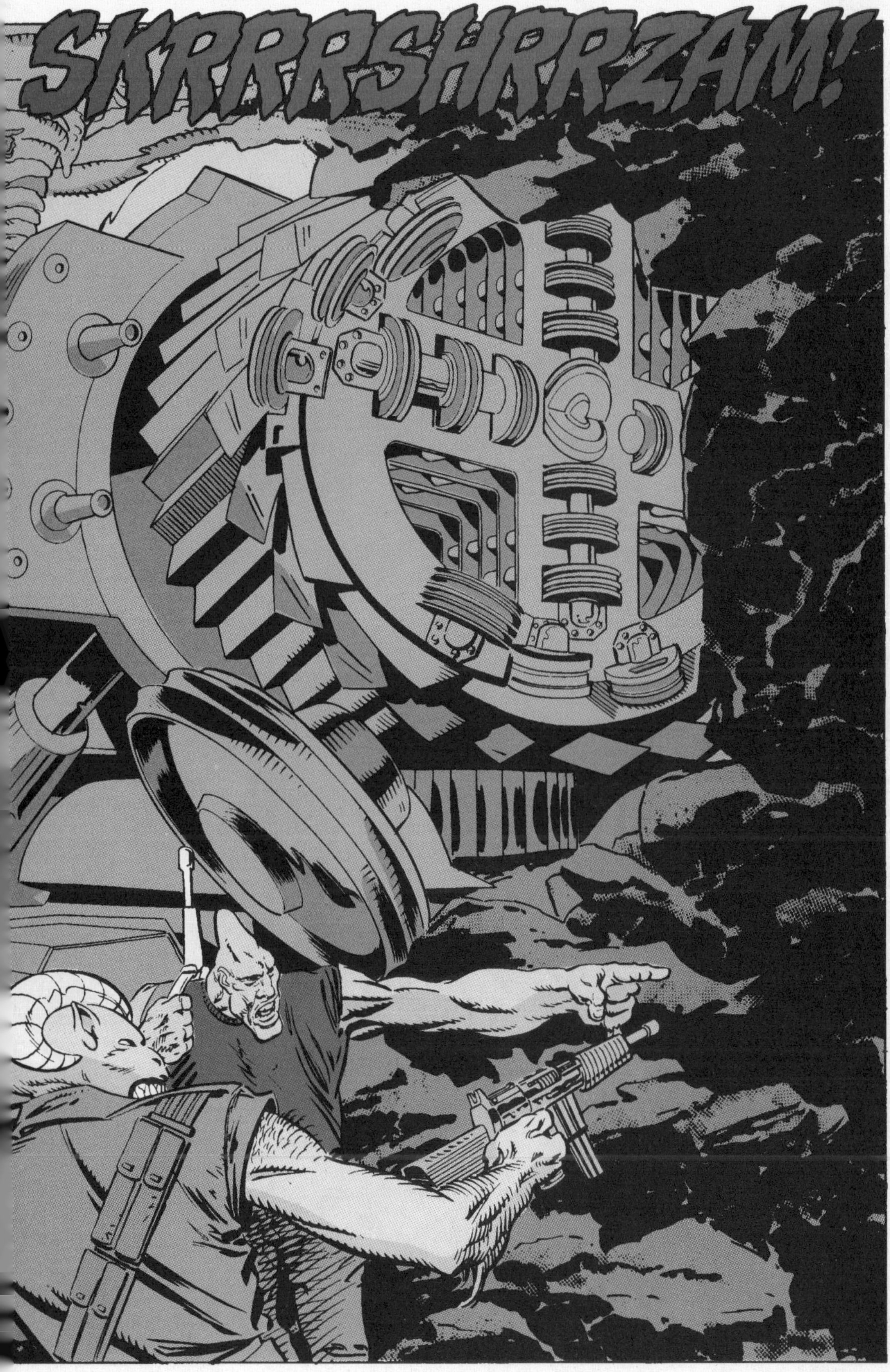
SKRRRSHRRZAM!

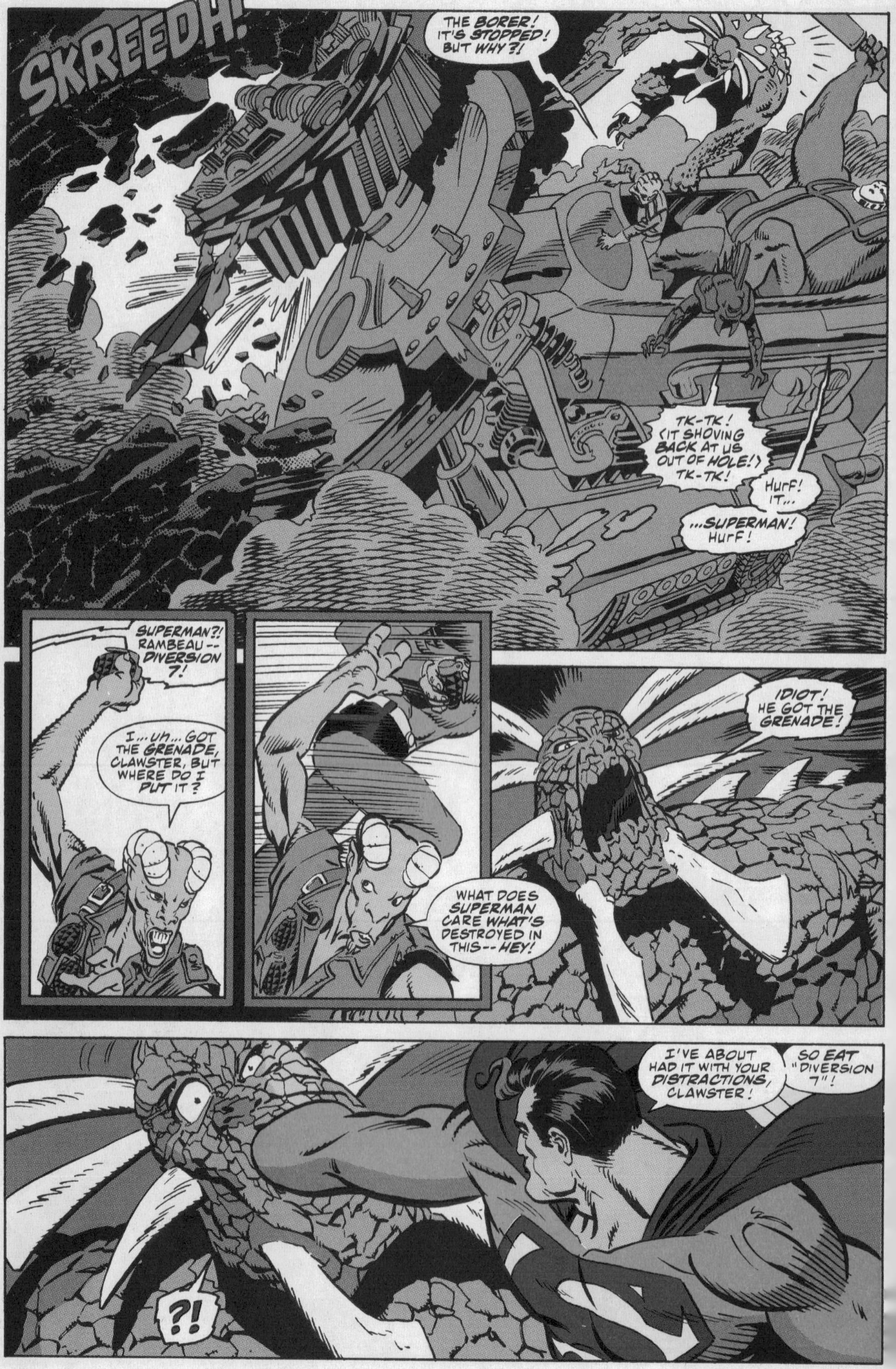
SKREEDH!
THE BORER! IT'S STOPPED! BUT WHY?!
TK-TK! ‹IT SHOVING BACK AT US OUT OF HOLE!› TK-TK!
HURF! IT...
...SUPERMAN! HURF!
SUPERMAN?! RAMBEAU-- DIVERSION 7!
I... UH... GOT THE GRENADE, CLAWSTER, BUT WHERE DO I PUT IT?
WHAT DOES SUPERMAN CARE WHAT'S DESTROYED IN THIS--HEY!
IDIOT! HE GOT THE GRENADE!
I'VE ABOUT HAD IT WITH YOUR DISTRACTIONS, CLAWSTER!
SO EAT "DIVERSION 7"!
?!

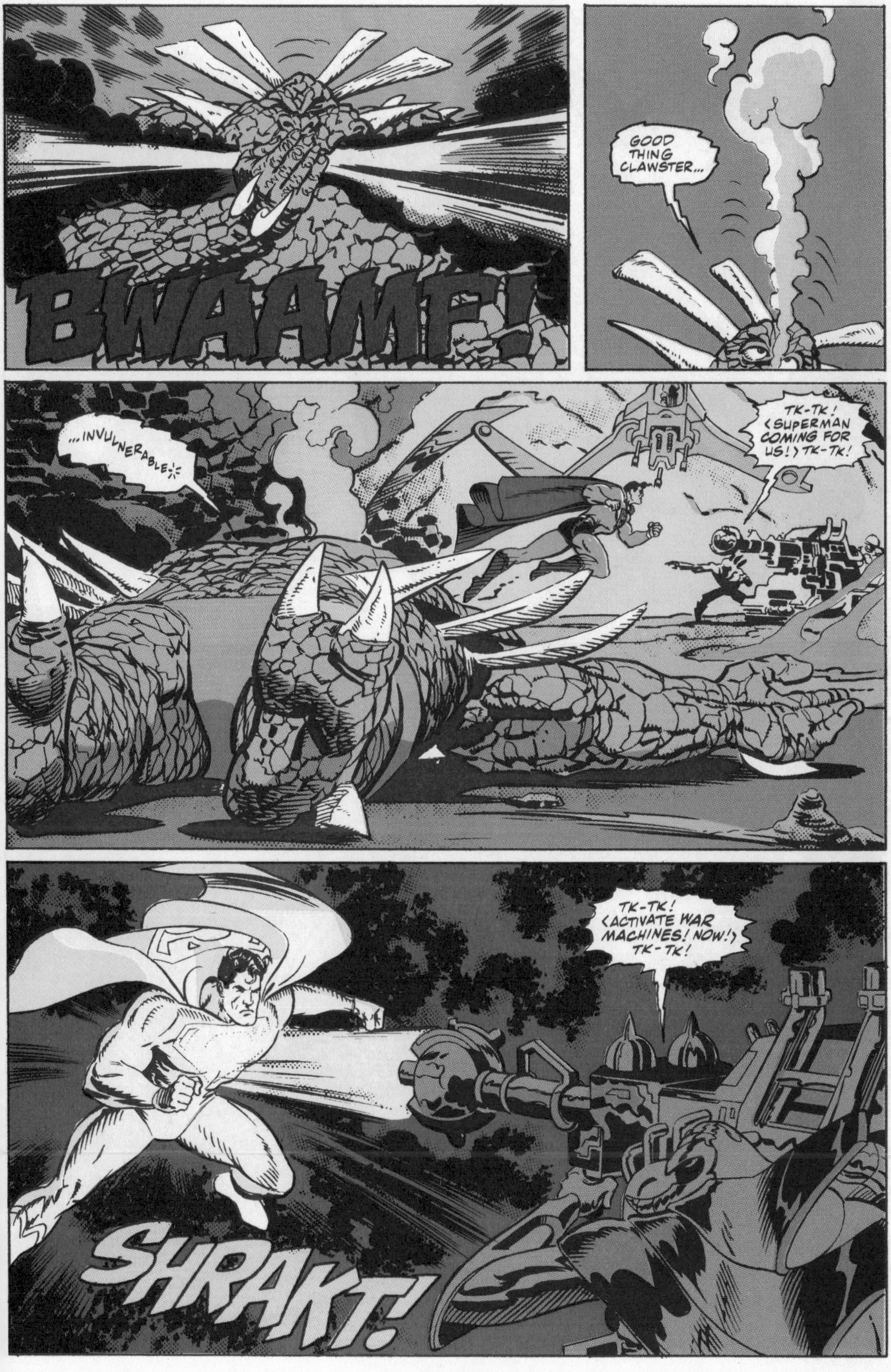
BWAAMF!
GOOD THING CLAWSTER...
...INVULNERABLE!
TK-TK! ‹SUPERMAN COMING FOR US!› TK-TK!
TK-TK! ‹ACTIVATE WAR MACHINES! NOW!› TK-TK!
SHRAKT!

MISSED MY CHANCE TO STOP THEM ONCE...

WHAKT!

WON'T MAKE THAT MISTAKE AGAIN!

¿WHUFF!¿ ¿HUFF!¿ <THAT--> <--SMARTS!>

POUND!

KRAZZZZH!

WHAM

KRL'LI'S UNCONSCIOUS! THE BATTLE SEEMS TO BE GOING AGAINST US!

PERHAPS, AFTER ALL, DISCRETION WOULD BE THE BETTER PART OF VALOR!

COME BACK HERE, WAR WORLDER!

WHERE'S THE LADY REPORTER YOU'RE HOLDING CAPTIVE?

C-CAPTIVE? SURELY, SUPERMAN, YOU KNOW... WE WARWORLDERS DON'T TAKE CAPTIVES!

WHERE IS SHE?

CHARLIE TOOK HER TO THE EAST TUNNEL! BY NOW, SHE'S DEAD!

W-WHAT ARE YOU GOING TO DO?

POUND YOU UP TO YOUR NECK INTO THE ROCK FLOOR!

AND MAYBE, IF YOU'RE WRONG, I MIGHT JUST BOTHER TO DIG YOU OUT AGAIN!

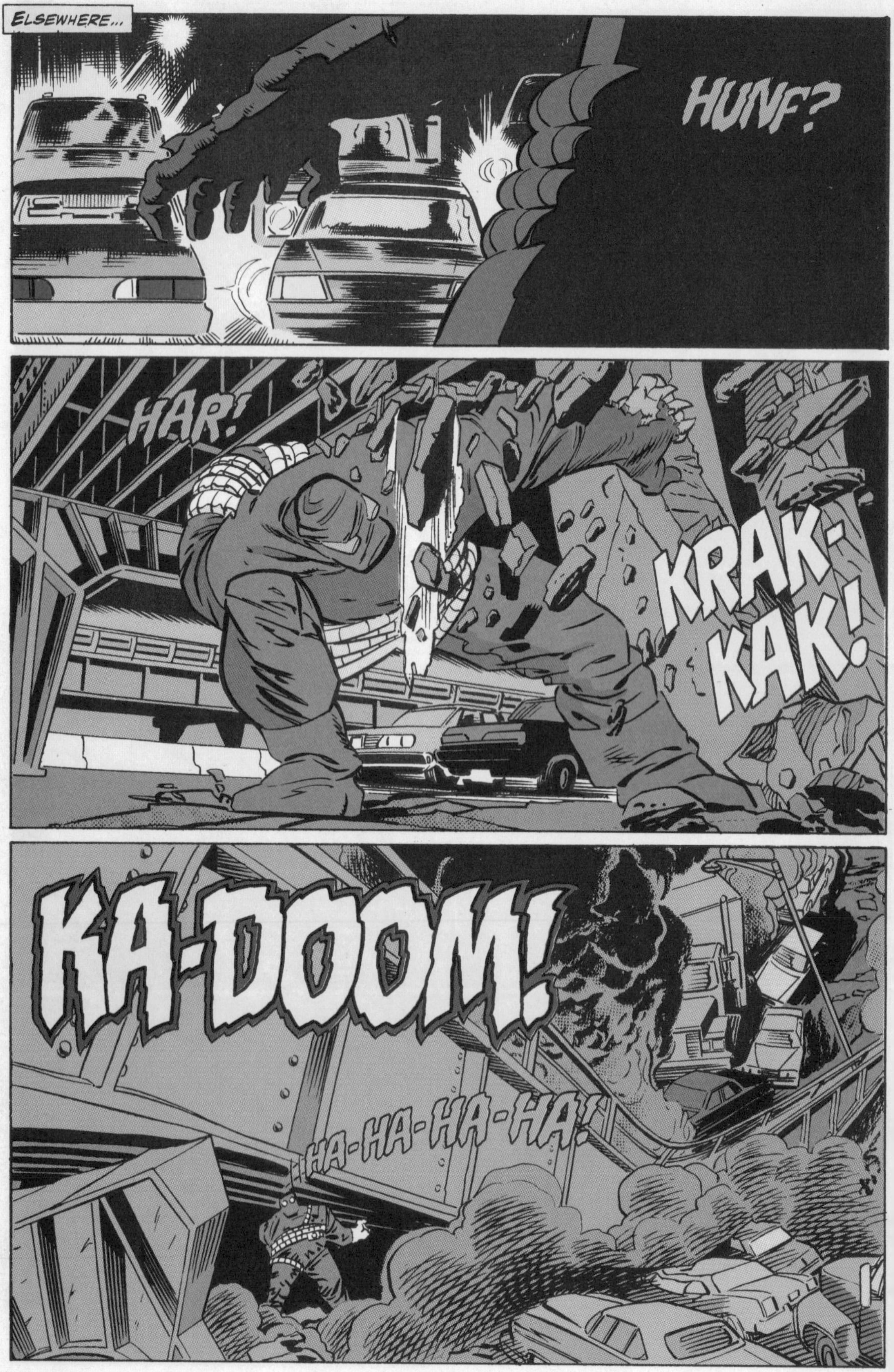
ELSEWHERE...
HUNF?
HAR!
KRAK-KAK!
KA-DOOM!
HA-HA-HA-HA!

THE JAILS ON THE SURFACE WON'T *HOLD* THESE GUYS!

WE'LL HOLD A *TRIAL* AND DEAL WITH THEM IN *UNDERWORLD.*

BUT... YOU DON'T HAVE TO *STAY* DOWN HERE, YOU KNOW.

THERE'S A PLACE FOR YOU AND YOUR FRIENDS IN *METROPOLIS.*

YOU *KIDDIN',* RIGHT?

AIN'T NUTHIN' FOR *US* ON THE SURFACE, AN' *CHARLIE* AN' *ME'RE* HUMAN.

AN' IT'S NOT LIKE MY FRIENDS GOT MARKETABLE SKILLS OR NUTHIN'. NAH...

...WE *JAWED* 'BOUT IT BEFORE, AN' WE DECIDED TA STAY IN THE *TUNNELS.*

WHAT ABOUT *YOU,* CHARLIE?

I COULD TRY TO GET YOU A JOB AT THE *PLANET.* YOU'RE PRETTY GOOD AT FERRETING OUT *INFORMATION.*

THANKS, MISS LANE. BUT I'LL TAKE MY CHANCES HERE.

THEN... MAYBE YOU CAN BE OUR *UNDERWORLD CORRESPONDENT?*

DEAL!

YA KNOW, GRUB, THERE'S WORSE DOWN HERE THAN THE WAR-WORLDERS.

YOU THINK I SHOULD *TELL* 'EM ... MY DUTY AS A *CORRESPONDENT* AN' ALL?

NAH, BLOODTHIRST IS *OUR* PROBLEM. BUT IT'S GOOD TO KNOW IF WE CAN'T HANDLE 'IM...

...WE CAN CALL IN *SUPERMAN!*

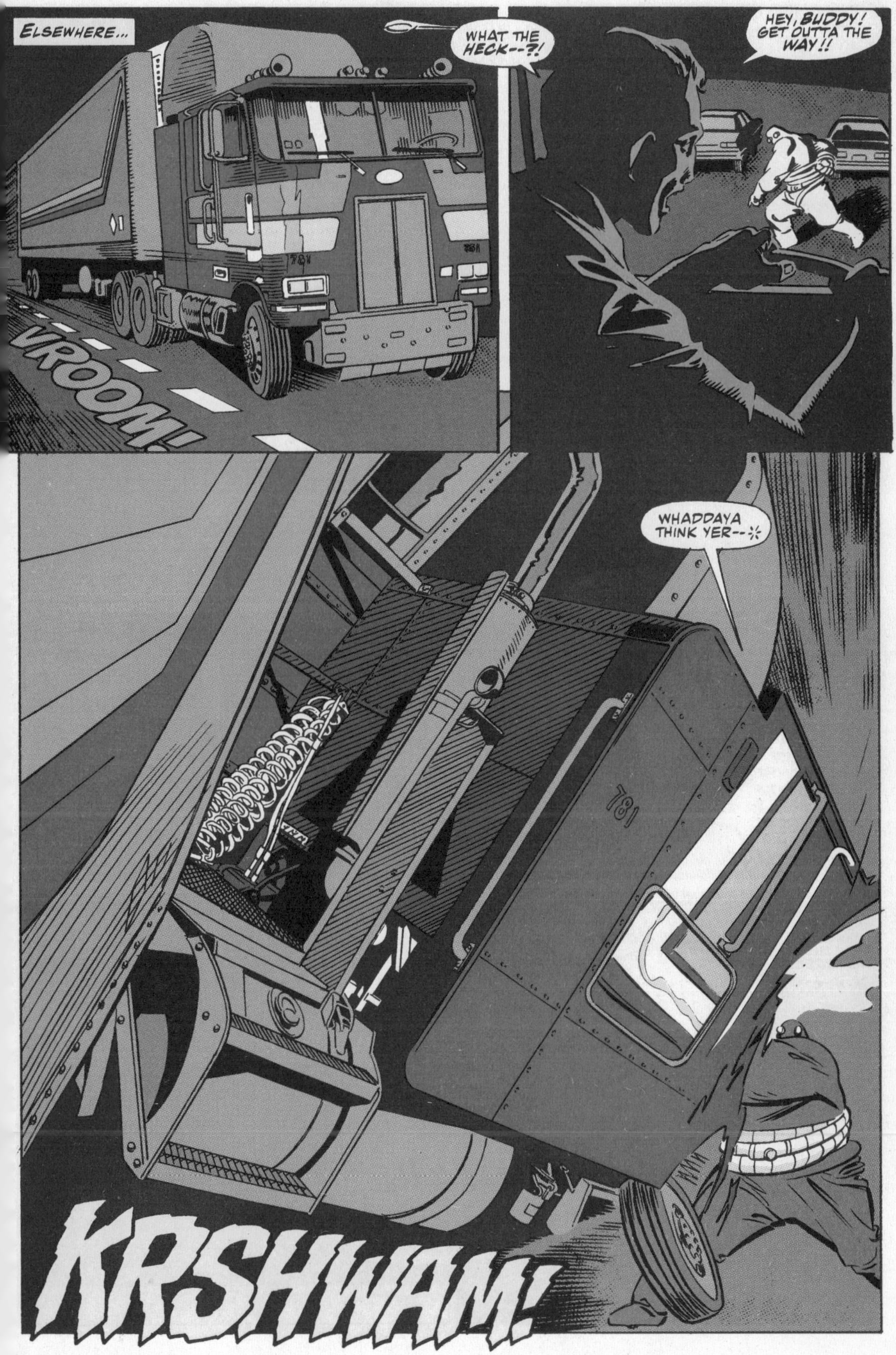
ELSEWHERE...
WHAT THE HECK--?!
VROOM!
HEY, BUDDY! GET OUTTA THE WAY!!
WHADDAYA THINK YER--
KRSHWAM!

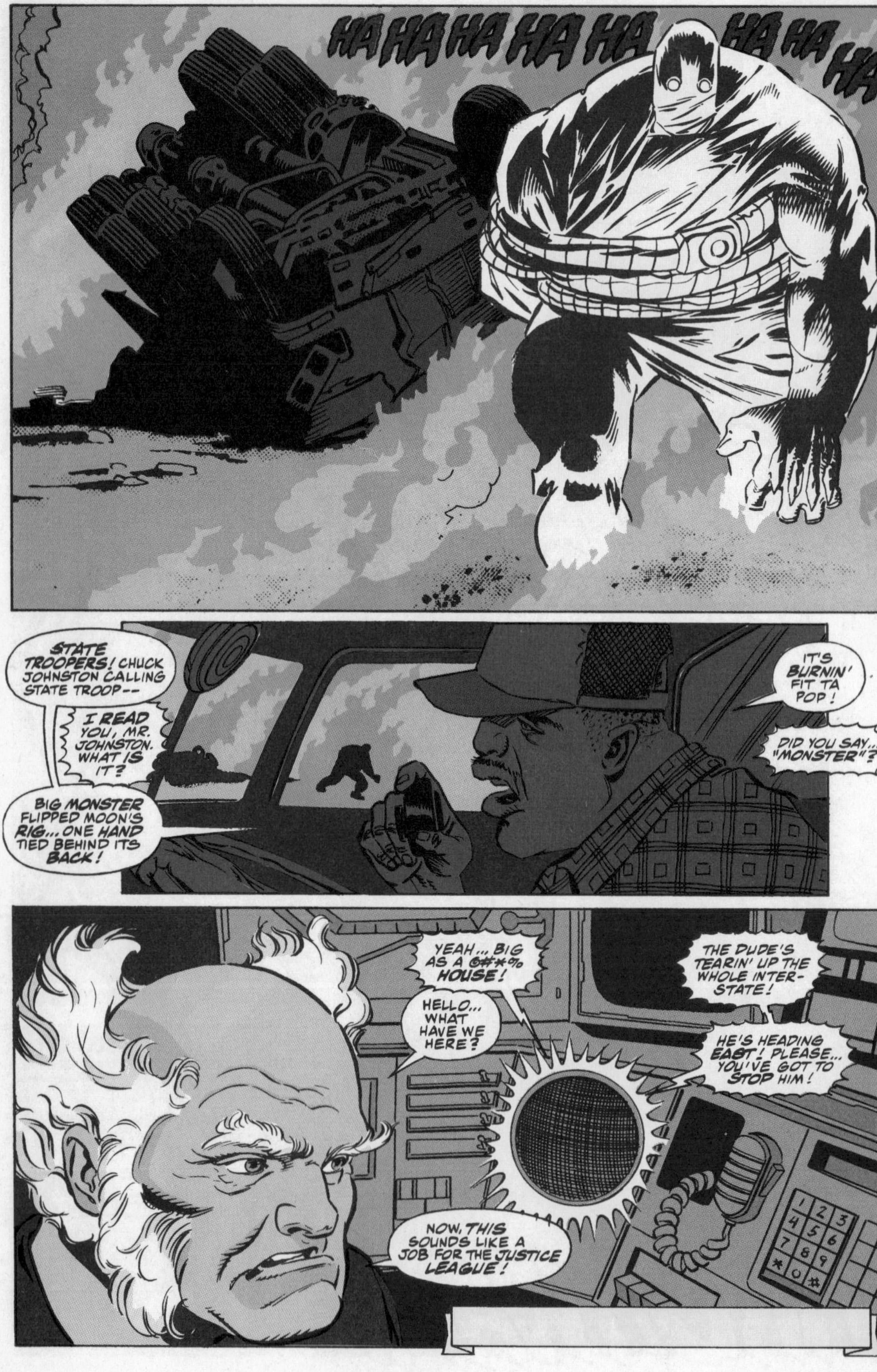
HA HA HA HA HA HA HA HA HA
STATE TROOPERS! CHUCK JOHNSTON CALLING STATE TROOP--
I READ YOU, MR. JOHNSTON. WHAT IS IT?
BIG MONSTER FLIPPED MOON'S RIG... ONE HAND TIED BEHIND ITS BACK!
IT'S BURNIN' FIT TA POP!
DID YOU SAY... "MONSTER"?
YEAH... BIG AS A @#*% HOUSE!
HELLO... WHAT HAVE WE HERE?
THE DUDE'S TEARIN' UP THE WHOLE INTER-STATE!
HE'S HEADING EAST! PLEASE... YOU'VE GOT TO STOP HIM!
NOW, THIS SOUNDS LIKE A JOB FOR THE JUSTICE LEAGUE!

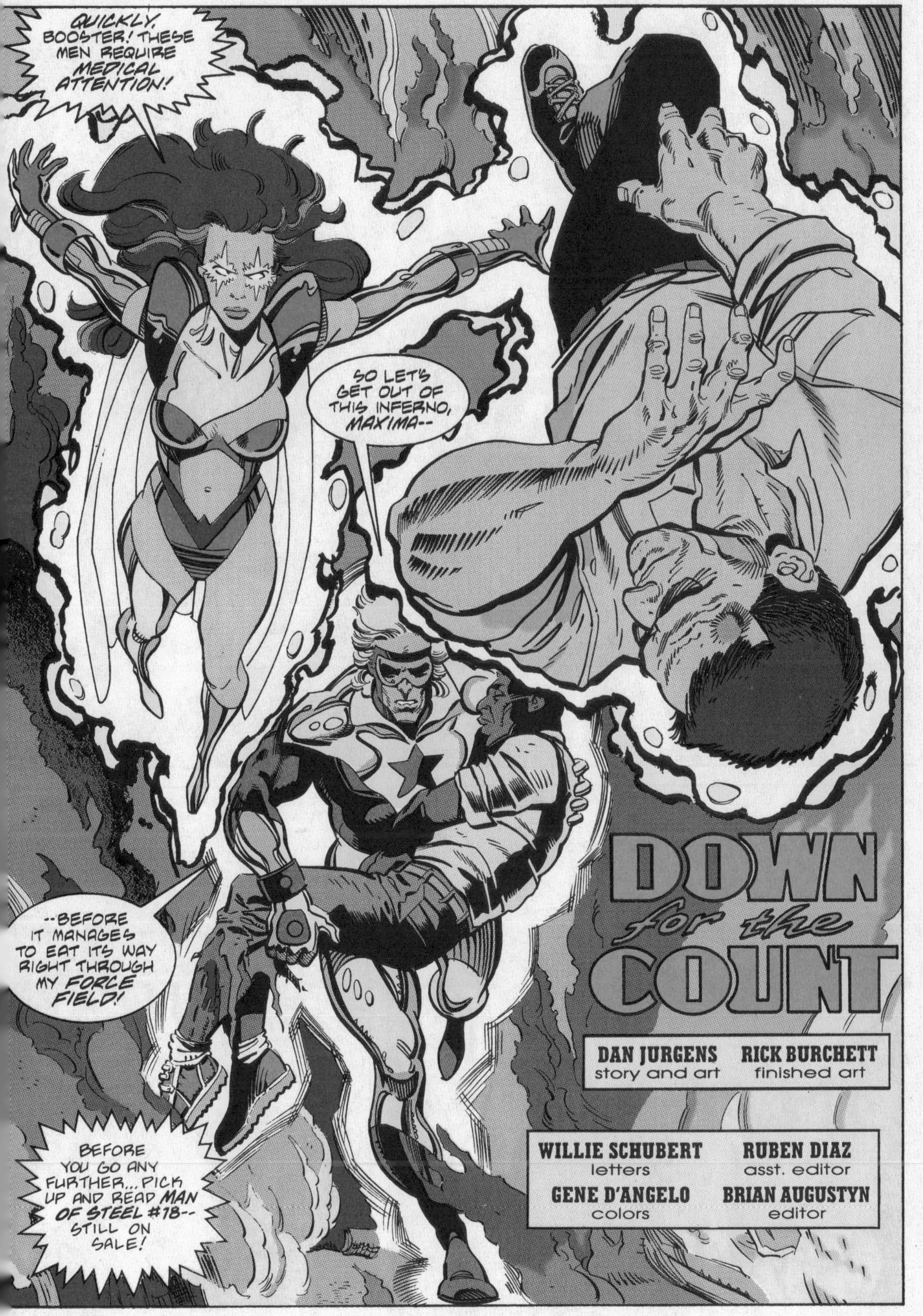
QUICKLY, BOOSTER! THESE MEN REQUIRE MEDICAL ATTENTION!
SO LET'S GET OUT OF THIS INFERNO, MAXIMA--
--BEFORE IT MANAGES TO EAT ITS WAY RIGHT THROUGH MY FORCE FIELD!
BEFORE YOU GO ANY FURTHER... PICK UP AND READ MAN OF STEEL #18-- STILL ON SALE!
DOWN for the COUNT
DAN JURGENS story and art
RICK BURCHETT finished art
WILLIE SCHUBERT letters
RUBEN DIAZ asst. editor
GENE D'ANGELO colors
BRIAN AUGUSTYN editor

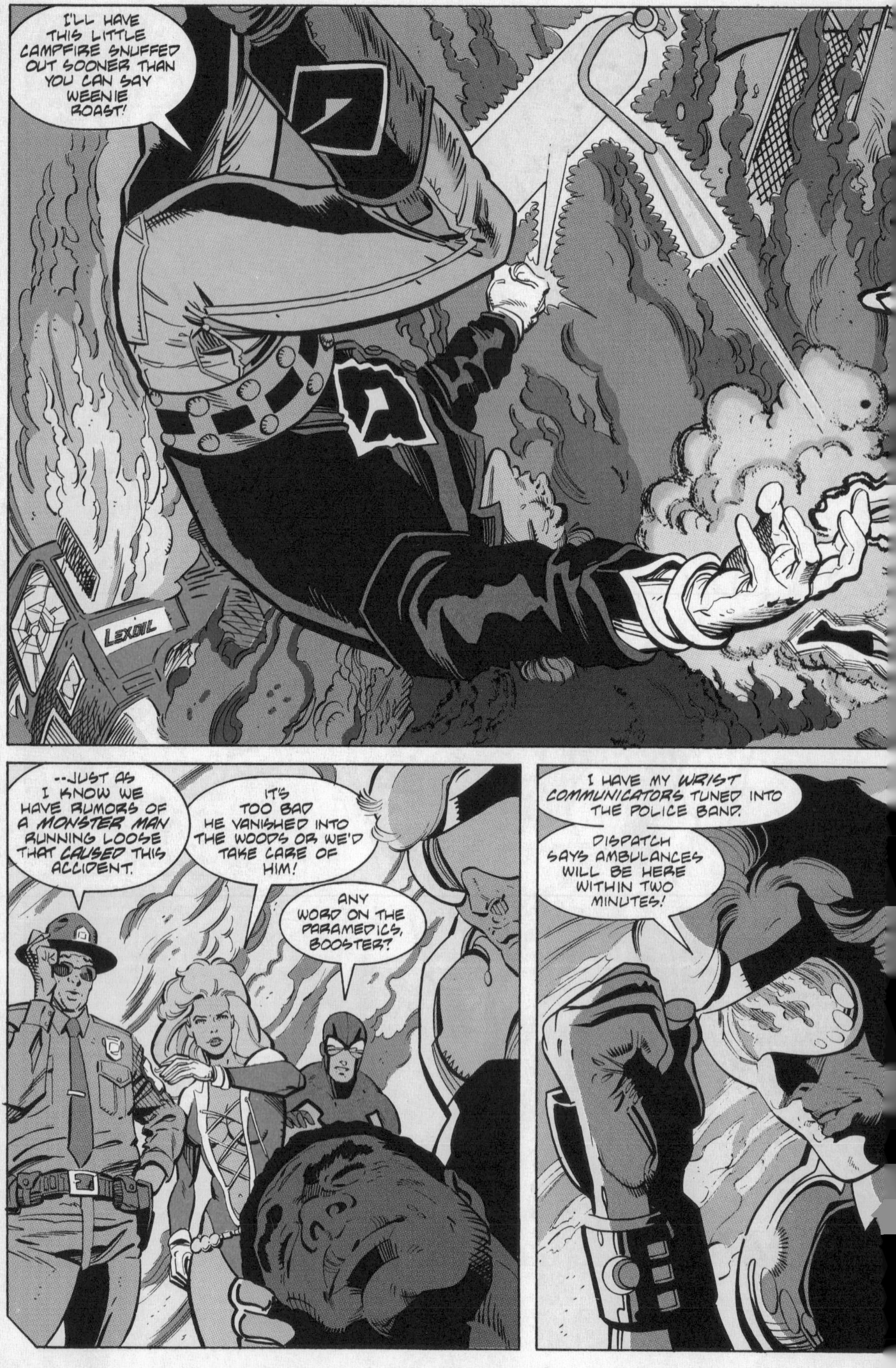
I'LL HAVE THIS LITTLE CAMPFIRE SNUFFED OUT SOONER THAN YOU CAN SAY WEENIE ROAST!
LEXOIL
--JUST AS I KNOW WE HAVE RUMORS OF A MONSTER MAN RUNNING LOOSE THAT CAUSED THIS ACCIDENT.
IT'S TOO BAD HE VANISHED INTO THE WOODS OR WE'D TAKE CARE OF HIM!
ANY WORD ON THE PARAMEDICS, BOOSTER?
I HAVE MY WRIST COMMUNICATORS TUNED INTO THE POLICE BAND.
DISPATCH SAYS AMBULANCES WILL BE HERE WITHIN TWO MINUTES!

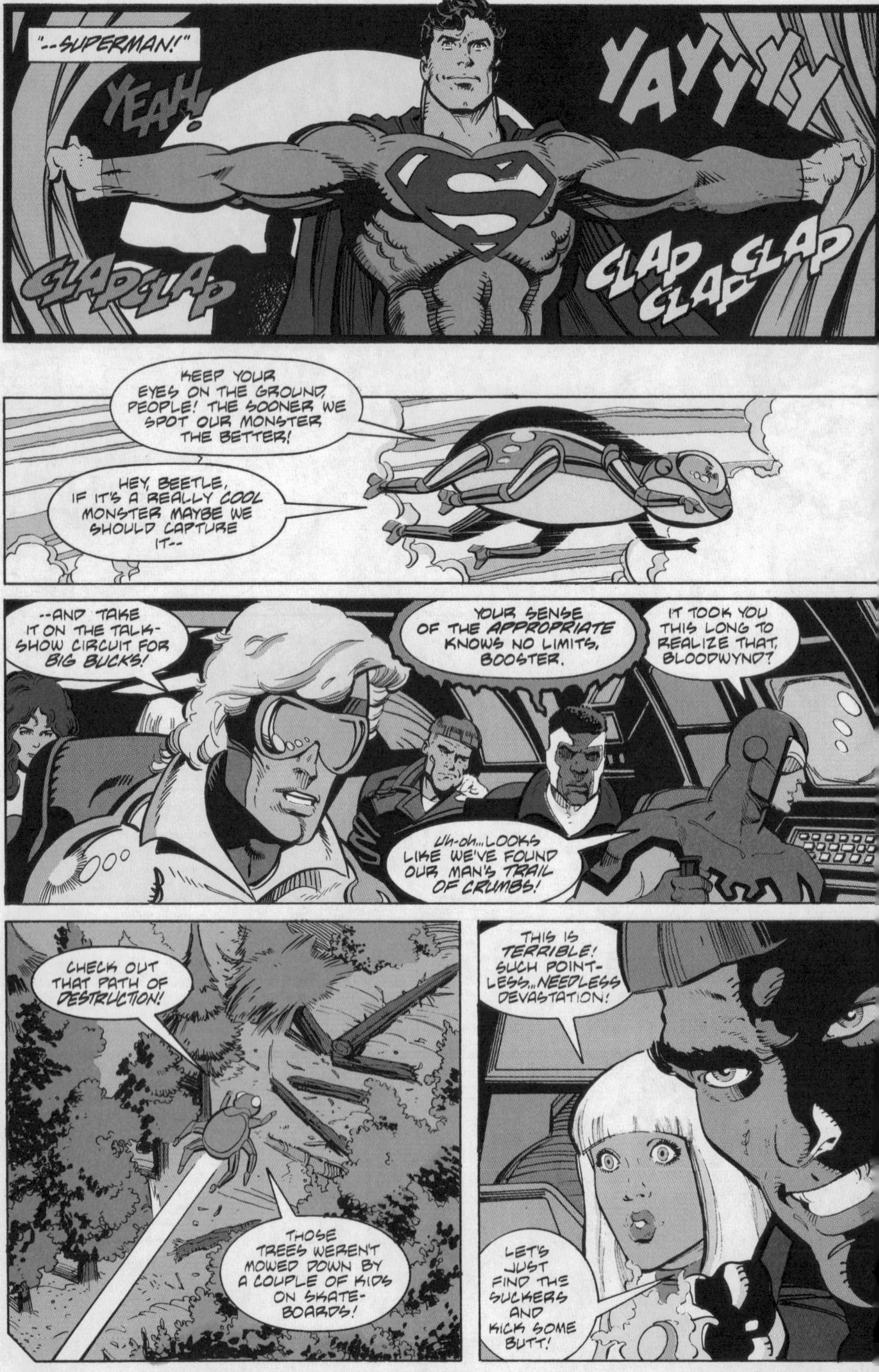
"--SUPERMAN!"
YEAH!
YAYYYY
CLAP CLAP
CLAP CLAP CLAP
KEEP YOUR EYES ON THE GROUND, PEOPLE! THE SOONER WE SPOT OUR MONSTER THE BETTER!
HEY, BEETLE, IF IT'S A REALLY COOL MONSTER MAYBE WE SHOULD CAPTURE IT--
--AND TAKE IT ON THE TALK-SHOW CIRCUIT FOR BIG BUCKS!
YOUR SENSE OF THE APPROPRIATE KNOWS NO LIMITS, BOOSTER.
IT TOOK YOU THIS LONG TO REALIZE THAT, BLOODWYND?
UH-OH... LOOKS LIKE WE'VE FOUND OUR MAN'S TRAIL OF CRUMBS!
CHECK OUT THAT PATH OF DESTRUCTION!
THOSE TREES WEREN'T MOWED DOWN BY A COUPLE OF KIDS ON SKATE-BOARDS!
THIS IS TERRIBLE! SUCH POINT-LESS... NEEDLESS DEVASTATION!
LET'S JUST FIND THE SUCKERS AND KICK SOME BUTT!

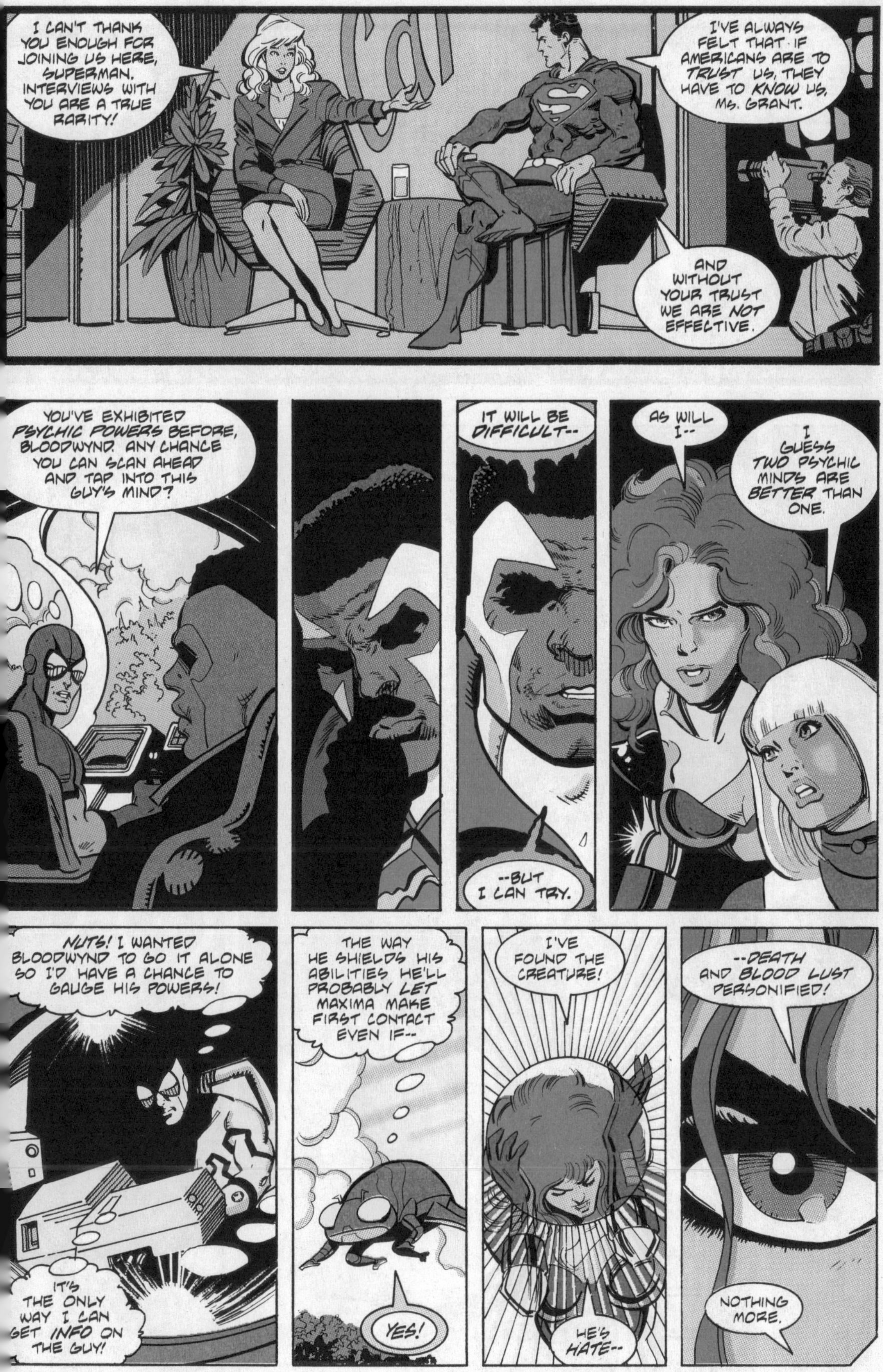

I CAN'T THANK YOU ENOUGH FOR JOINING US HERE, SUPERMAN. INTERVIEWS WITH YOU ARE A TRUE RARITY!
I'VE ALWAYS FELT THAT IF AMERICANS ARE TO TRUST US, THEY HAVE TO KNOW US, MS. GRANT.
AND WITHOUT YOUR TRUST WE ARE NOT EFFECTIVE.
YOU'VE EXHIBITED PSYCHIC POWERS BEFORE, BLOODWYND. ANY CHANCE YOU CAN SCAN AHEAD AND TAP INTO THIS GUY'S MIND?
IT WILL BE DIFFICULT--
--BUT I CAN TRY.
AS WILL I--
I GUESS TWO PSYCHIC MINDS ARE BETTER THAN ONE.
NUTS! I WANTED BLOODWYND TO GO IT ALONE SO I'D HAVE A CHANCE TO GAUGE HIS POWERS!
IT'S THE ONLY WAY I CAN GET INFO ON THE GUY!
THE WAY HE SHIELDS HIS ABILITIES HE'LL PROBABLY LET MAXIMA MAKE FIRST CONTACT EVEN IF--
YES!
I'VE FOUND THE CREATURE!
HE'S HATE--
--DEATH AND BLOOD LUST PERSONIFIED!
NOTHING MORE.

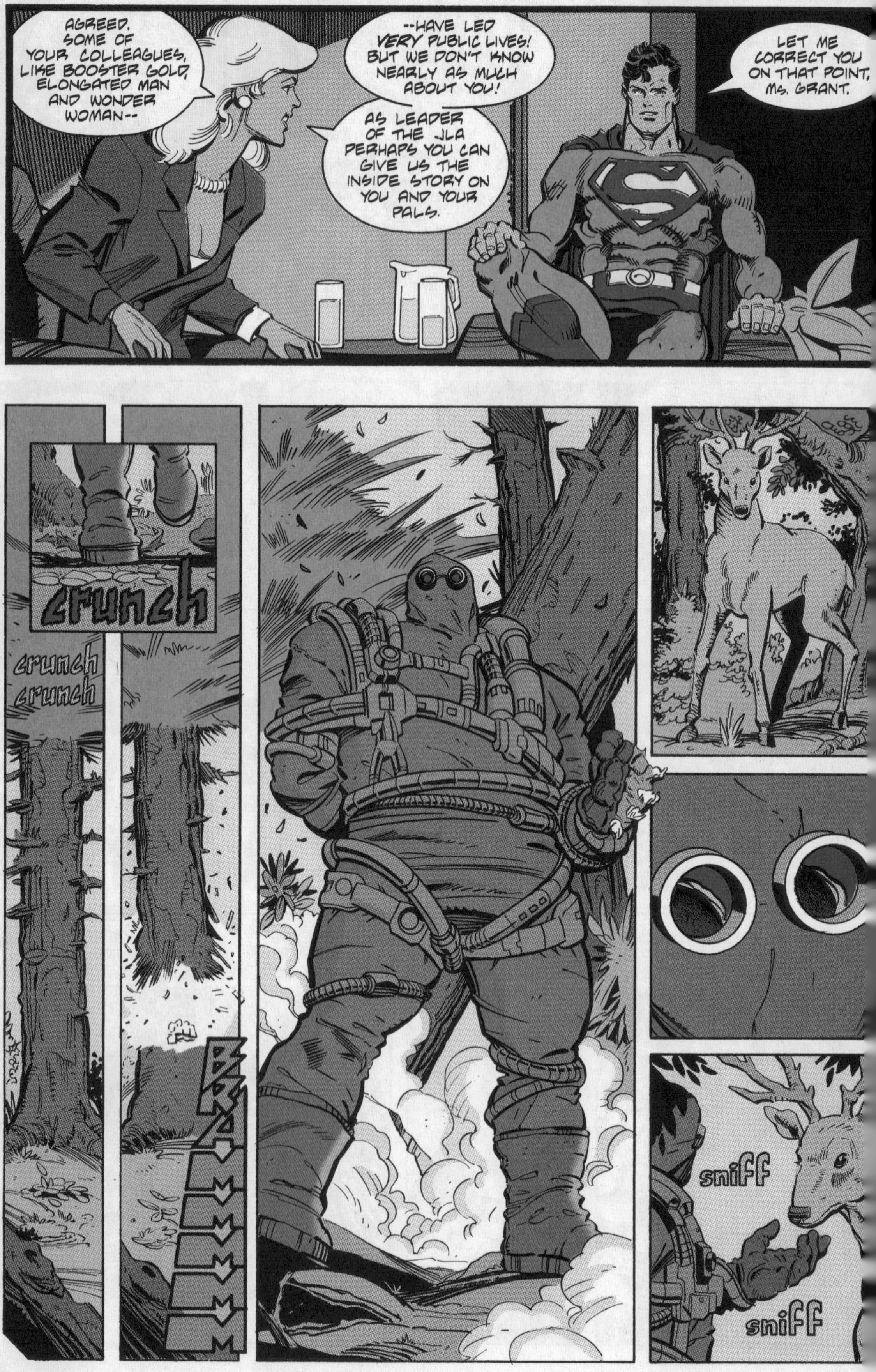
AGREED. SOME OF YOUR COLLEAGUES, LIKE BOOSTER GOLD, ELONGATED MAN AND WONDER WOMAN--
--HAVE LED VERY PUBLIC LIVES! BUT WE DON'T KNOW NEARLY AS MUCH ABOUT YOU!
AS LEADER OF THE JLA PERHAPS YOU CAN GIVE US THE INSIDE STORY ON YOU AND YOUR PALS.
LET ME CORRECT YOU ON THAT POINT, MS. GRANT.
crunch
crunch
crunch
sniff
sniff

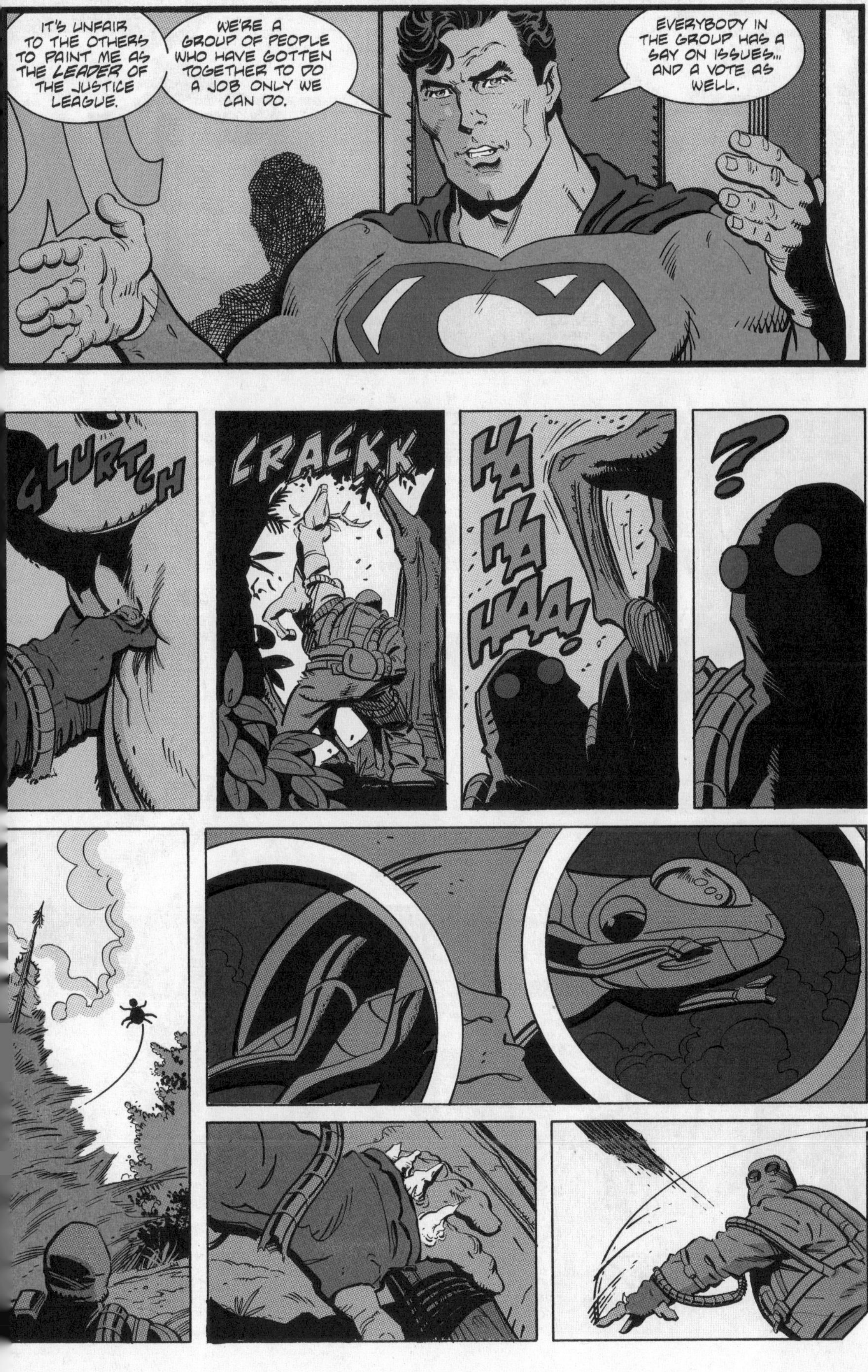
IT'S UNFAIR TO THE OTHERS TO PAINT ME AS THE LEADER OF THE JUSTICE LEAGUE.
WE'RE A GROUP OF PEOPLE WHO HAVE GOTTEN TOGETHER TO DO A JOB ONLY WE CAN DO.
EVERYBODY IN THE GROUP HAS A SAY ON ISSUES... AND A VOTE AS WELL.
GLURTCH
CRACKK
HA HA HAA!
?

CAMERA ONE

SURELY YOU'VE BEEN A GREATER INFLUENCE THAN THAT!

RESPECTED OBSERVERS SUGGEST YOU'VE PROVIDED A QUALITY OF STRENGTH AND FOCUS THE LEAGUE PREVIOUSLY LACKED.

CAMERA TWO

THEY WERE A TALENTED, *DEDICATED* BUNCH LONG BEFORE I JOINED, MS. GRANT.

I'M PROUD TO BE IN THEIR RANKS.

YO, BEETLE! RADAR SHOWS A PROJECTILE COMING--

SHRAK

EVERYBODY ASSUME CRASH POSITIONS!

I'M GONNA FIND THE GUY WHO *WHACKED* US AND SEW HIS EYELIDS SHUT!

OUR HYDRAULICS ARE SHREDDED! WE'RE GOING *DOWN!*

BETTER GIVE THE *NON-FLYERS* A HAND FIRST!

AND YOU BETTER MAKE IT *QUICK!*

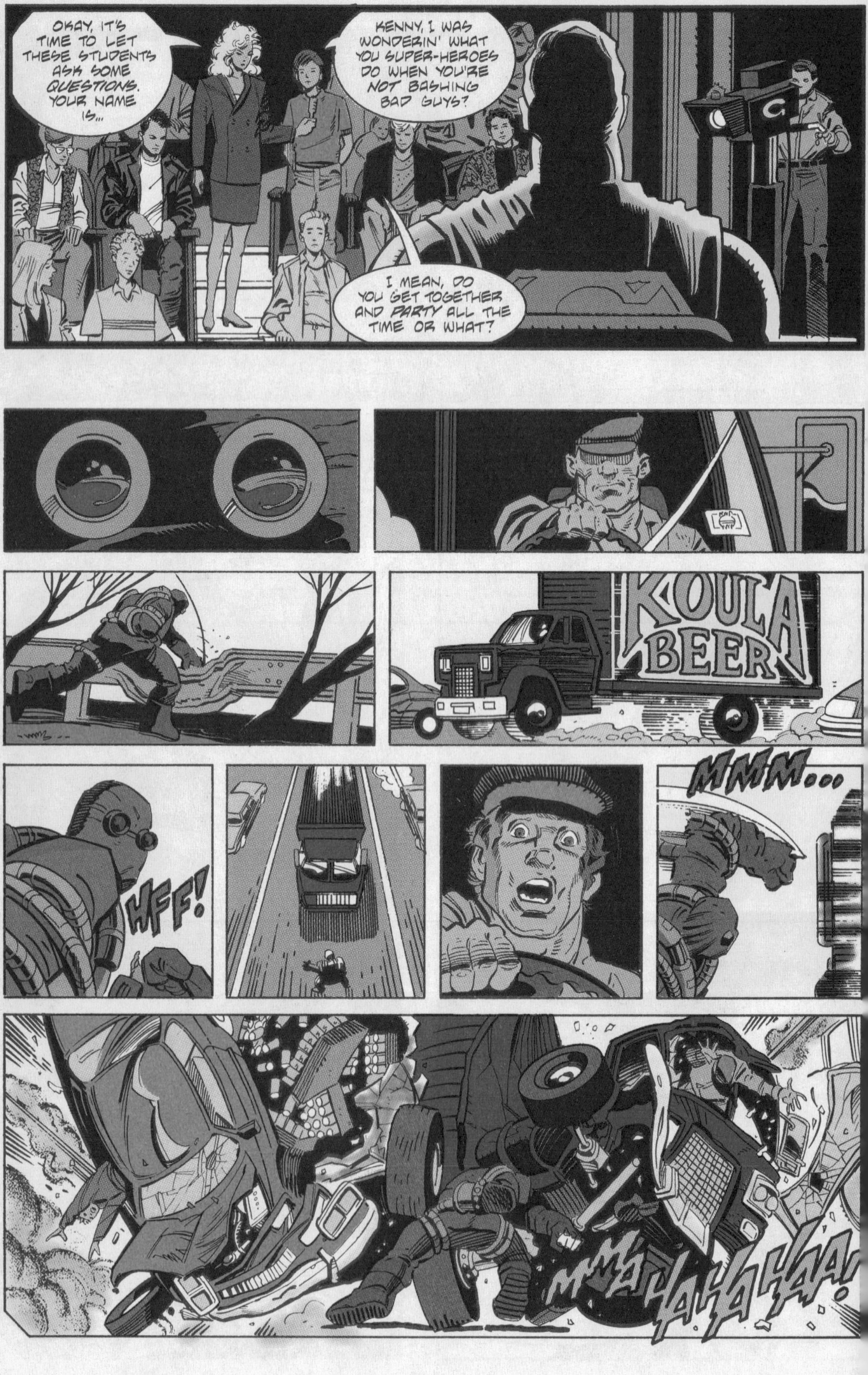
OKAY, IT'S TIME TO LET THESE STUDENTS ASK SOME QUESTIONS. YOUR NAME IS...
KENNY, I WAS WONDERIN' WHAT YOU SUPER-HEROES DO WHEN YOU'RE NOT BASHING BAD GUYS?
I MEAN, DO YOU GET TOGETHER AND PARTY ALL THE TIME OR WHAT?
KOULA BEER
HFF!
MMM...
MMAHAHAHA!

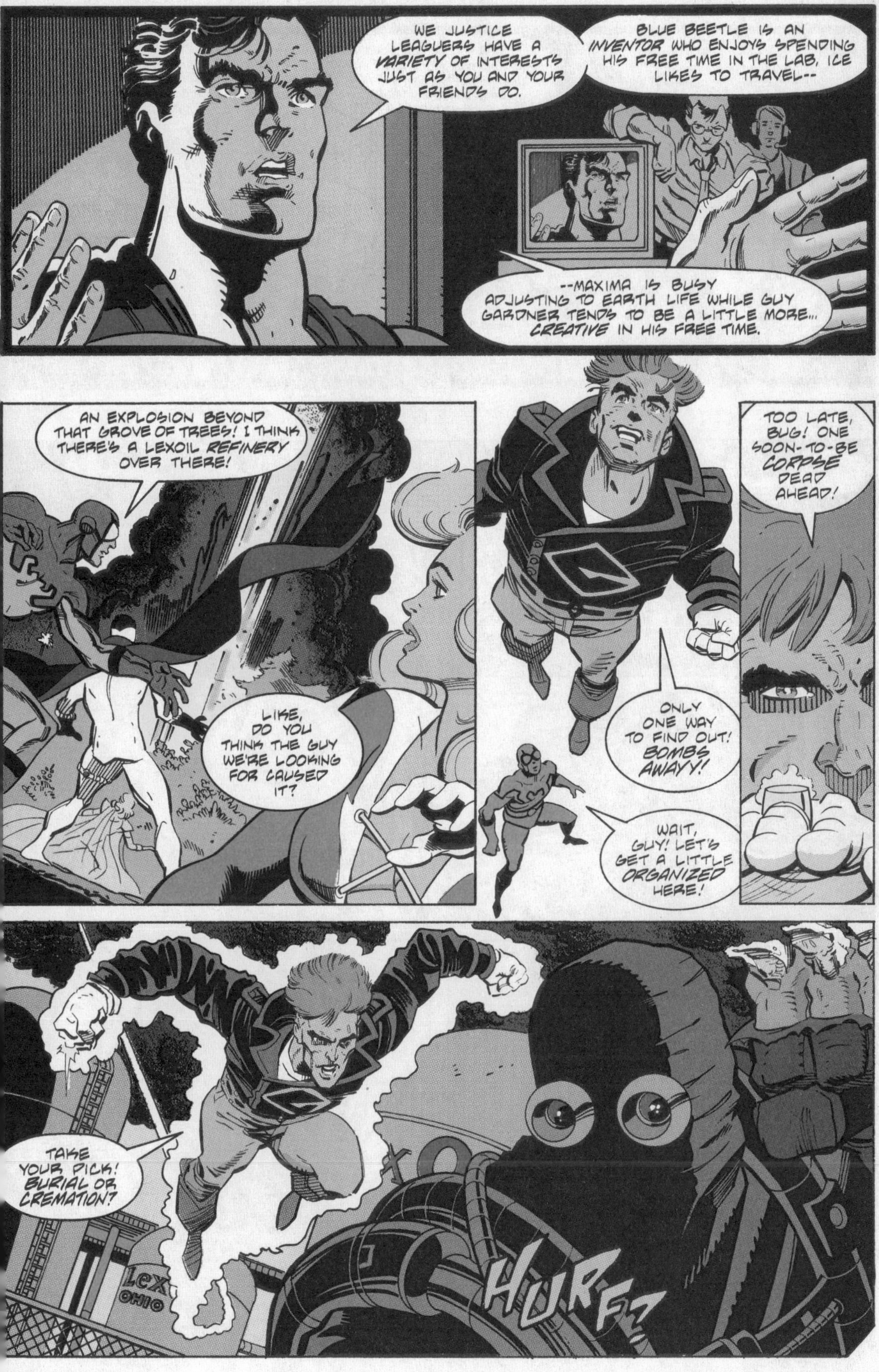
WE JUSTICE LEAGUERS HAVE A VARIETY OF INTERESTS JUST AS YOU AND YOUR FRIENDS DO.
BLUE BEETLE IS AN INVENTOR WHO ENJOYS SPENDING HIS FREE TIME IN THE LAB. ICE LIKES TO TRAVEL--
--MAXIMA IS BUSY ADJUSTING TO EARTH LIFE WHILE GUY GARDNER TENDS TO BE A LITTLE MORE... CREATIVE IN HIS FREE TIME.
AN EXPLOSION BEYOND THAT GROVE OF TREES! I THINK THERE'S A LEXOIL REFINERY OVER THERE!
LIKE, DO YOU THINK THE GUY WE'RE LOOKING FOR CAUSED IT?
ONLY ONE WAY TO FIND OUT! BOMBS AWAY!
WAIT, GUY! LET'S GET A LITTLE ORGANIZED HERE!
TOO LATE, BUG! ONE SOON-TO-BE CORPSE DEAD AHEAD!
TAKE YOUR PICK! BURIAL OR CREMATION?
LEX OHIO
HURF?

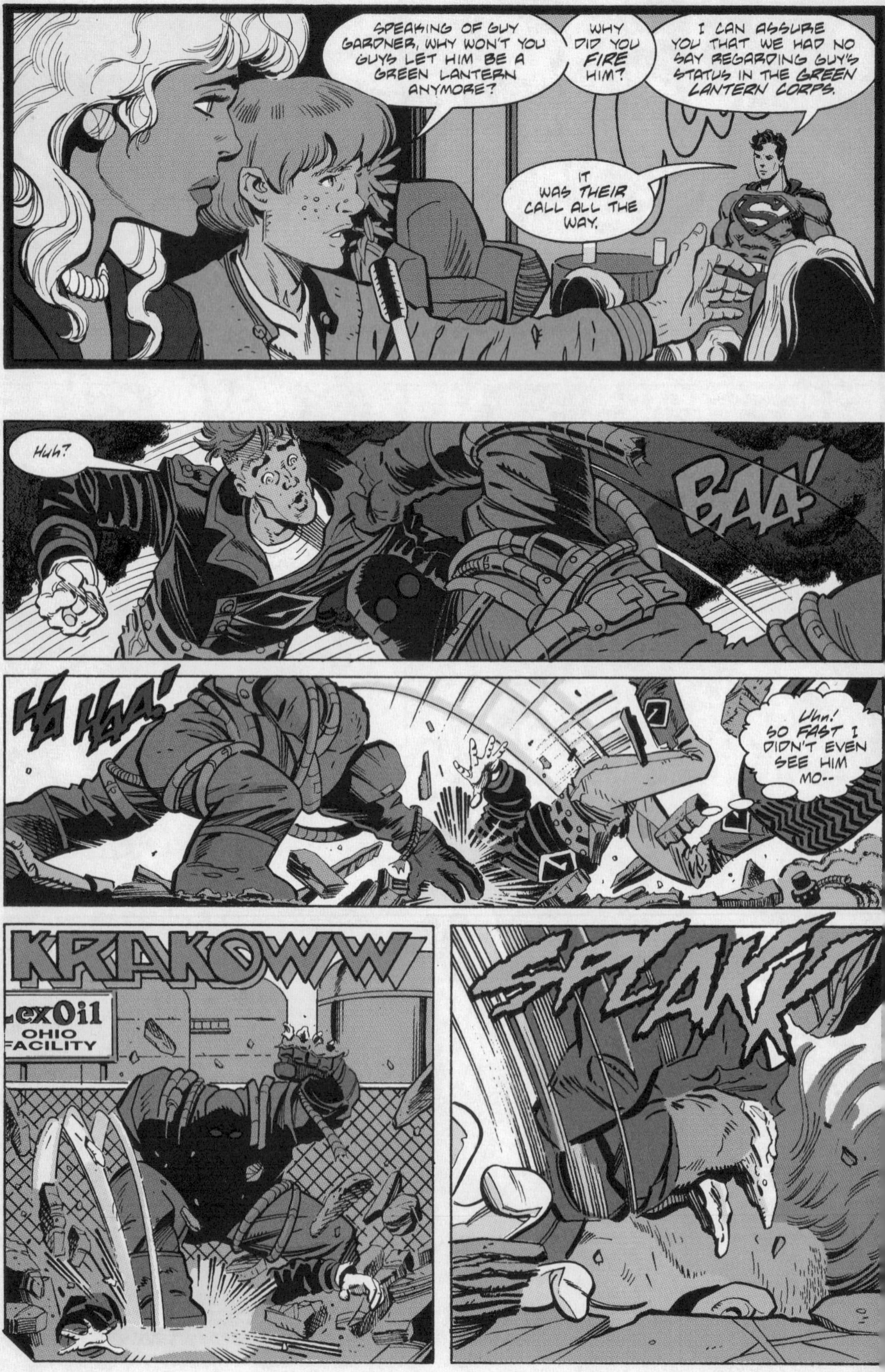
SPEAKING OF GUY GARDNER, WHY WON'T YOU GUYS LET HIM BE A GREEN LANTERN ANYMORE?
WHY DID YOU FIRE HIM?
I CAN ASSURE YOU THAT WE HAD NO SAY REGARDING GUY'S STATUS IN THE GREEN LANTERN CORPS.
IT WAS THEIR CALL ALL THE WAY.
Huh?
BAA!
HA HAA!
Uhn! SO FAST I DIDN'T EVEN SEE HIM MO--
KRAKOWW
LexOil
OHIO FACILITY

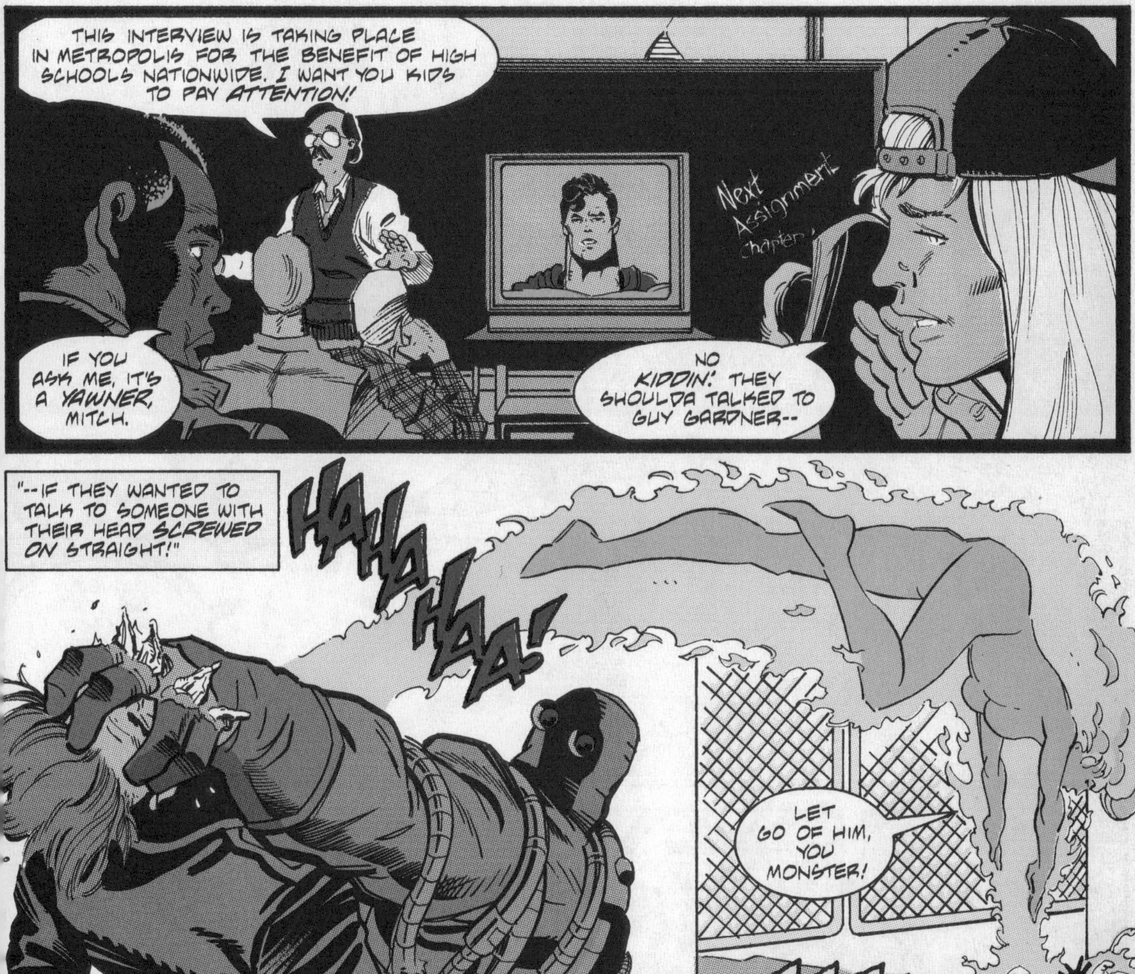
THIS INTERVIEW IS TAKING PLACE IN METROPOLIS FOR THE BENEFIT OF HIGH SCHOOLS NATIONWIDE. I WANT YOU KIDS TO PAY ATTENTION!
Next Assignment chapter
IF YOU ASK ME, IT'S A YAWNER, MITCH.
NO KIDDIN'! THEY SHOULDA TALKED TO GUY GARDNER--
"--IF THEY WANTED TO TALK TO SOMEONE WITH THEIR HEAD SCREWED ON STRAIGHT!"
HAHAHAHAA!
LET GO OF HIM, YOU MONSTER!
EEF!
THAT FREAKIN' THING'S POWERFUL! NEVER HAD A CHANCE TO FIGHT BACK!
CAN'T BREATHE...
CAN'T...
...EVEN...
...THINK...

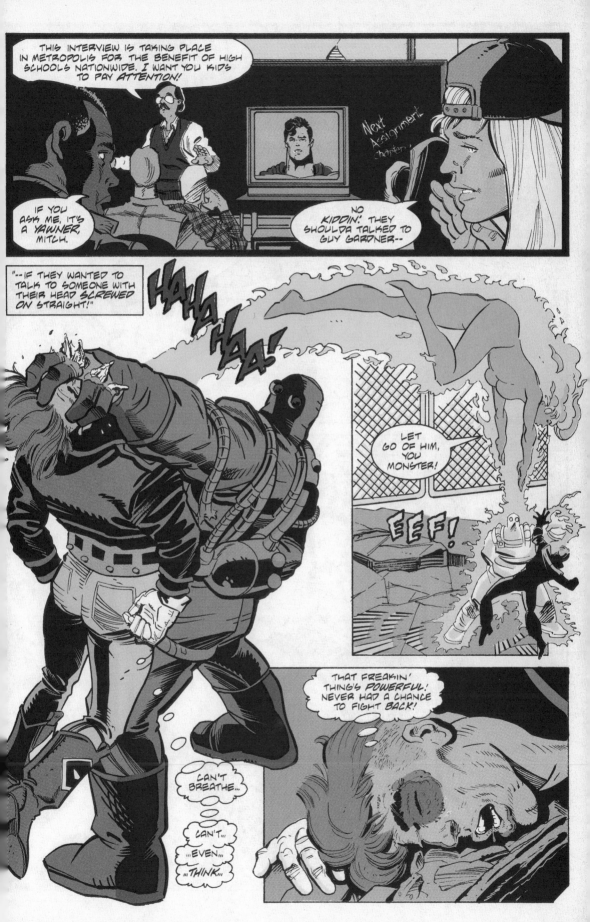

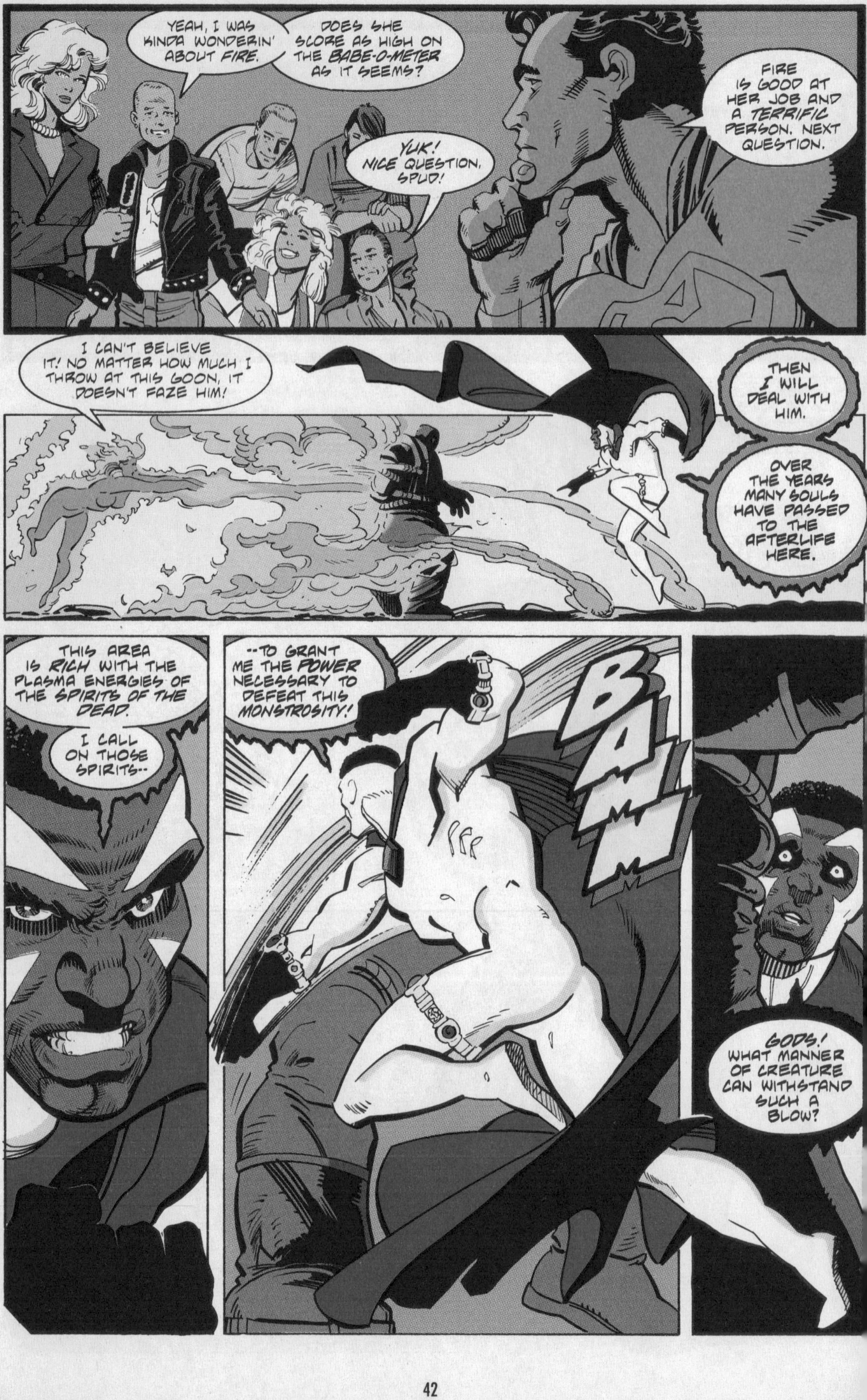
YEAH, I WAS KINDA WONDERIN' ABOUT FIRE.
DOES SHE SCORE AS HIGH ON THE BABE-O-METER AS IT SEEMS?
YUK! NICE QUESTION, SPUD!
FIRE IS GOOD AT HER JOB AND A TERRIFIC PERSON. NEXT QUESTION.
I CAN'T BELIEVE IT! NO MATTER HOW MUCH I THROW AT THIS GOON, IT DOESN'T FAZE HIM!
THEN I WILL DEAL WITH HIM.
OVER THE YEARS MANY SOULS HAVE PASSED TO THE AFTERLIFE HERE.
THIS AREA IS RICH WITH THE PLASMA ENERGIES OF THE SPIRITS OF THE DEAD.
I CALL ON THOSE SPIRITS--
--TO GRANT ME THE POWER NECESSARY TO DEFEAT THIS MONSTROSITY!
BAMM
GODS! WHAT MANNER OF CREATURE CAN WITHSTAND SUCH A BLOW?

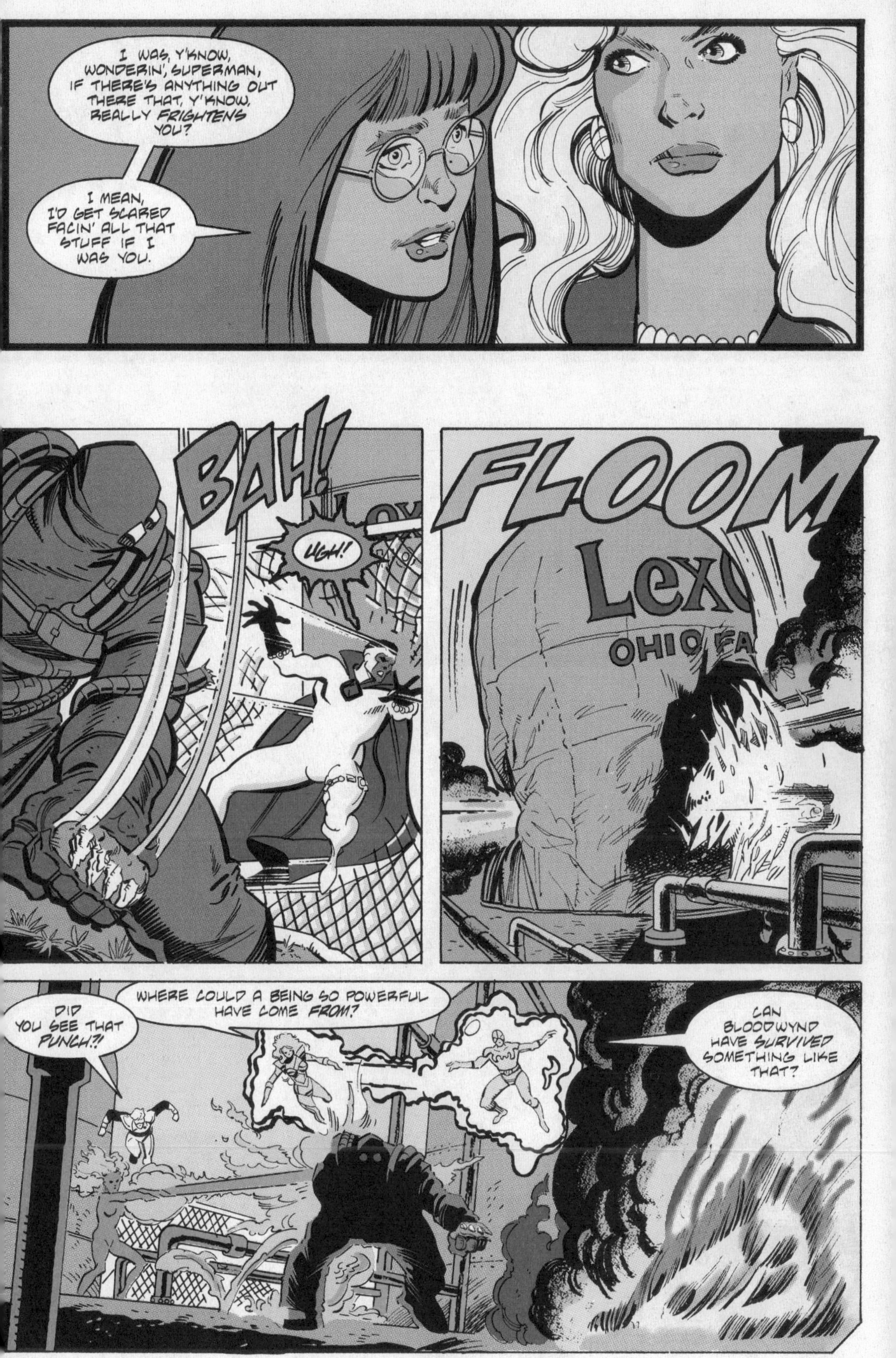

I WAS, Y'KNOW, WONDERIN', SUPERMAN, IF THERE'S ANYTHING OUT THERE THAT, Y'KNOW, REALLY FRIGHTENS YOU?
I MEAN, I'D GET SCARED FACIN' ALL THAT STUFF IF I WAS YOU.
BAH!
UGH!
FLOOM
Lex
OHIO FA
DID YOU SEE THAT PUNCH?!
WHERE COULD A BEING SO POWERFUL HAVE COME FROM?
CAN BLOODWYND HAVE SURVIVED SOMETHING LIKE THAT?

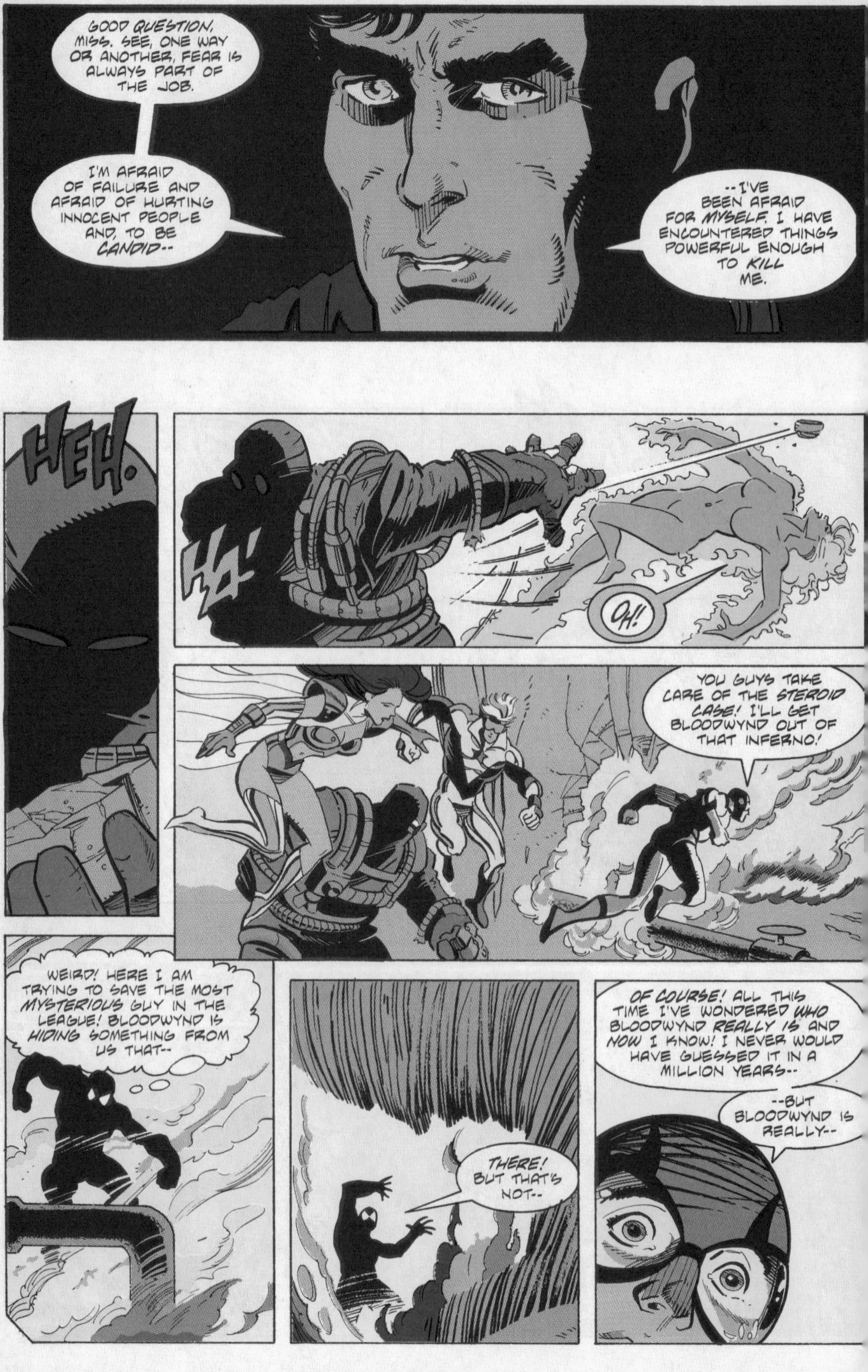
GOOD QUESTION, MISS. SEE, ONE WAY OR ANOTHER, FEAR IS ALWAYS PART OF THE JOB.
I'M AFRAID OF FAILURE AND AFRAID OF HURTING INNOCENT PEOPLE AND, TO BE CANDID--
--I'VE BEEN AFRAID FOR MYSELF. I HAVE ENCOUNTERED THINGS POWERFUL ENOUGH TO KILL ME.
HEH.
HA!
OH!
YOU GUYS TAKE CARE OF THE STEROID CASE! I'LL GET BLOODWYND OUT OF THAT INFERNO!
WEIRD! HERE I AM TRYING TO SAVE THE MOST MYSTERIOUS GUY IN THE LEAGUE! BLOODWYND IS HIDING SOMETHING FROM US THAT--
THERE! BUT THAT'S NOT--
OF COURSE! ALL THIS TIME I'VE WONDERED WHO BLOODWYND REALLY IS AND NOW I KNOW! I NEVER WOULD HAVE GUESSED IT IN A MILLION YEARS--
--BUT BLOODWYND IS REALLY--

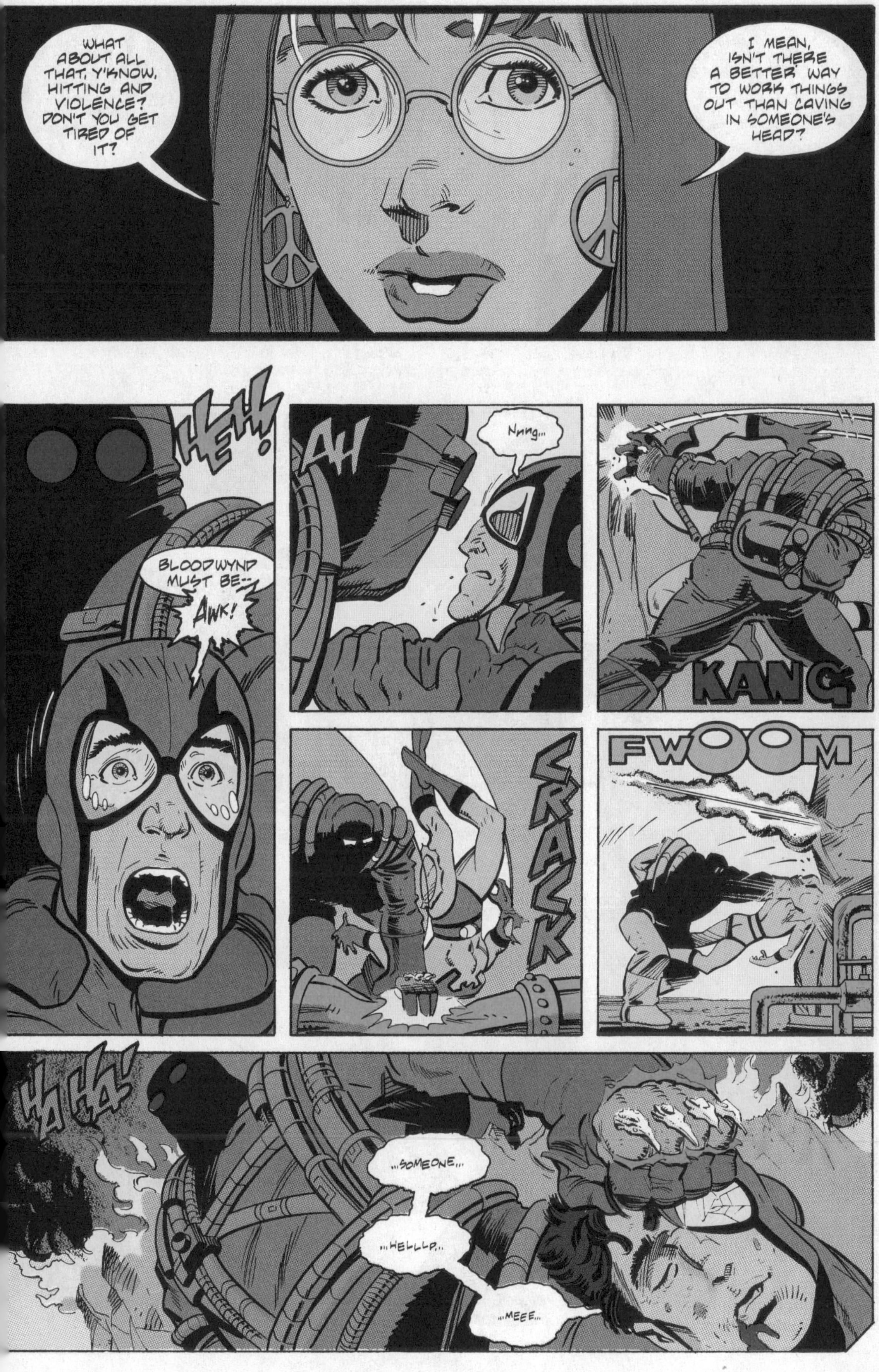
WHAT ABOUT ALL THAT, Y'KNOW, HITTING AND VIOLENCE? DON'T YOU GET TIRED OF IT?
I MEAN, ISN'T THERE A BETTER WAY TO WORK THINGS OUT THAN CAVING IN SOMEONE'S HEAD?
HEH!
BLOODWYND MUST BE--
AWK!
AH
Nnng...
KANG
CRACK
FWOOM
HA HA!
...SOMEONE...
...HELLLP...
...MEEE...

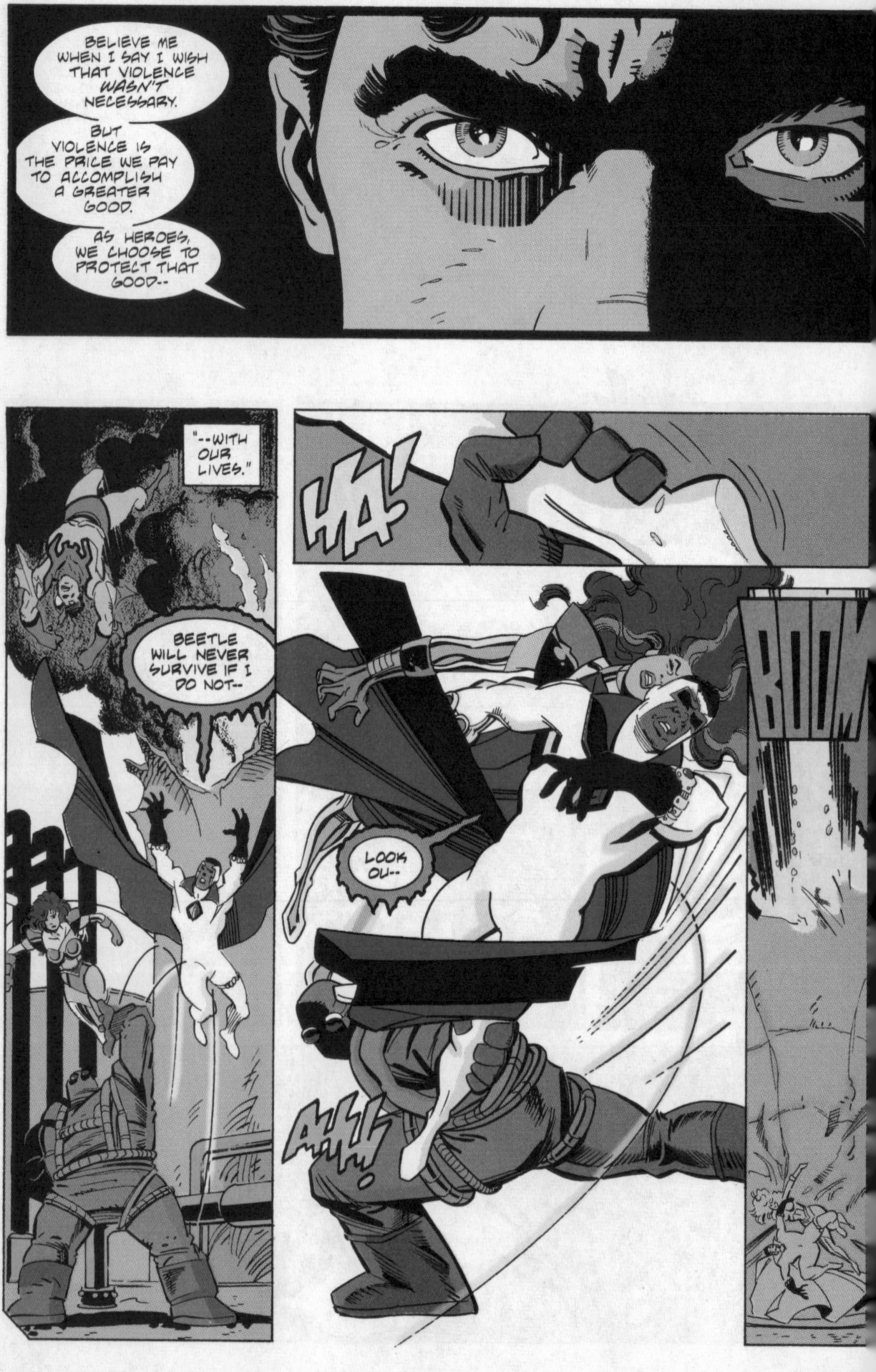
BELIEVE ME WHEN I SAY I WISH THAT VIOLENCE WASN'T NECESSARY.
BUT VIOLENCE IS THE PRICE WE PAY TO ACCOMPLISH A GREATER GOOD.
AS HEROES, WE CHOOSE TO PROTECT THAT GOOD--
"--WITH OUR LIVES."
BEETLE WILL NEVER SURVIVE IF I DO NOT--
HA!
BOOM
LOOK OU--
AH!

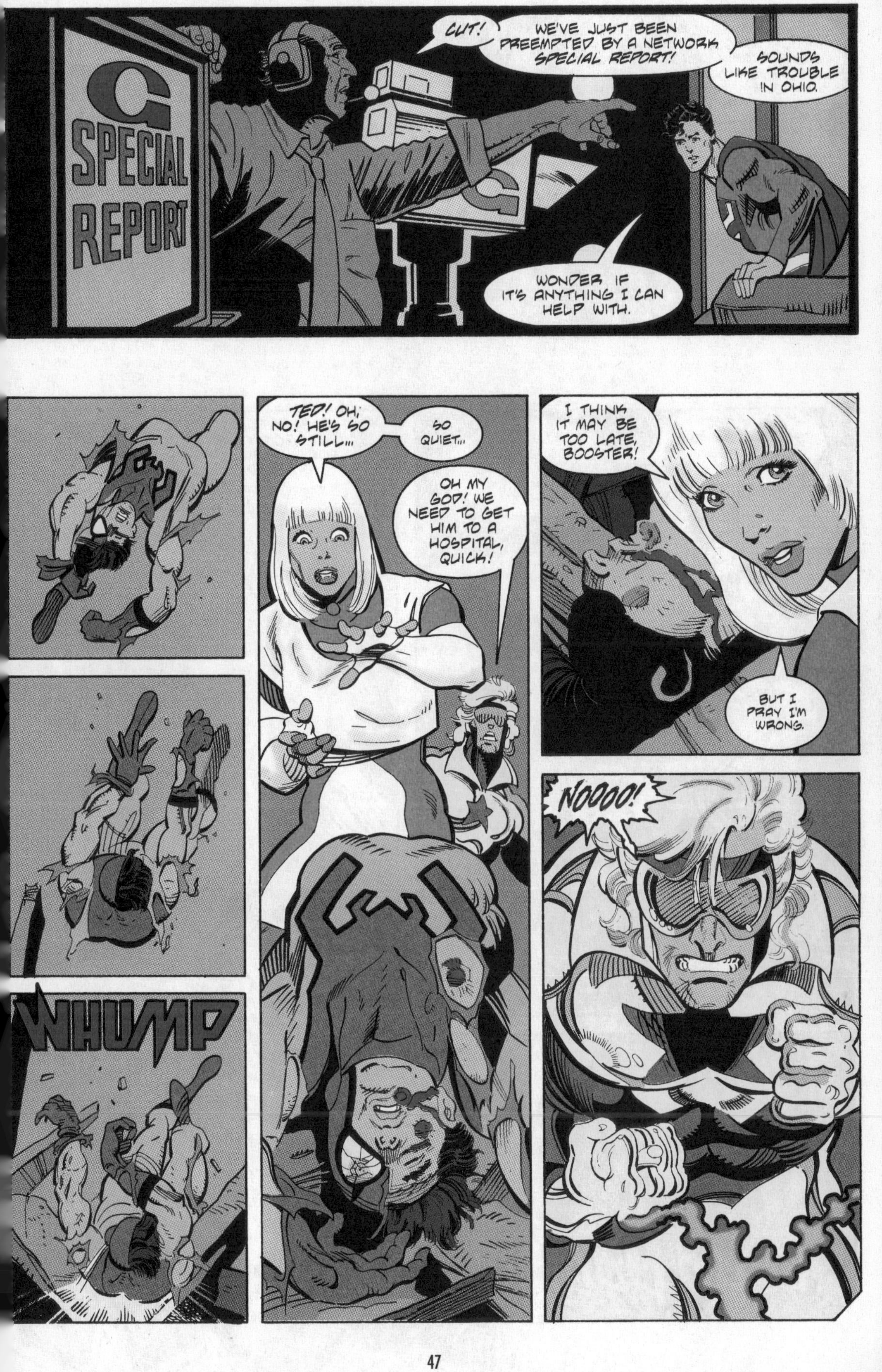

SPECIAL REPORT
CUT!
WE'VE JUST BEEN PREEMPTED BY A NETWORK SPECIAL REPORT!
SOUNDS LIKE TROUBLE IN OHIO.
WONDER IF IT'S ANYTHING I CAN HELP WITH.
TED! OH, NO! HE'S SO STILL...
SO QUIET...
OH MY GOD! WE NEED TO GET HIM TO A HOSPITAL, QUICK!
I THINK IT MAY BE TOO LATE, BOOSTER!
BUT I PRAY I'M WRONG.
WHUMP
NOOOO!

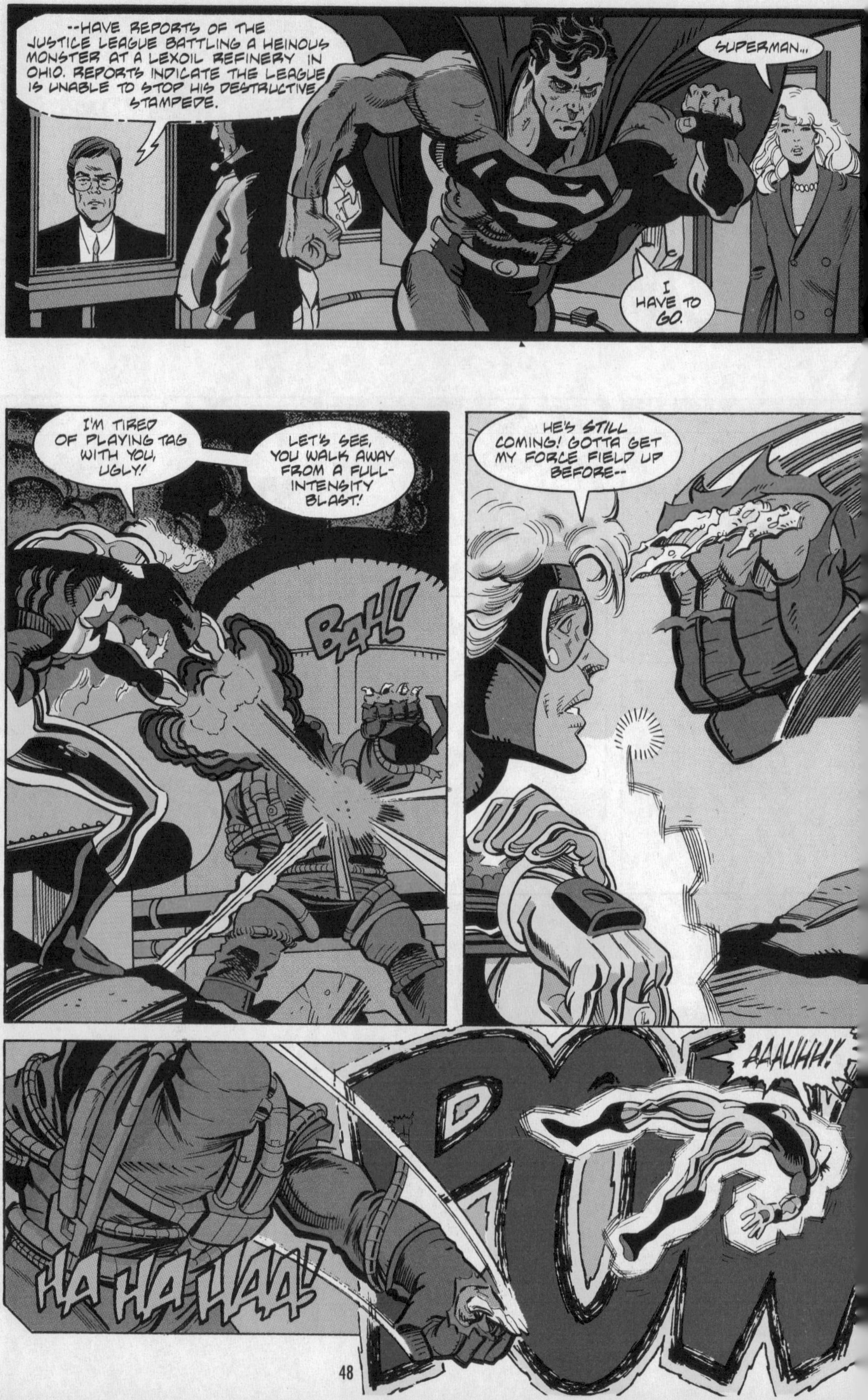
--HAVE REPORTS OF THE JUSTICE LEAGUE BATTLING A HEINOUS MONSTER AT A LEXOIL REFINERY IN OHIO. REPORTS INDICATE THE LEAGUE IS UNABLE TO STOP HIS DESTRUCTIVE STAMPEDE.
SUPERMAN...
I HAVE TO GO.
I'M TIRED OF PLAYING TAG WITH YOU, UGLY!
LET'S SEE, YOU WALK AWAY FROM A FULL-INTENSITY BLAST!
BAH!
HE'S STILL COMING! GOTTA GET MY FORCE FIELD UP BEFORE--
AAAUHH!
POW
HA HA HAA!

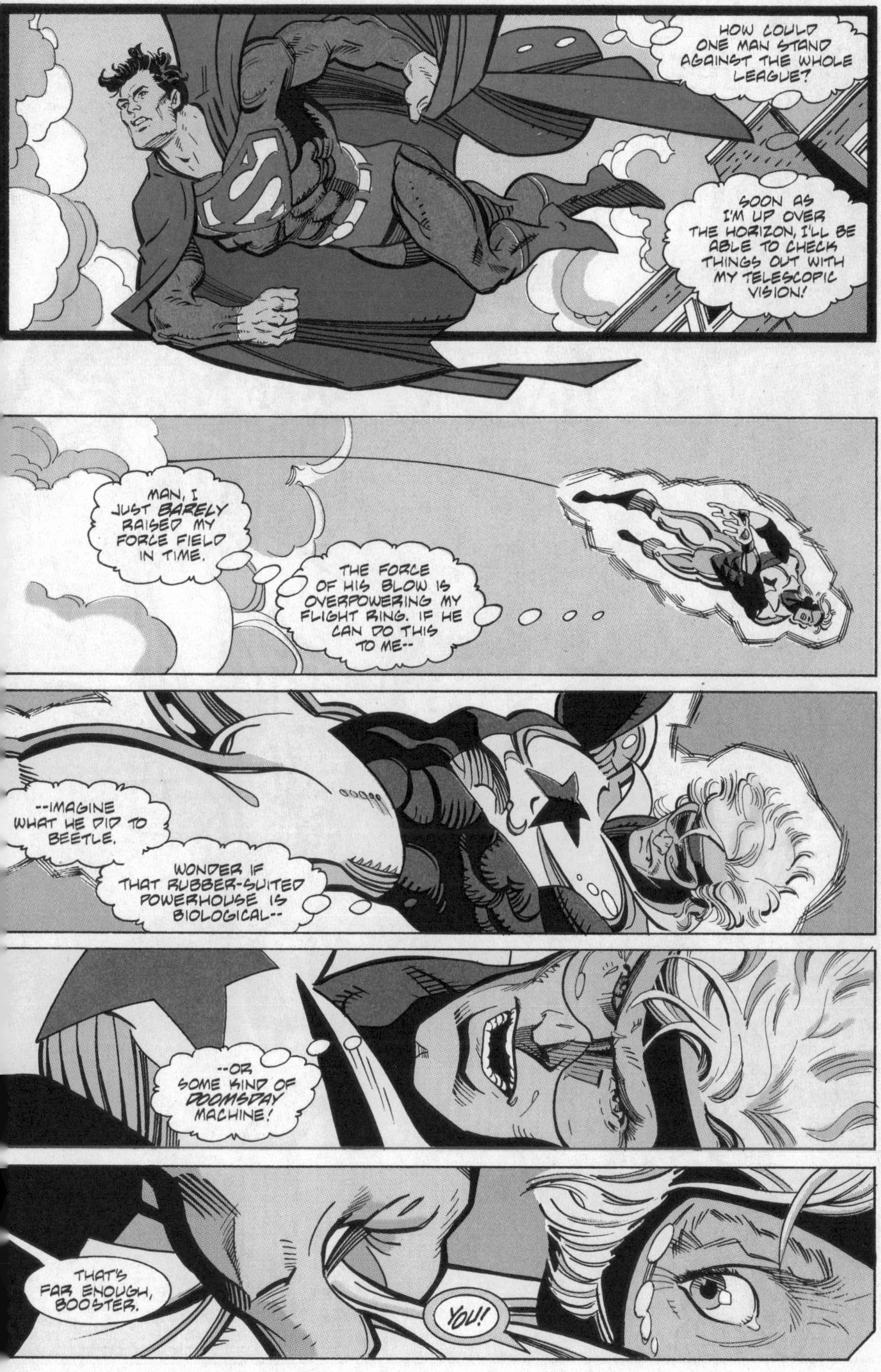
HOW COULD ONE MAN STAND AGAINST THE WHOLE LEAGUE?
SOON AS I'M UP OVER THE HORIZON, I'LL BE ABLE TO CHECK THINGS OUT WITH MY TELESCOPIC VISION!
MAN, I JUST BARELY RAISED MY FORCE FIELD IN TIME.
THE FORCE OF HIS BLOW IS OVERPOWERING MY FLIGHT RING. IF HE CAN DO THIS TO ME--
--IMAGINE WHAT HE DID TO BEETLE.
WONDER IF THAT RUBBER-SUITED POWERHOUSE IS BIOLOGICAL--
--OR SOME KIND OF DOOMSDAY MACHINE!
THAT'S FAR ENOUGH, BOOSTER.
YOU!

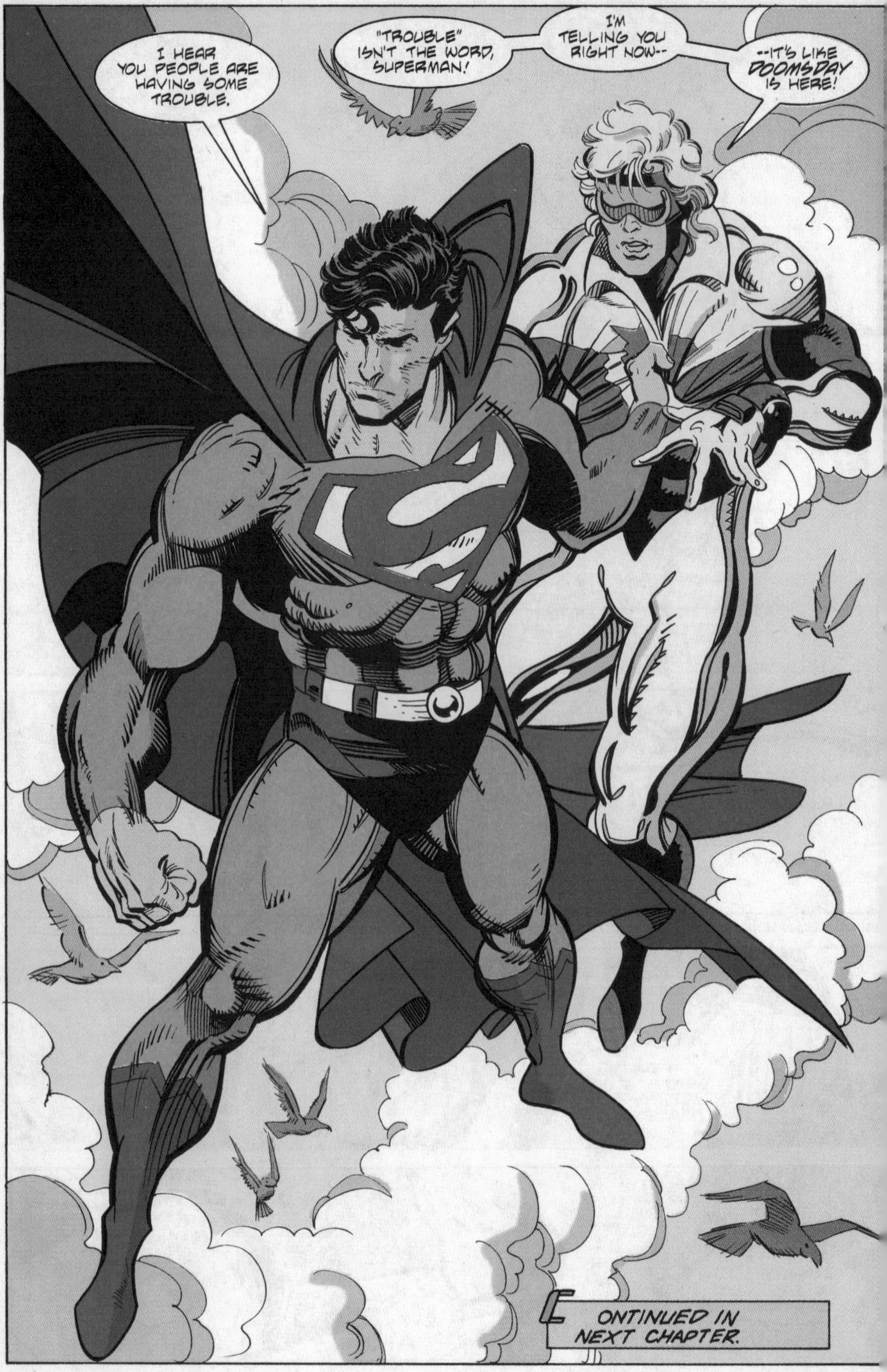

I HEAR YOU PEOPLE ARE HAVING SOME TROUBLE.
"TROUBLE" ISN'T THE WORD, SUPERMAN!
I'M TELLING YOU RIGHT NOW--
--IT'S LIKE DOOMSDAY IS HERE!
CONTINUED IN NEXT CHAPTER.

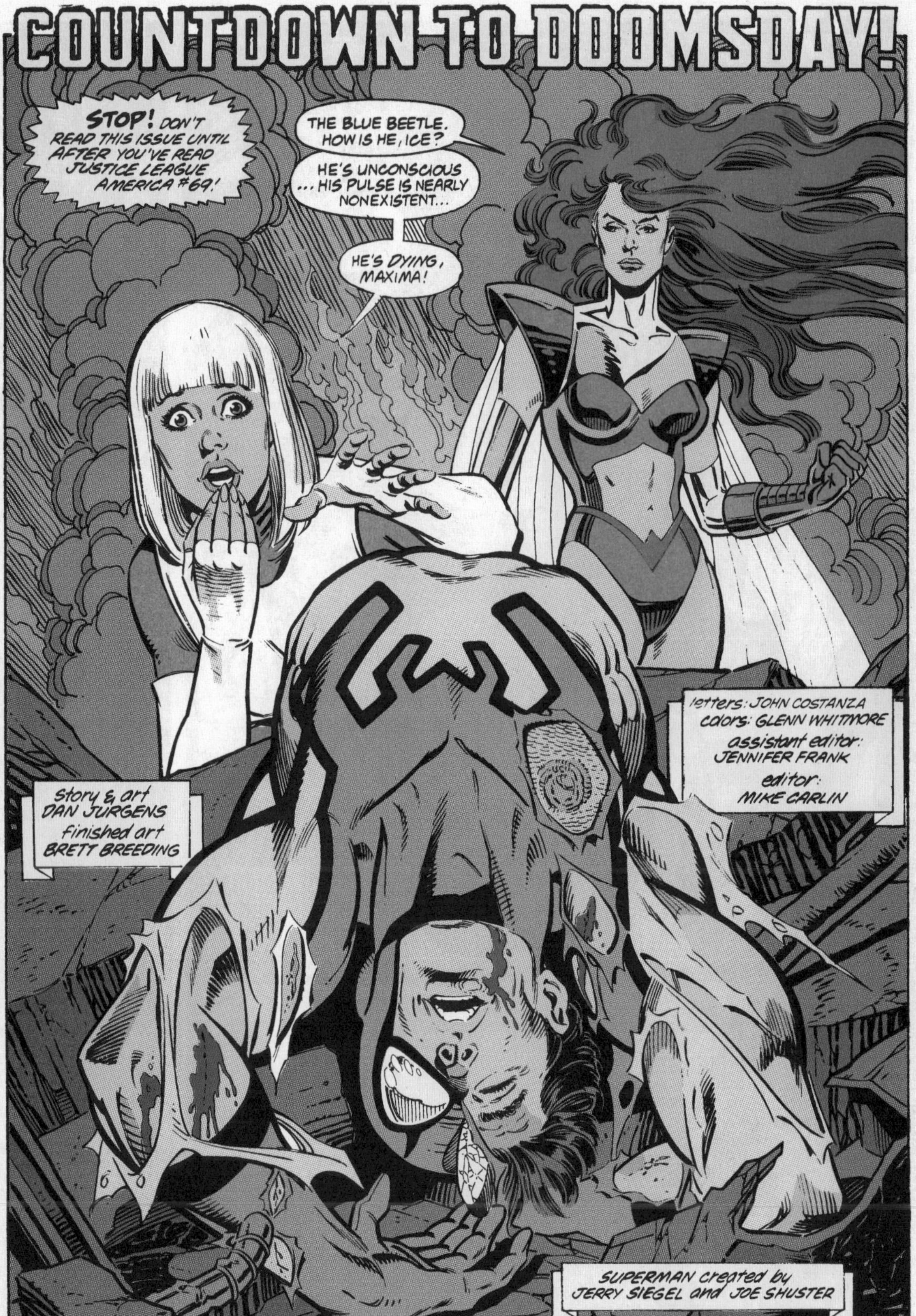

COUNTDOWN TO DOOMSDAY!
STOP! DON'T READ THIS ISSUE UNTIL AFTER YOU'VE READ JUSTICE LEAGUE AMERICA #69!
THE BLUE BEETLE. HOW IS HE, ICE?
HE'S UNCONSCIOUS ... HIS PULSE IS NEARLY NONEXISTENT...
HE'S DYING, MAXIMA!
story & art DAN JURGENS finished art BRETT BREEDING
letters: JOHN COSTANZA colors: GLENN WHITMORE assistant editor: JENNIFER FRANK editor: MIKE CARLIN
SUPERMAN created by JERRY SIEGEL and JOE SHUSTER

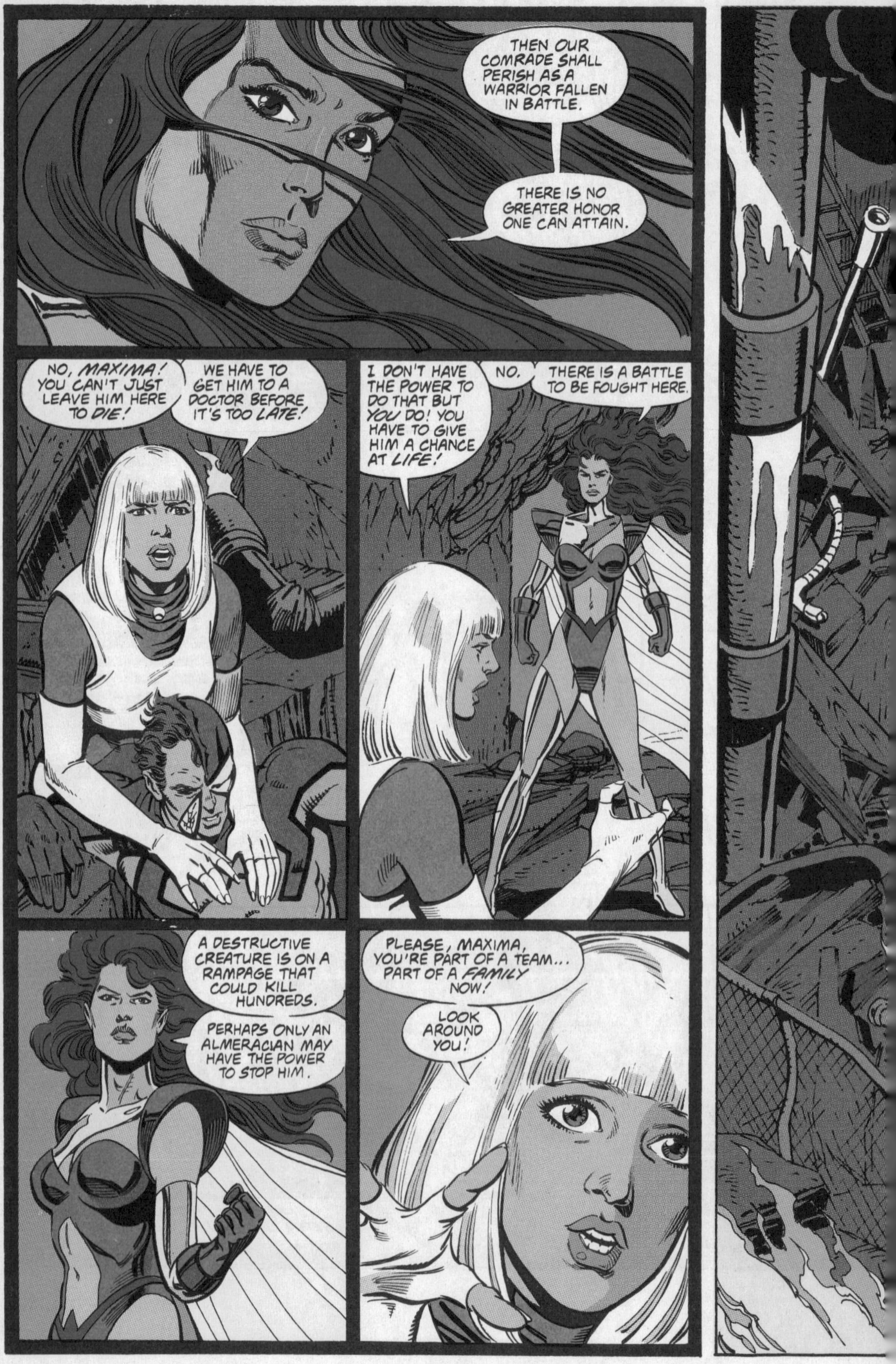
THEN OUR COMRADE SHALL PERISH AS A WARRIOR FALLEN IN BATTLE.
THERE IS NO GREATER HONOR ONE CAN ATTAIN.
NO, MAXIMA! YOU CAN'T JUST LEAVE HIM HERE TO DIE!
WE HAVE TO GET HIM TO A DOCTOR BEFORE IT'S TOO LATE!
I DON'T HAVE THE POWER TO DO THAT BUT YOU DO! YOU HAVE TO GIVE HIM A CHANCE AT LIFE!
NO.
THERE IS A BATTLE TO BE FOUGHT HERE.
A DESTRUCTIVE CREATURE IS ON A RAMPAGE THAT COULD KILL HUNDREDS.
PERHAPS ONLY AN ALMERACIAN MAY HAVE THE POWER TO STOP HIM.
PLEASE, MAXIMA, YOU'RE PART OF A TEAM... PART OF A FAMILY NOW!
LOOK AROUND YOU!

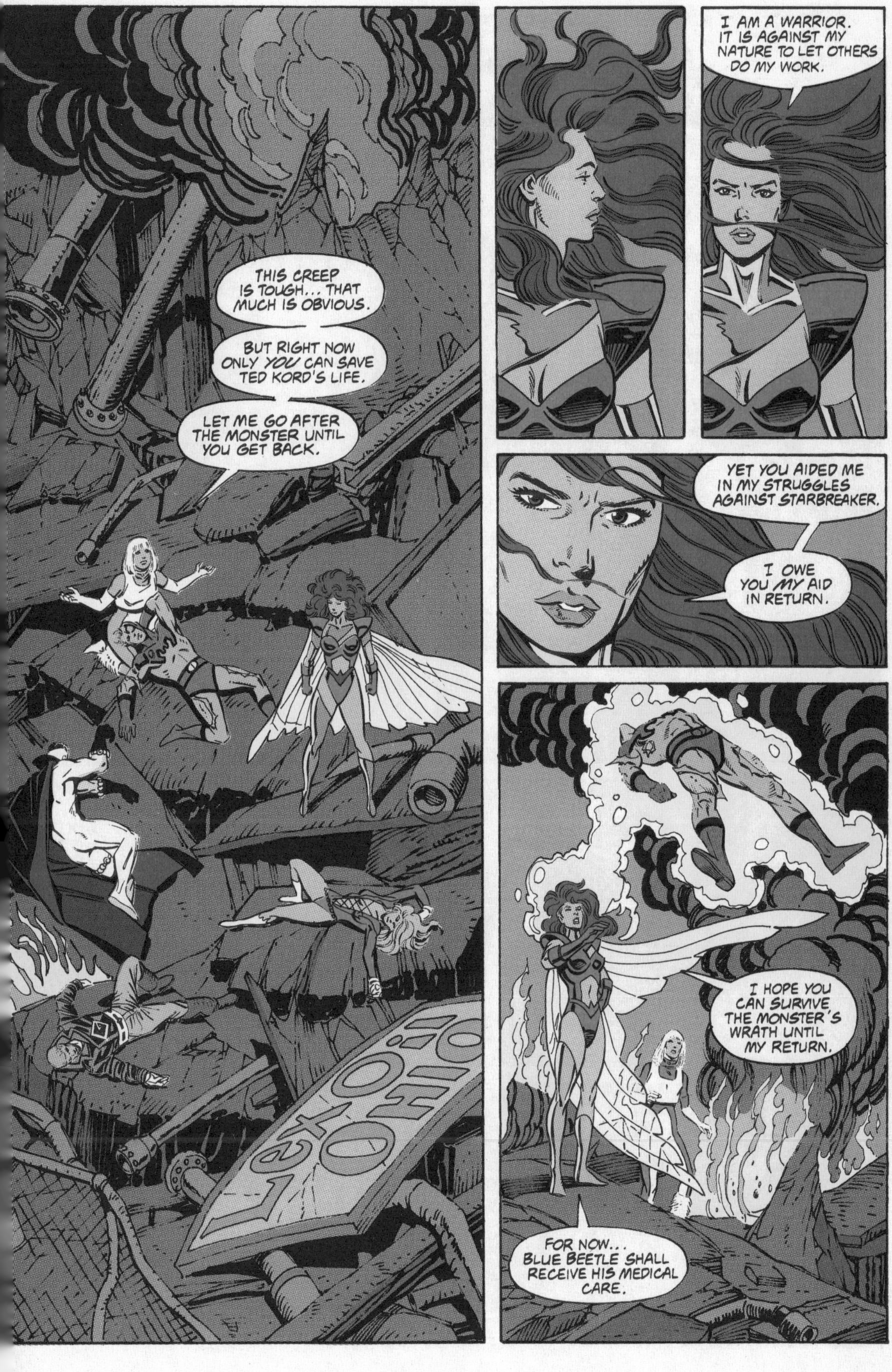
THIS CREEP IS TOUGH... THAT MUCH IS OBVIOUS.
BUT RIGHT NOW ONLY YOU CAN SAVE TED KORD'S LIFE.
LET ME GO AFTER THE MONSTER UNTIL YOU GET BACK.
I AM A WARRIOR. IT IS AGAINST MY NATURE TO LET OTHERS DO MY WORK.
YET YOU AIDED ME IN MY STRUGGLES AGAINST STARBREAKER.
I OWE YOU MY AID IN RETURN.
I HOPE YOU CAN SURVIVE THE MONSTER'S WRATH UNTIL MY RETURN.
FOR NOW... BLUE BEETLE SHALL RECEIVE HIS MEDICAL CARE.

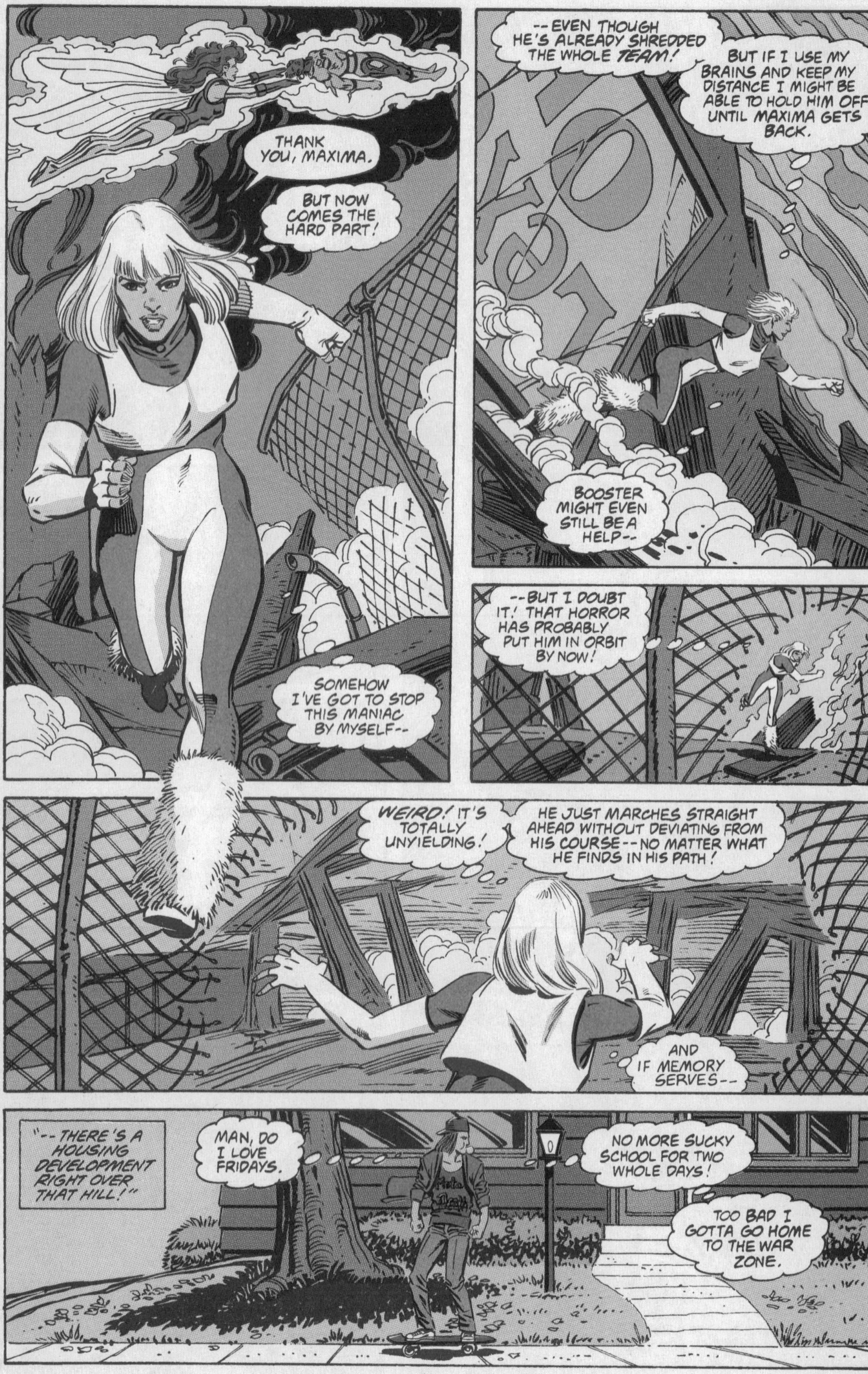

THANK YOU, MAXIMA.
BUT NOW COMES THE HARD PART!
SOMEHOW I'VE GOT TO STOP THIS MANIAC BY MYSELF--
--EVEN THOUGH HE'S ALREADY SHREDDED THE WHOLE TEAM!
BUT IF I USE MY BRAINS AND KEEP MY DISTANCE I MIGHT BE ABLE TO HOLD HIM OFF UNTIL MAXIMA GETS BACK.
BOOSTER MIGHT EVEN STILL BE A HELP--
--BUT I DOUBT IT! THAT HORROR HAS PROBABLY PUT HIM IN ORBIT BY NOW!
WEIRD! IT'S TOTALLY UNYIELDING!
HE JUST MARCHES STRAIGHT AHEAD WITHOUT DEVIATING FROM HIS COURSE--NO MATTER WHAT HE FINDS IN HIS PATH!
AND IF MEMORY SERVES--
"--THERE'S A HOUSING DEVELOPMENT RIGHT OVER THAT HILL!"
MAN, DO I LOVE FRIDAYS.
NO MORE SUCKY SCHOOL FOR TWO WHOLE DAYS!
TOO BAD I GOTTA GO HOME TO THE WAR ZONE.

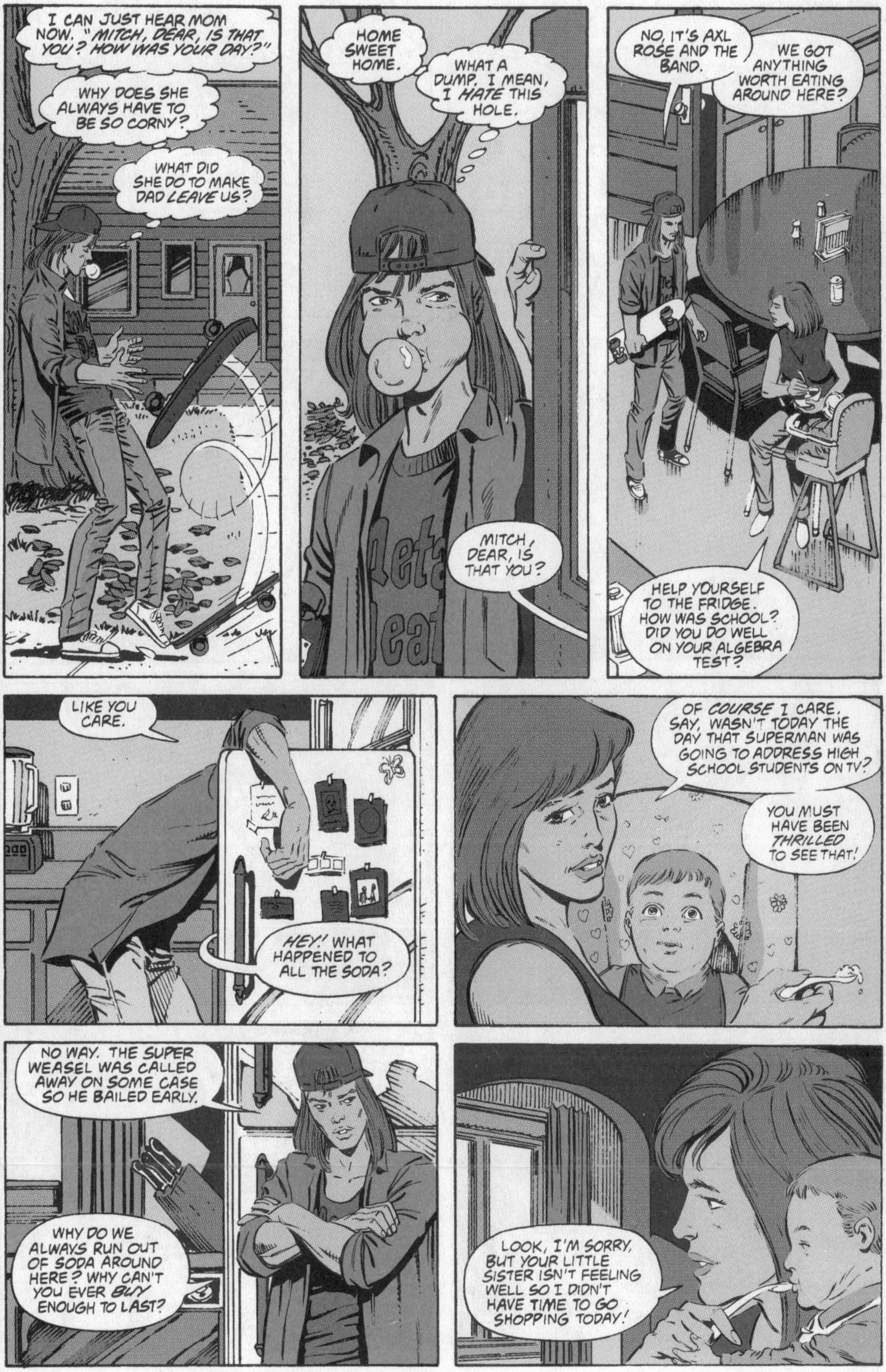
I CAN JUST HEAR MOM NOW. "MITCH, DEAR, IS THAT YOU? HOW WAS YOUR DAY?"
WHY DOES SHE ALWAYS HAVE TO BE SO CORNY?
WHAT DID SHE DO TO MAKE DAD LEAVE US?
HOME SWEET HOME.
WHAT A DUMP. I MEAN, I HATE THIS HOLE.
MITCH, DEAR, IS THAT YOU?
NO, IT'S AXL ROSE AND THE BAND.
WE GOT ANYTHING WORTH EATING AROUND HERE?
HELP YOURSELF TO THE FRIDGE. HOW WAS SCHOOL? DID YOU DO WELL ON YOUR ALGEBRA TEST?
LIKE YOU CARE.
HEY! WHAT HAPPENED TO ALL THE SODA?
OF COURSE I CARE. SAY, WASN'T TODAY THE DAY THAT SUPERMAN WAS GOING TO ADDRESS HIGH SCHOOL STUDENTS ON TV?
YOU MUST HAVE BEEN THRILLED TO SEE THAT!
NO WAY. THE SUPER WEASEL WAS CALLED AWAY ON SOME CASE SO HE BAILED EARLY.
WHY DO WE ALWAYS RUN OUT OF SODA AROUND HERE? WHY CAN'T YOU EVER BUY ENOUGH TO LAST?
LOOK, I'M SORRY, BUT YOUR LITTLE SISTER ISN'T FEELING WELL SO I DIDN'T HAVE TIME TO GO SHOPPING TODAY!

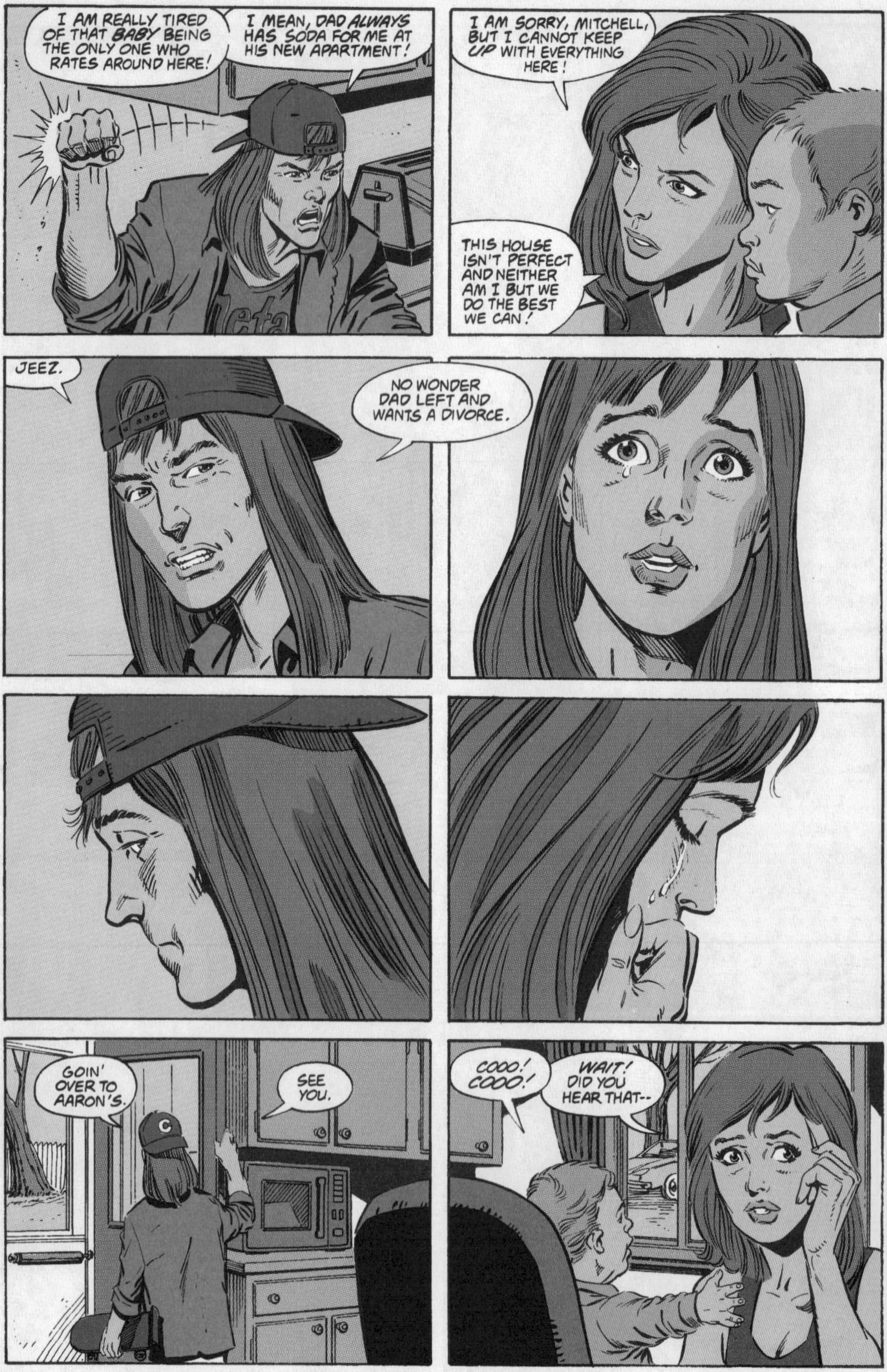
I AM REALLY TIRED OF THAT BABY BEING THE ONLY ONE WHO RATES AROUND HERE!
I MEAN, DAD ALWAYS HAS SODA FOR ME AT HIS NEW APARTMENT!
I AM SORRY, MITCHELL, BUT I CANNOT KEEP UP WITH EVERYTHING HERE!
THIS HOUSE ISN'T PERFECT AND NEITHER AM I BUT WE DO THE BEST WE CAN!
JEEZ.
NO WONDER DAD LEFT AND WANTS A DIVORCE.
GOIN' OVER TO AARON'S.
SEE YOU.
COOO! COOO!
WAIT! DID YOU HEAR THAT--

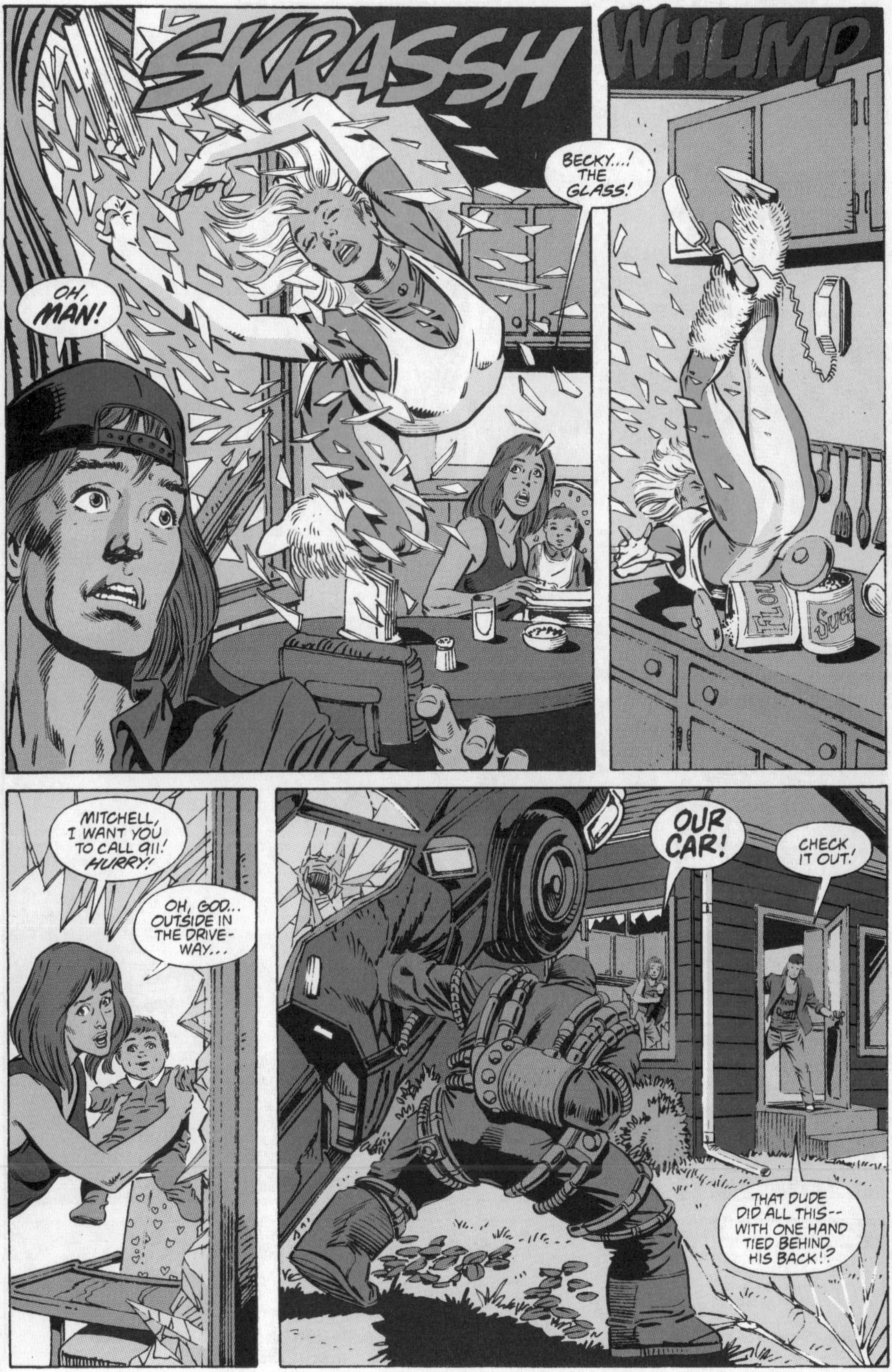

SKRASSH
OH, MAN!
BECKY...! THE GLASS!
WHUMP
FLOUR
SUGA
MITCHELL, I WANT YOU TO CALL 911! HURRY!
OH, GOD... OUTSIDE IN THE DRIVE-WAY...
OUR CAR!
CHECK IT OUT!
THAT DUDE DID ALL THIS-- WITH ONE HAND TIED BEHIND HIS BACK!?

58

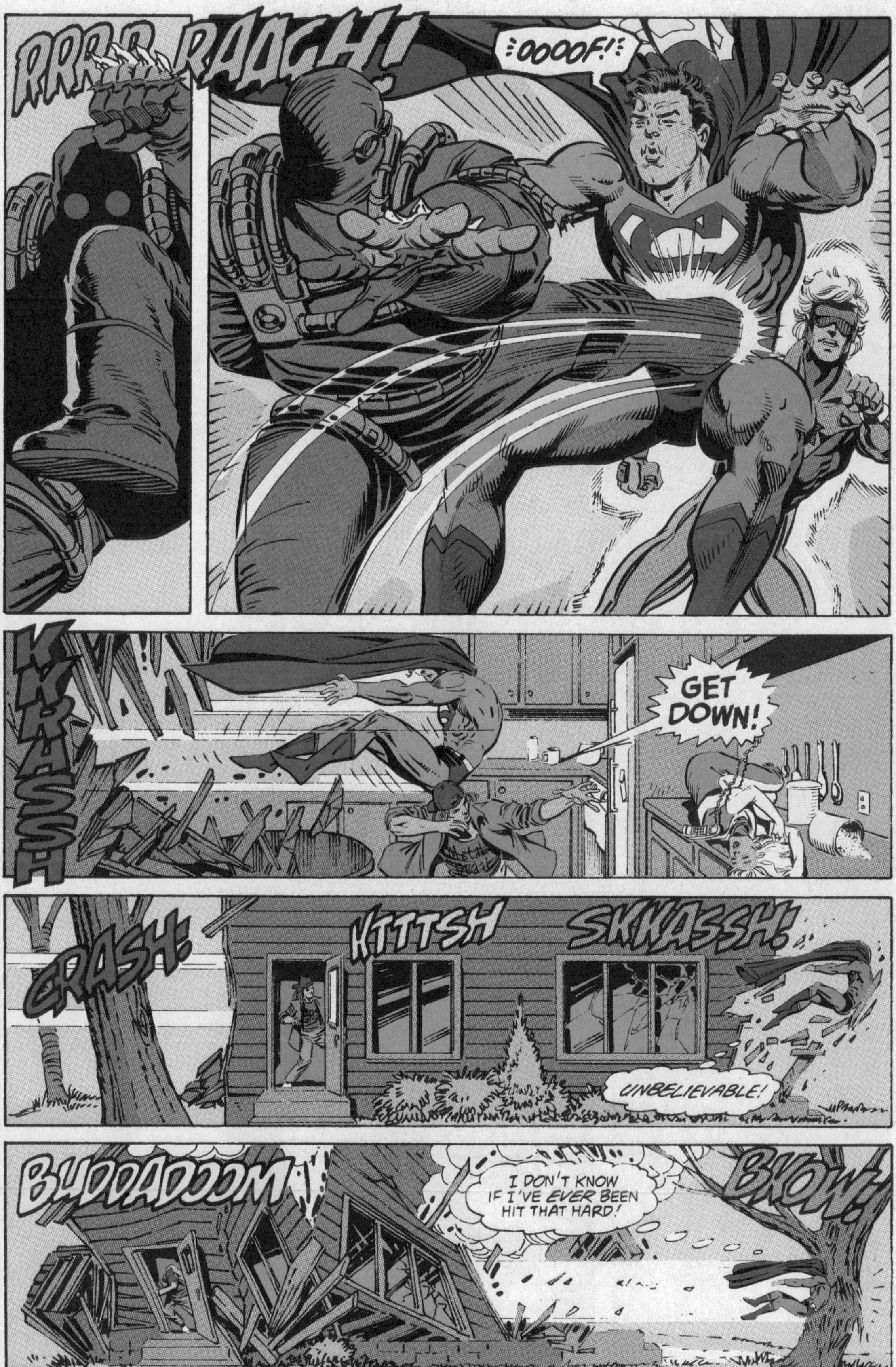
RRRR RAACH!
OOOOF!
KKRASSH
GET DOWN!
CRASH!
KTTTSH
SKWASSH!
UNBELIEVABLE!
BUDDADOOM
BKOW!
I DON'T KNOW IF I'VE EVER BEEN HIT THAT HARD!

HURRF!

:UHN!:

KRAKK!

NOO...

WH--WHERE'S THE REST OF THE LEAGUE?

BRAKODOM!

MA!

WHY?

WHY ARE YOU DOING THIS TO OUR HOUSE? WHAT DO YOU WANT FROM US?

HMF...

HA!

KRUNCH!

NO! NOT MY BABY!

PLEASE, NOT MY BABY!

61

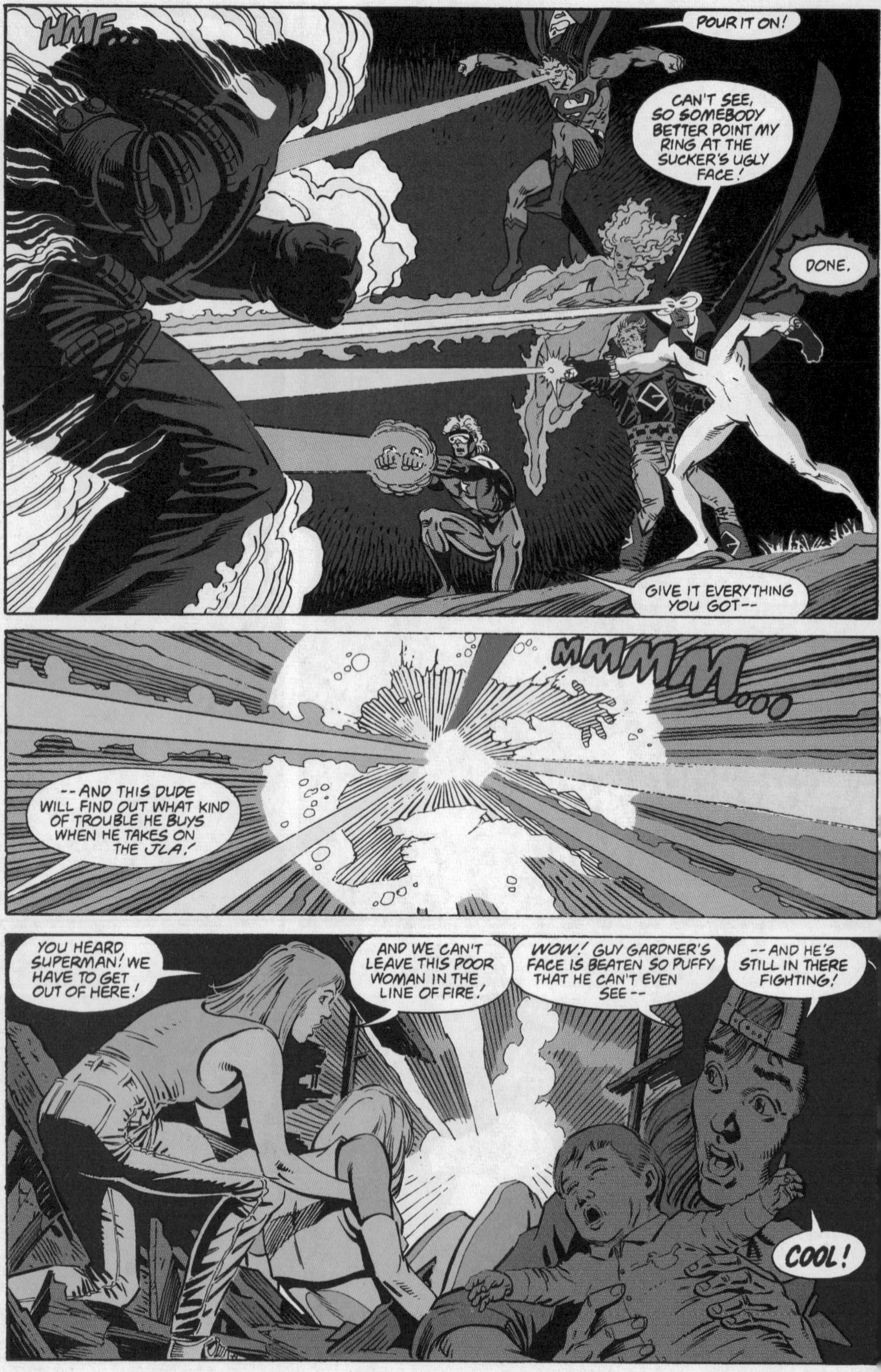

HMF...
POUR IT ON!
CAN'T SEE, SO SOMEBODY BETTER POINT MY RING AT THE SUCKER'S UGLY FACE!
DONE.
GIVE IT EVERYTHING YOU GOT--
MMMMM...
--AND THIS DUDE WILL FIND OUT WHAT KIND OF TROUBLE HE BUYS WHEN HE TAKES ON THE JLA!
YOU HEARD SUPERMAN! WE HAVE TO GET OUT OF HERE!
AND WE CAN'T LEAVE THIS POOR WOMAN IN THE LINE OF FIRE!
WOW! GUY GARDNER'S FACE IS BEATEN SO PUFFY THAT HE CAN'T EVEN SEE--
--AND HE'S STILL IN THERE FIGHTING!
COOL!

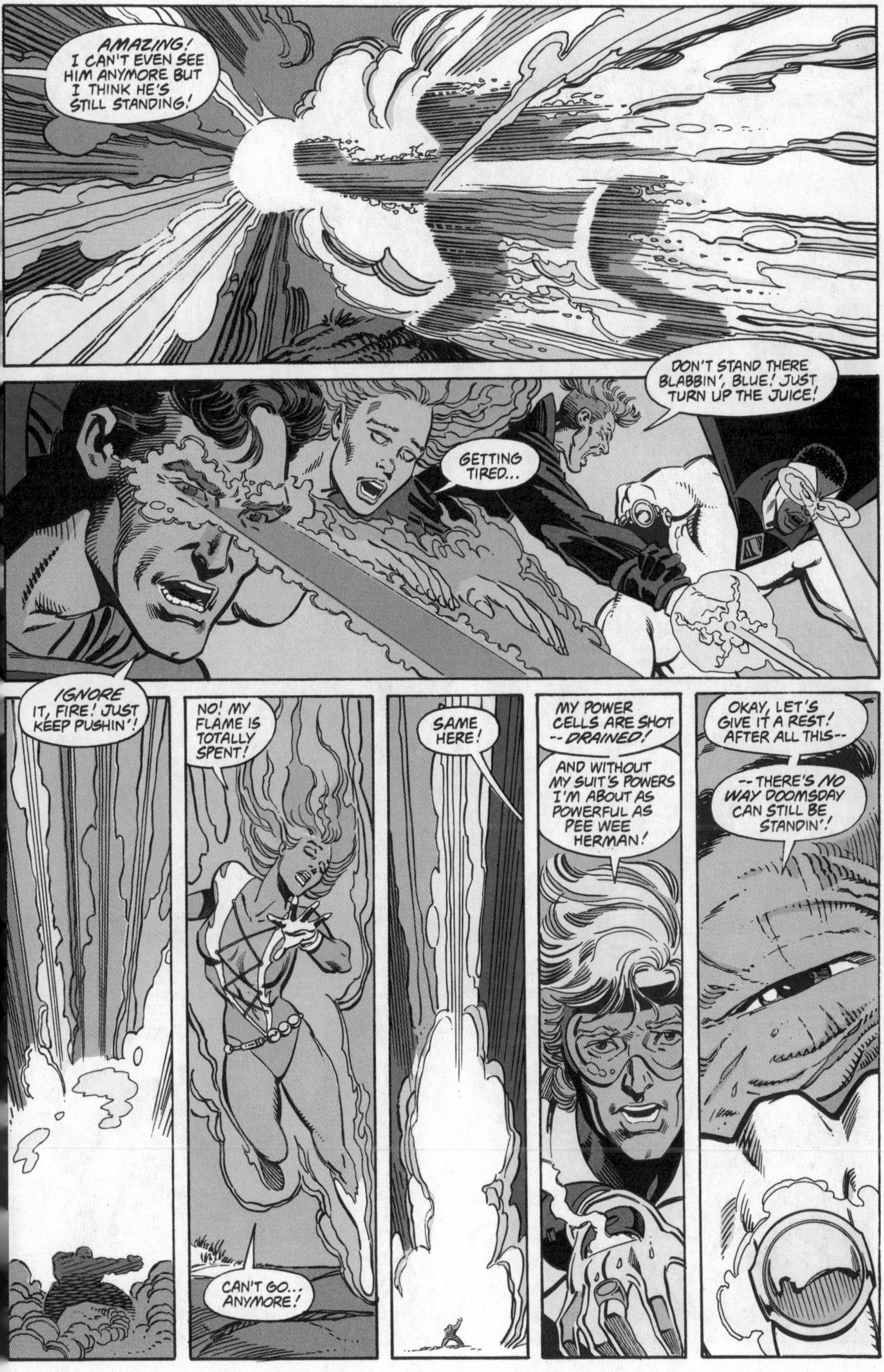
AMAZING! I CAN'T EVEN SEE HIM ANYMORE BUT I THINK HE'S STILL STANDING!
DON'T STAND THERE BLABBIN', BLUE! JUST TURN UP THE JUICE!
GETTING TIRED...
IGNORE IT, FIRE! JUST KEEP PUSHIN'!
NO! MY FLAME IS TOTALLY SPENT!
CAN'T GO... ANYMORE!
SAME HERE!
MY POWER CELLS ARE SHOT --DRAINED!
AND WITHOUT MY SUIT'S POWERS I'M ABOUT AS POWERFUL AS PEE WEE HERMAN!
OKAY, LET'S GIVE IT A REST! AFTER ALL THIS--
--THERE'S NO WAY DOOMSDAY CAN STILL BE STANDIN'!

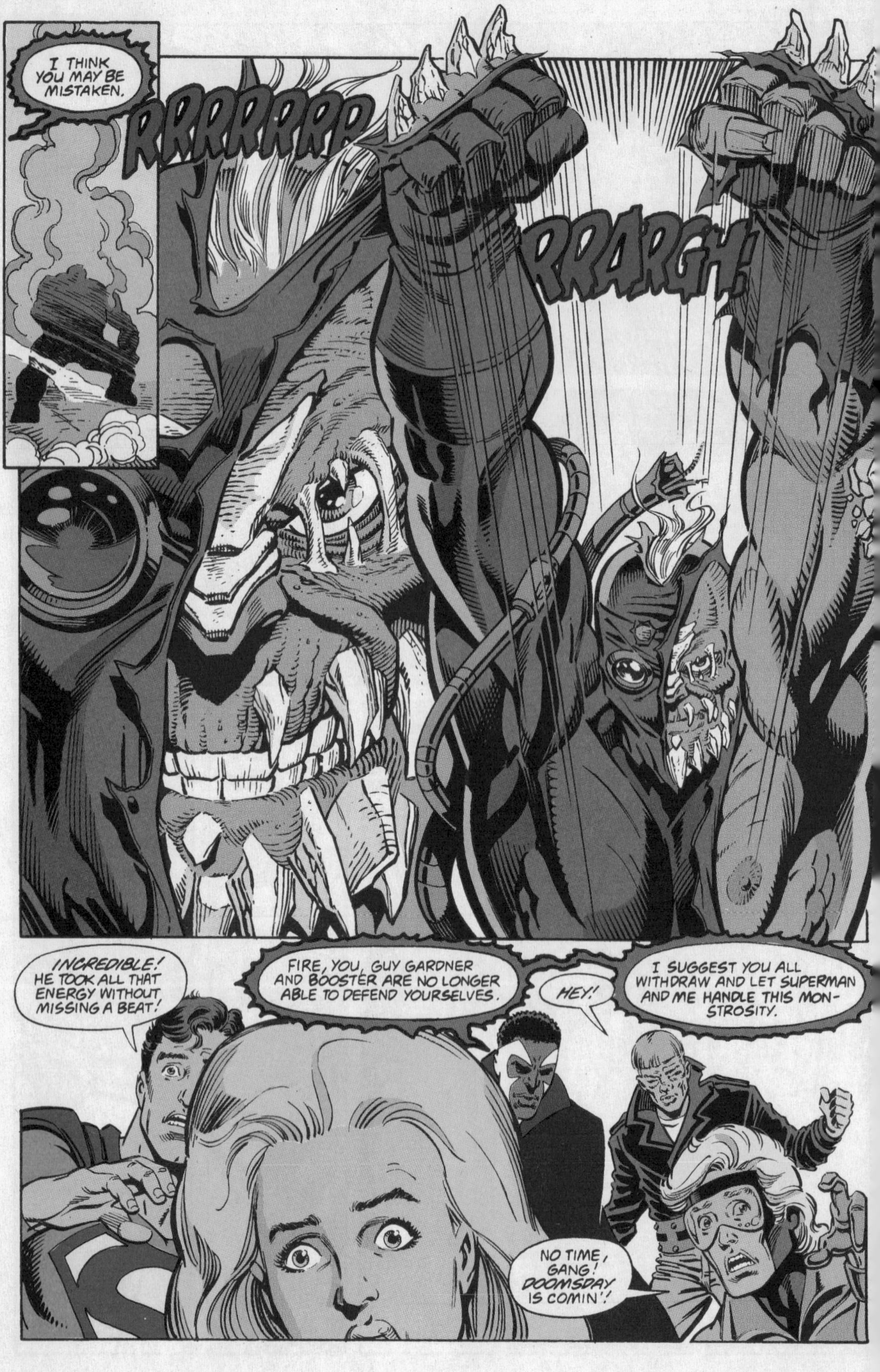

I THINK YOU MAY BE MISTAKEN.
RRRRRRRR
RRARGH!
INCREDIBLE! HE TOOK ALL THAT ENERGY WITHOUT MISSING A BEAT!
FIRE, YOU, GUY GARDNER AND BOOSTER ARE NO LONGER ABLE TO DEFEND YOURSELVES.
HEY!
I SUGGEST YOU ALL WITHDRAW AND LET SUPERMAN AND ME HANDLE THIS MONSTROSITY.
NO TIME, GANG! DOOMSDAY IS COMIN'!

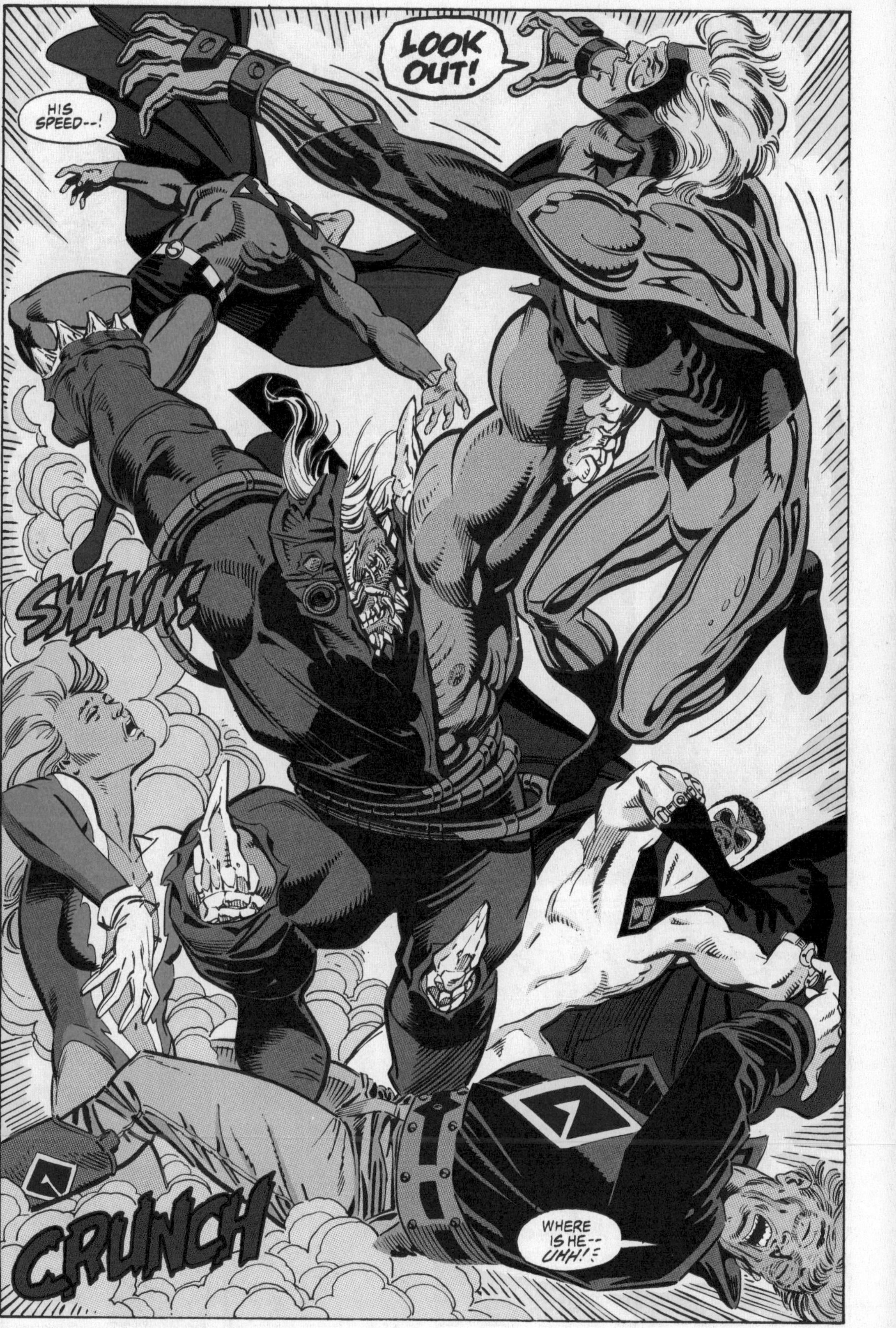
HIS SPEED--!
LOOK OUT!
SWAKK!
WHERE IS HE-- UHH!
CRUNCH

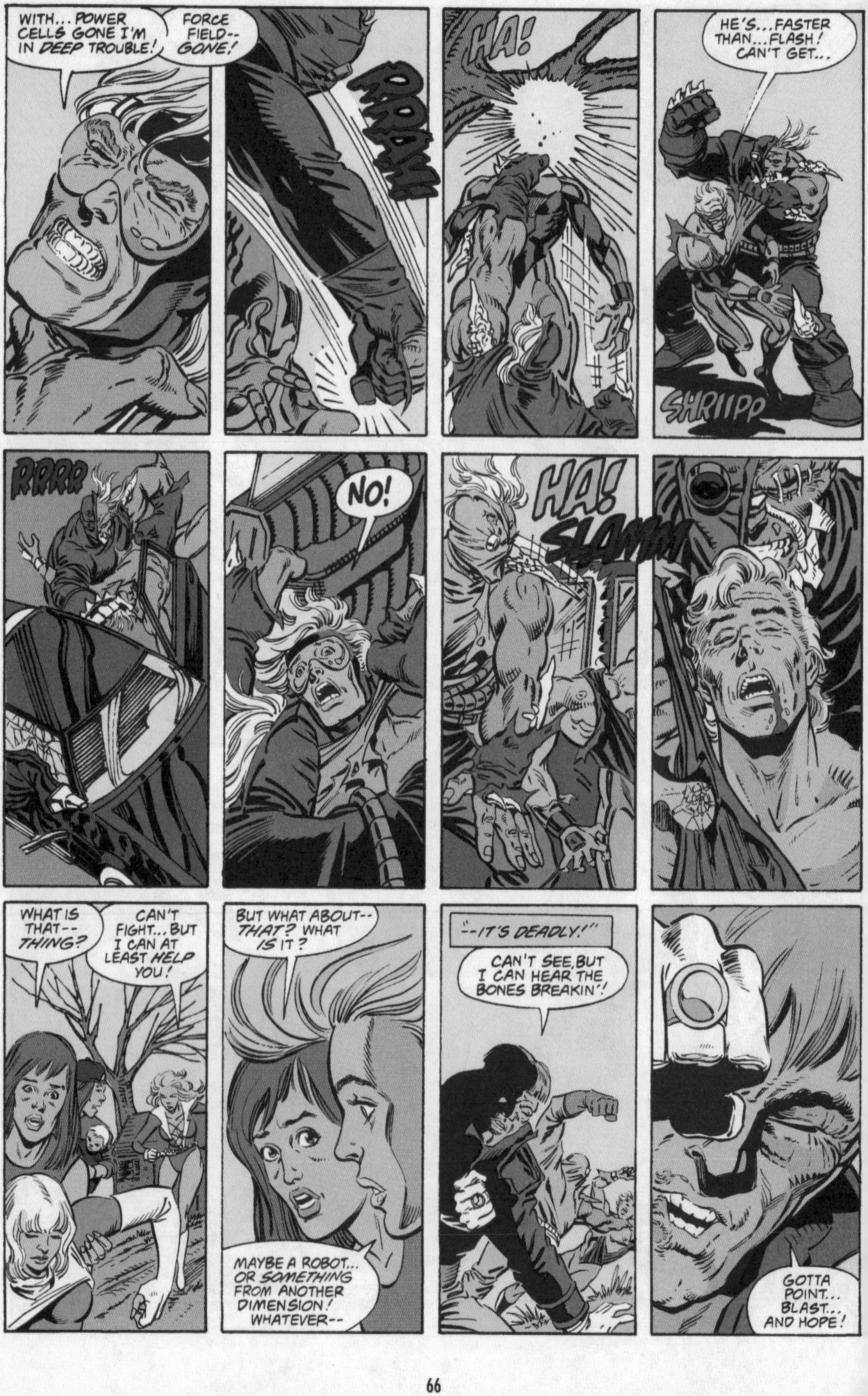

WITH... POWER CELLS GONE I'M IN DEEP TROUBLE!
FORCE FIELD-- GONE!
RRRAW
HA!
HE'S... FASTER THAN... FLASH! CAN'T GET...
SHRIIPP
RRRR
NO!
HA!
SLAMM
WHAT IS THAT-- THING?
CAN'T FIGHT... BUT I CAN AT LEAST HELP YOU!
BUT WHAT ABOUT-- THAT? WHAT IS IT?
MAYBE A ROBOT... OR SOMETHING FROM ANOTHER DIMENSION! WHATEVER--
"--IT'S DEADLY!"
CAN'T SEE, BUT I CAN HEAR THE BONES BREAKIN'!
GOTTA POINT... BLAST... AND HOPE!

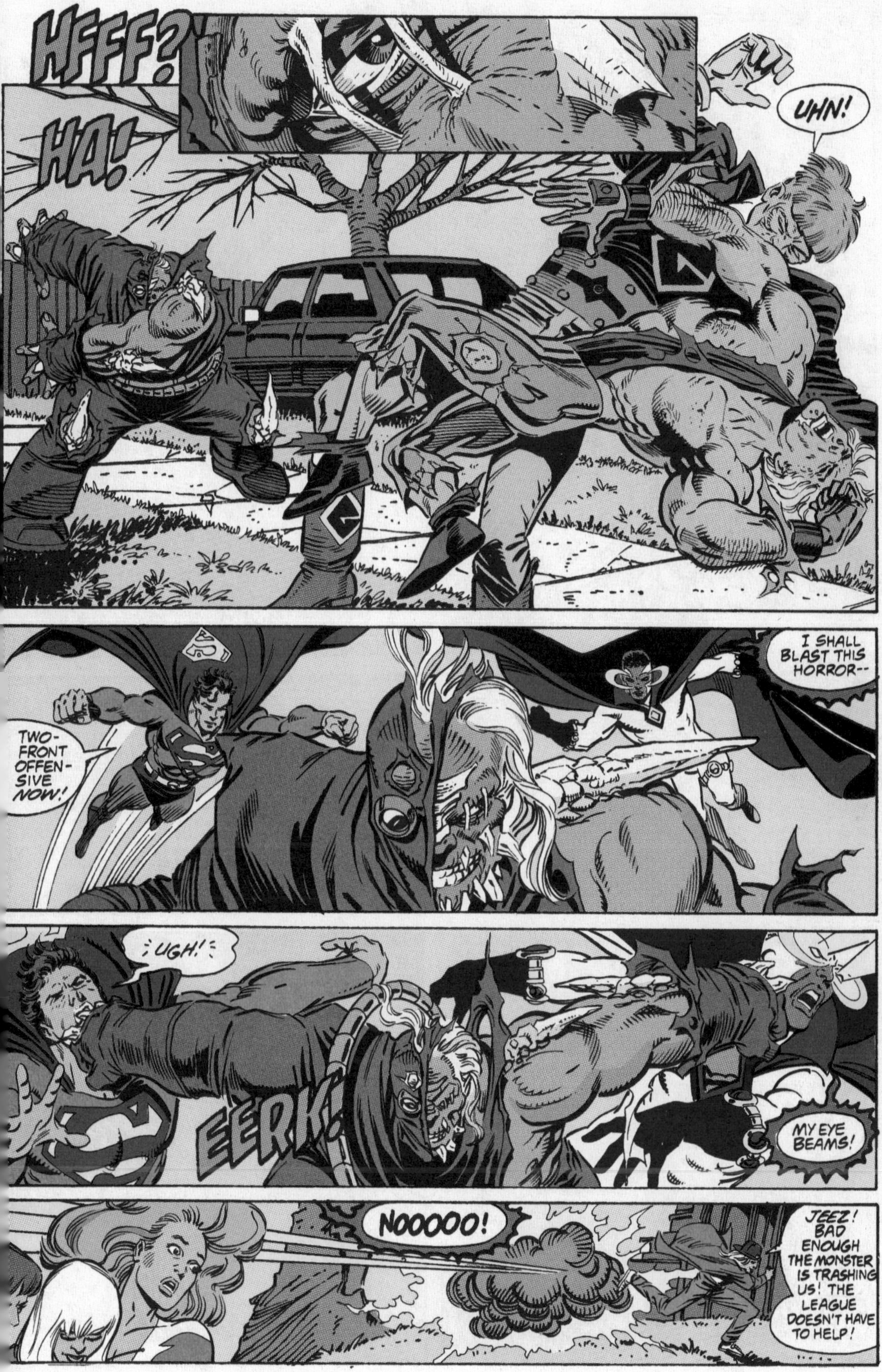
HFFF?
HA!
UHN!
TWO-FRONT OFFEN-SIVE NOW!
I SHALL BLAST THIS HORROR--
UGH!
EERK!
MY EYE BEAMS!
NOOOOO!
JEEZ! BAD ENOUGH THE MONSTER IS TRASHING US! THE LEAGUE DOESN'T HAVE TO HELP!

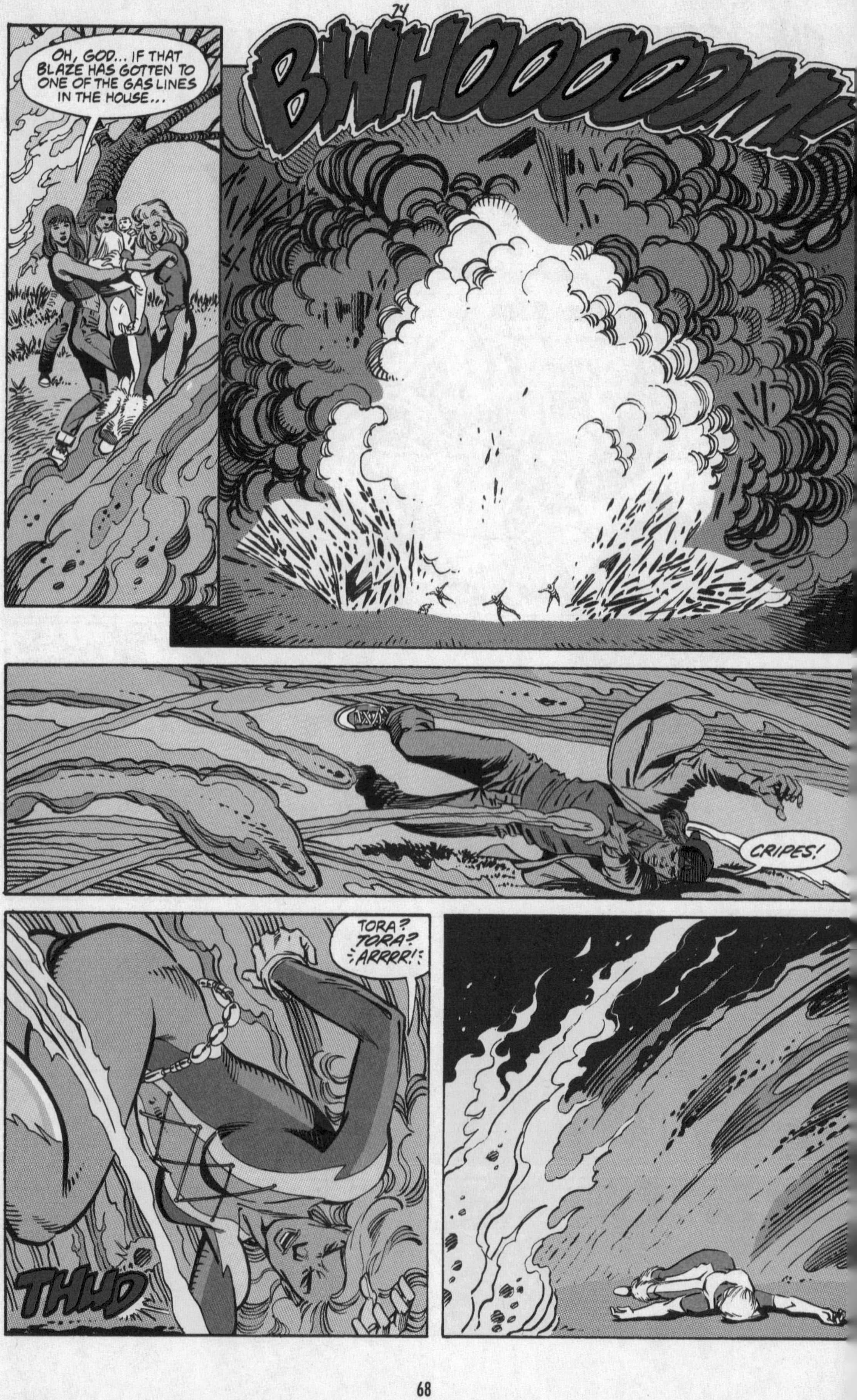
24
OH, GOD... IF THAT BLAZE HAS GOTTEN TO ONE OF THE GAS LINES IN THE HOUSE...
BWHOOOOOM!
CRIPES!
TORA? TORA? ARRRR!
THUD

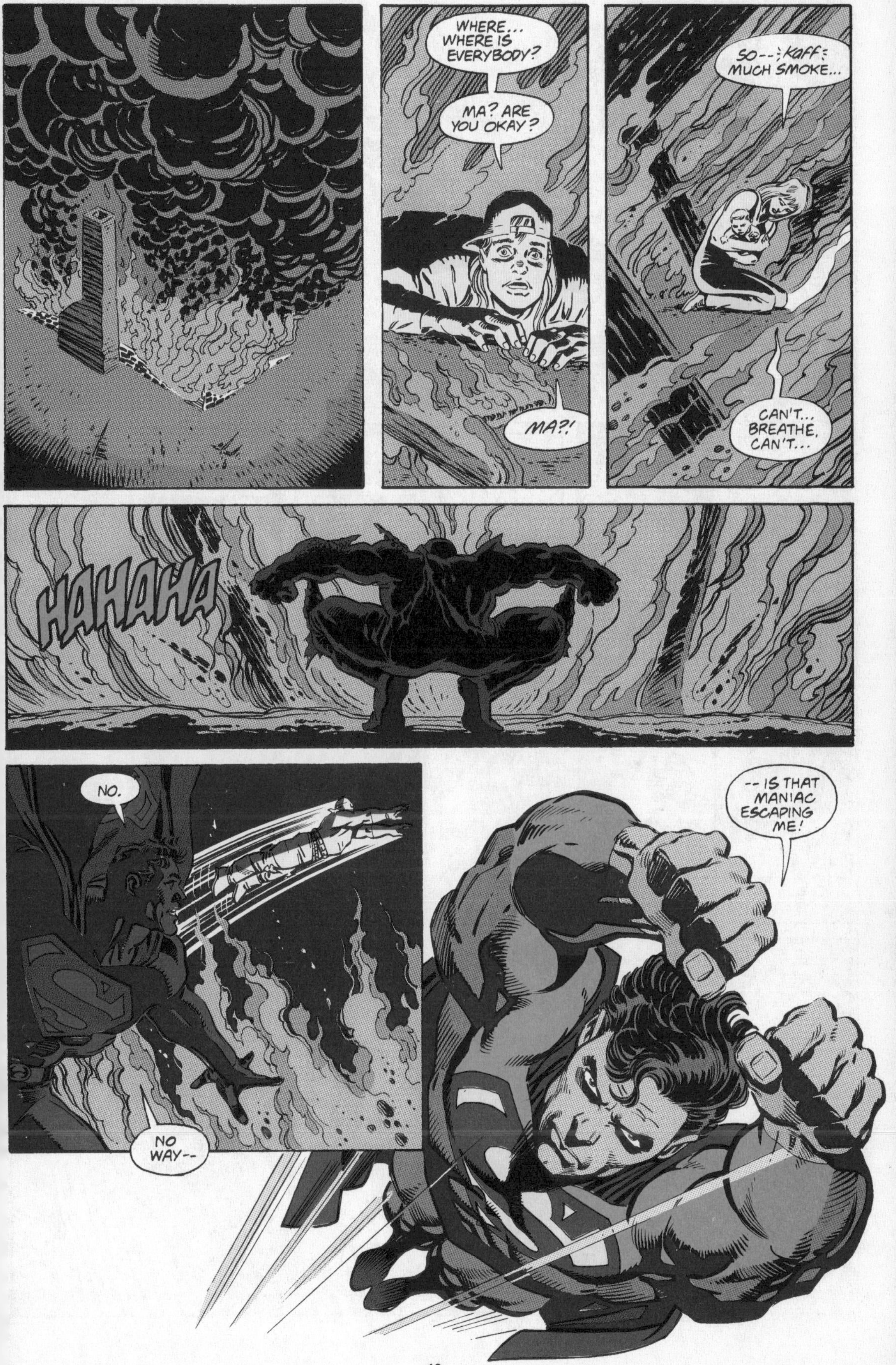
WHERE... WHERE IS EVERYBODY?
MA? ARE YOU OKAY?
MA?!
SO--kaff MUCH SMOKE...
CAN'T... BREATHE, CAN'T...
HAHAHA
NO.
NO WAY--
--IS THAT MANIAC ESCAPING ME!

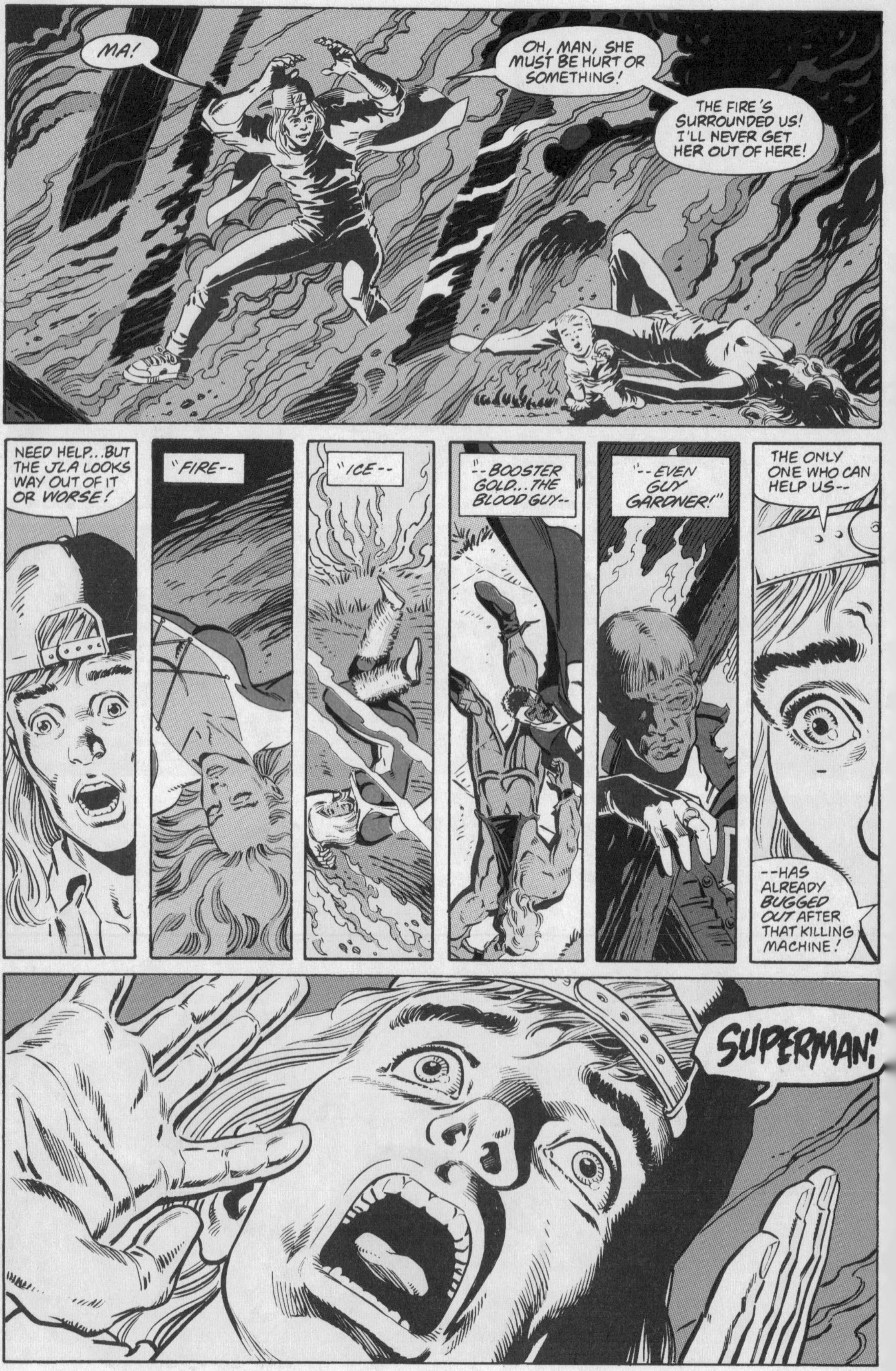
MA!
OH, MAN, SHE MUST BE HURT OR SOMETHING!
THE FIRE'S SURROUNDED US! I'LL NEVER GET HER OUT OF HERE!
NEED HELP...BUT THE JLA LOOKS WAY OUT OF IT OR WORSE!
"FIRE--
"ICE--
"--BOOSTER GOLD...THE BLOOD GUY--
"--EVEN GUY GARDNER!"
THE ONLY ONE WHO CAN HELP US--
--HAS ALREADY BUGGED OUT AFTER THAT KILLING MACHINE!
SUPERMAN!

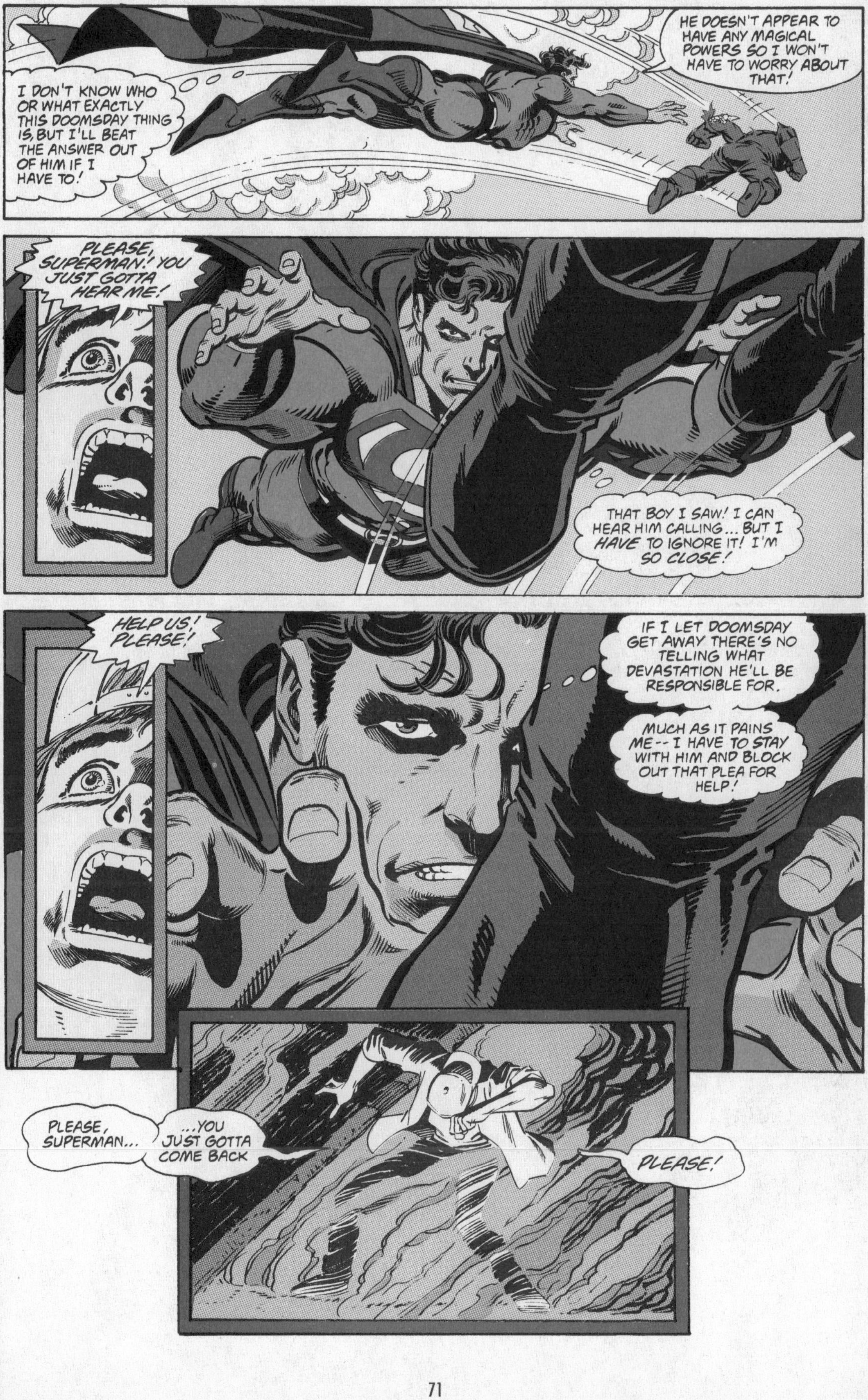
I DON'T KNOW WHO OR WHAT EXACTLY THIS DOOMSDAY THING IS, BUT I'LL BEAT THE ANSWER OUT OF HIM IF I HAVE TO!
HE DOESN'T APPEAR TO HAVE ANY MAGICAL POWERS SO I WON'T HAVE TO WORRY ABOUT THAT!
PLEASE, SUPERMAN! YOU JUST GOTTA HEAR ME!
THAT BOY I SAW! I CAN HEAR HIM CALLING... BUT I HAVE TO IGNORE IT! I'M SO CLOSE!
HELP US! PLEASE!
IF I LET DOOMSDAY GET AWAY THERE'S NO TELLING WHAT DEVASTATION HE'LL BE RESPONSIBLE FOR.
MUCH AS IT PAINS ME -- I HAVE TO STAY WITH HIM AND BLOCK OUT THAT PLEA FOR HELP!
PLEASE, SUPERMAN...
...YOU JUST GOTTA COME BACK
PLEASE!

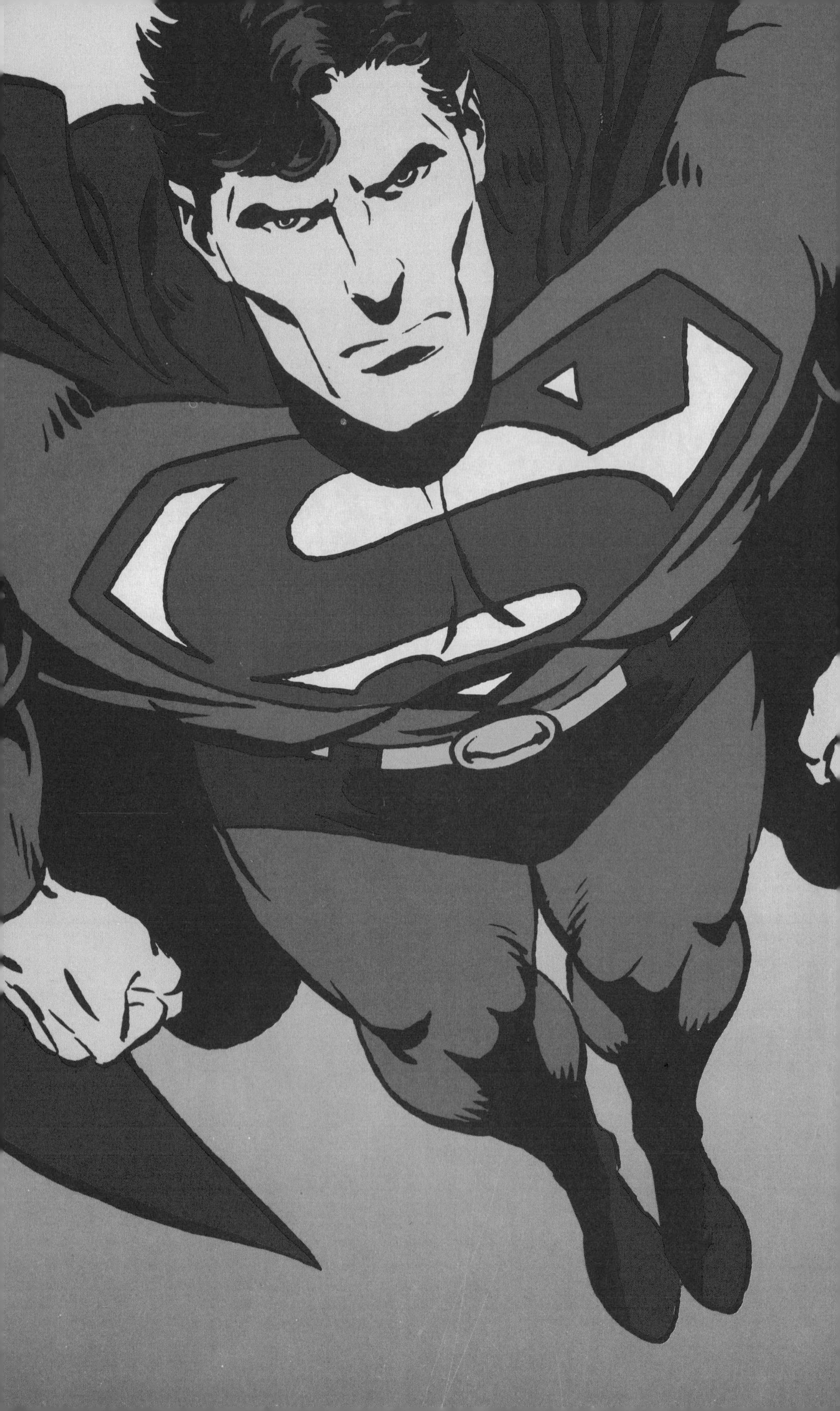

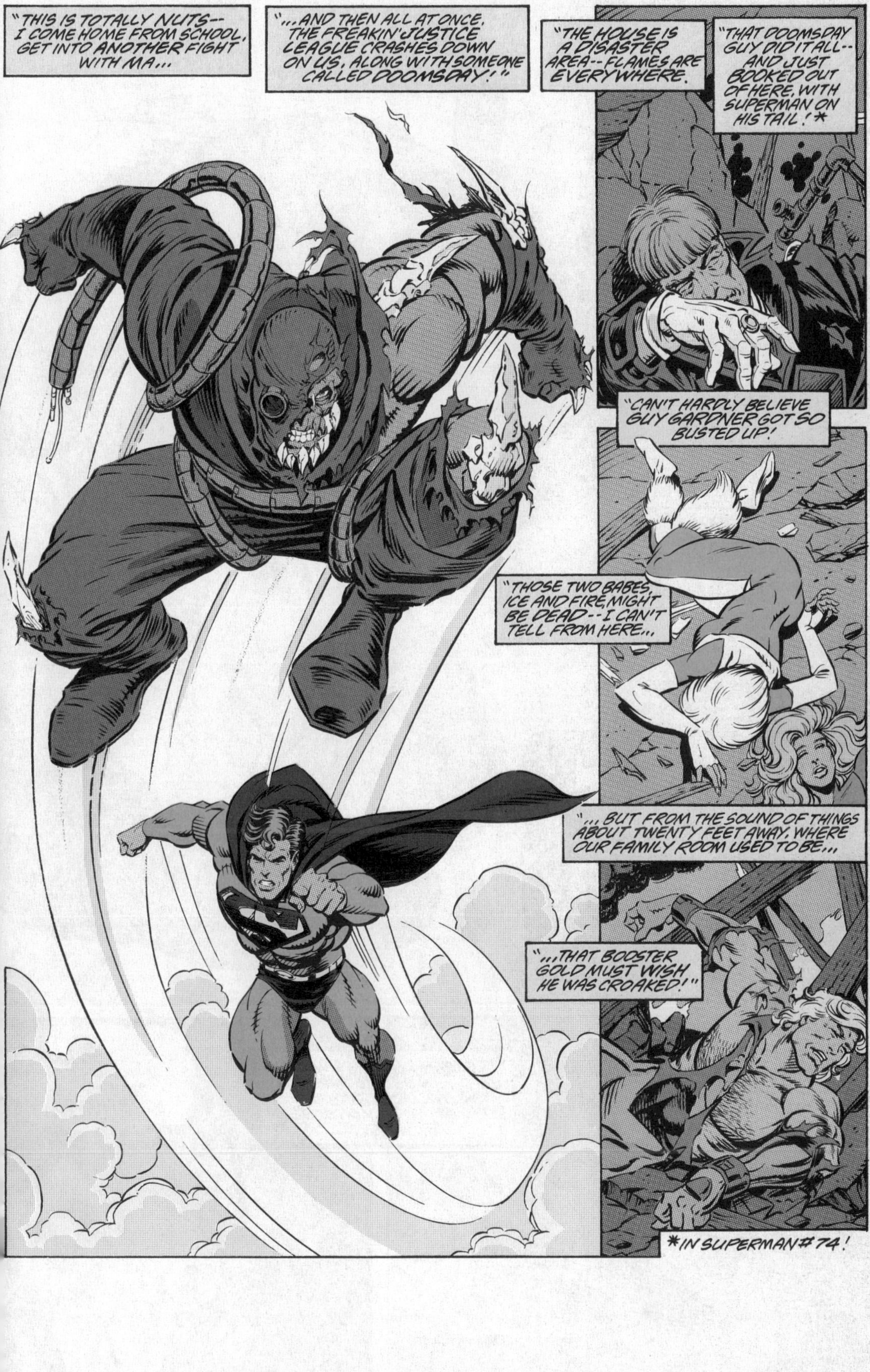
"THIS IS TOTALLY NUTS-- I COME HOME FROM SCHOOL, GET INTO ANOTHER FIGHT WITH MA...
"...AND THEN ALL AT ONCE, THE FREAKIN' JUSTICE LEAGUE CRASHES DOWN ON US, ALONG WITH SOMEONE CALLED DOOMSDAY!"
"THE HOUSE IS A DISASTER AREA-- FLAMES ARE EVERYWHERE.
"THAT DOOMSDAY GUY DID IT ALL-- AND JUST BOOKED OUT OF HERE, WITH SUPERMAN ON HIS TAIL! *
"CAN'T HARDLY BELIEVE GUY GARDNER GOT SO BUSTED UP!
"THOSE TWO BABES, ICE AND FIRE, MIGHT BE DEAD-- I CAN'T TELL FROM HERE...
"... BUT FROM THE SOUND OF THINGS ABOUT TWENTY FEET AWAY, WHERE OUR FAMILY ROOM USED TO BE...
"...THAT BOOSTER GOLD MUST WISH HE WAS CROAKED!"
*IN SUPERMAN #74!

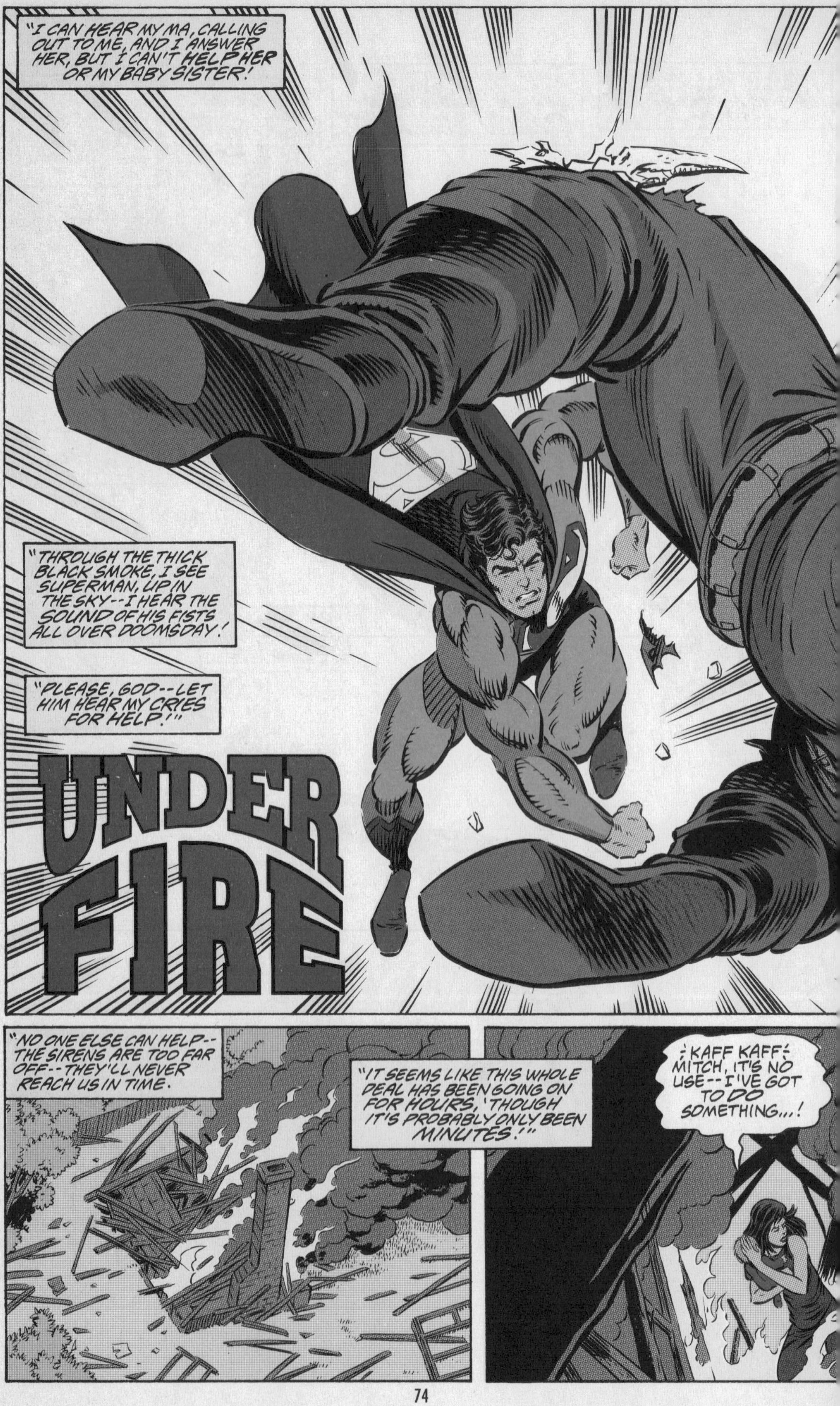
"I CAN HEAR MY MA, CALLING OUT TO ME, AND I ANSWER HER, BUT I CAN'T HELP HER OR MY BABY SISTER!
"THROUGH THE THICK BLACK SMOKE, I SEE SUPERMAN, UP IN THE SKY--I HEAR THE SOUND OF HIS FISTS ALL OVER DOOMSDAY!
"PLEASE, GOD--LET HIM HEAR MY CRIES FOR HELP!"
UNDER FIRE
"NO ONE ELSE CAN HELP--THE SIRENS ARE TOO FAR OFF--THEY'LL NEVER REACH US IN TIME.
"IT SEEMS LIKE THIS WHOLE DEAL HAS BEEN GOING ON FOR HOURS, 'THOUGH IT'S PROBABLY ONLY BEEN MINUTES!"
:KAFF KAFF: MITCH, IT'S NO USE--I'VE GOT TO DO SOMETHING...!

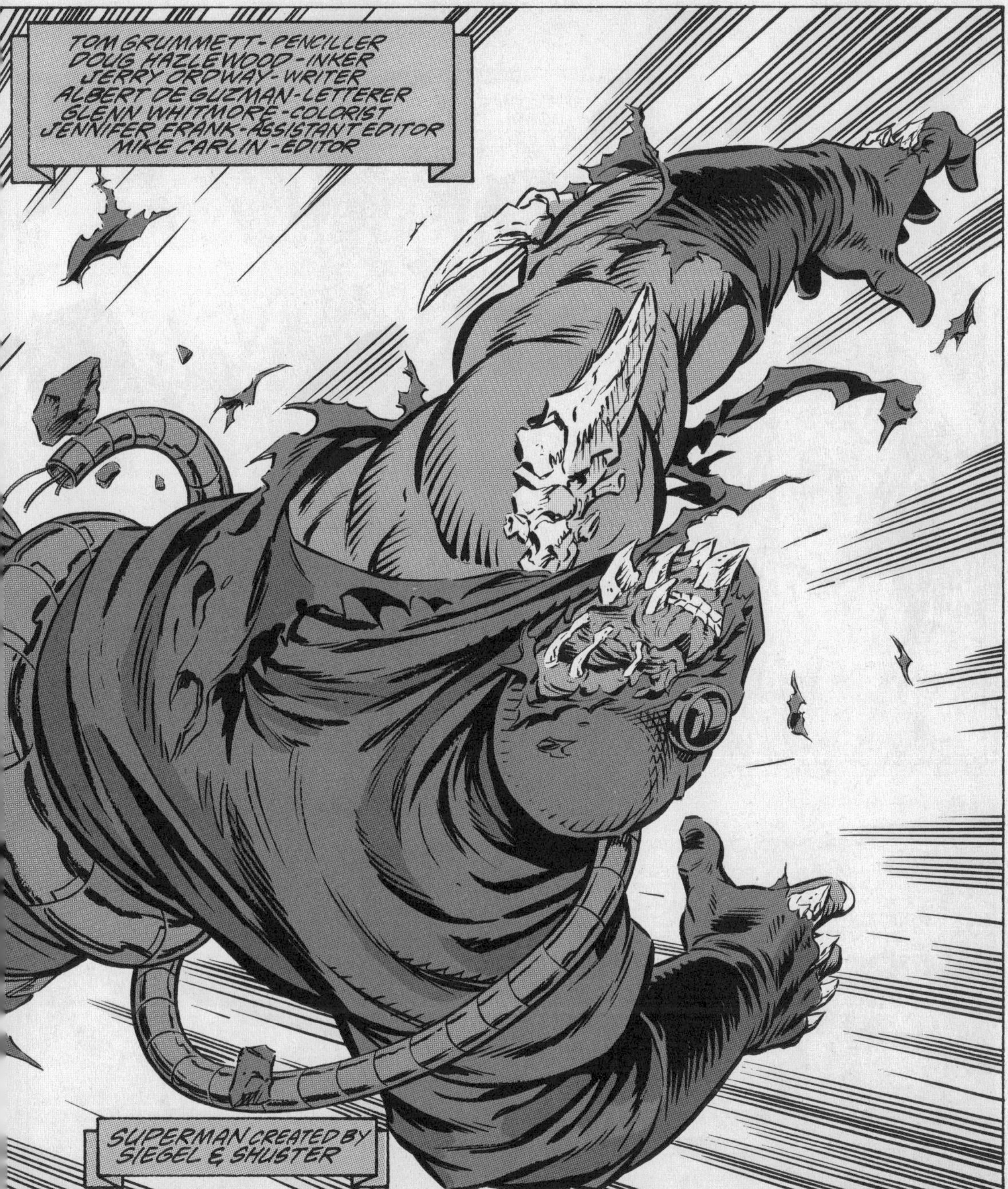
TOM GRUMMETT-PENCILLER
DOUG HAZLEWOOD-INKER
JERRY ORDWAY-WRITER
ALBERT DE GUZMAN-LETTERER
GLENN WHITMORE-COLORIST
JENNIFER FRANK-ASSISTANT EDITOR
MIKE CARLIN-EDITOR
SUPERMAN CREATED BY SIEGEL & SHUSTER

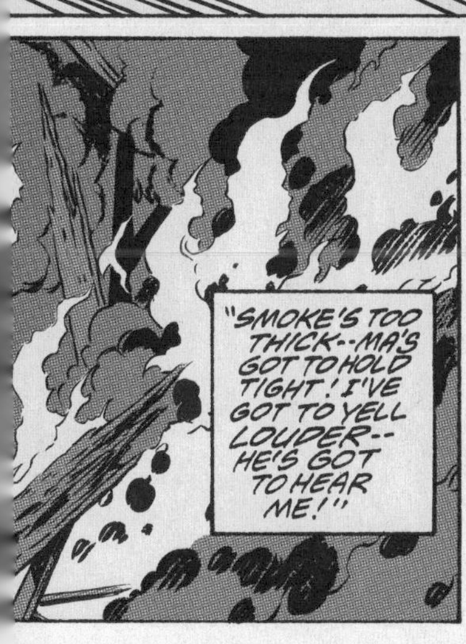
"SMOKE'S TOO THICK--MA'S GOT TO HOLD TIGHT! I'VE GOT TO YELL LOUDER--HE'S GOT TO HEAR ME!"

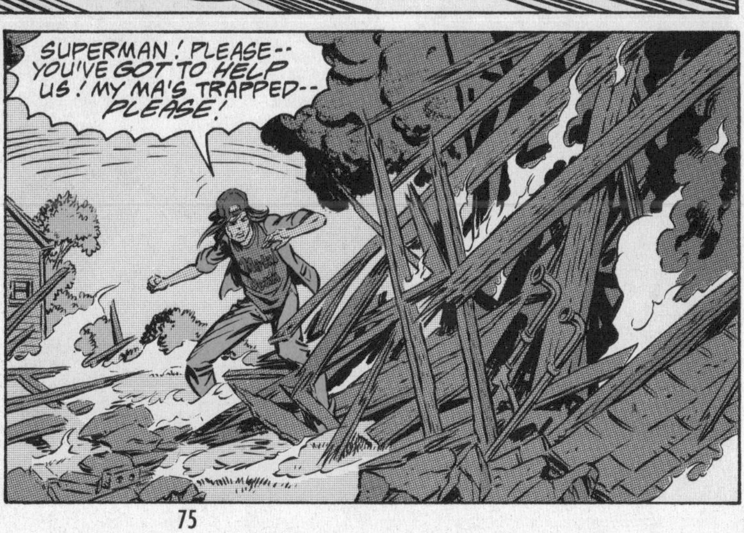
SUPERMAN! PLEASE--YOU'VE GOT TO HELP US! MY MA'S TRAPPED--PLEASE!

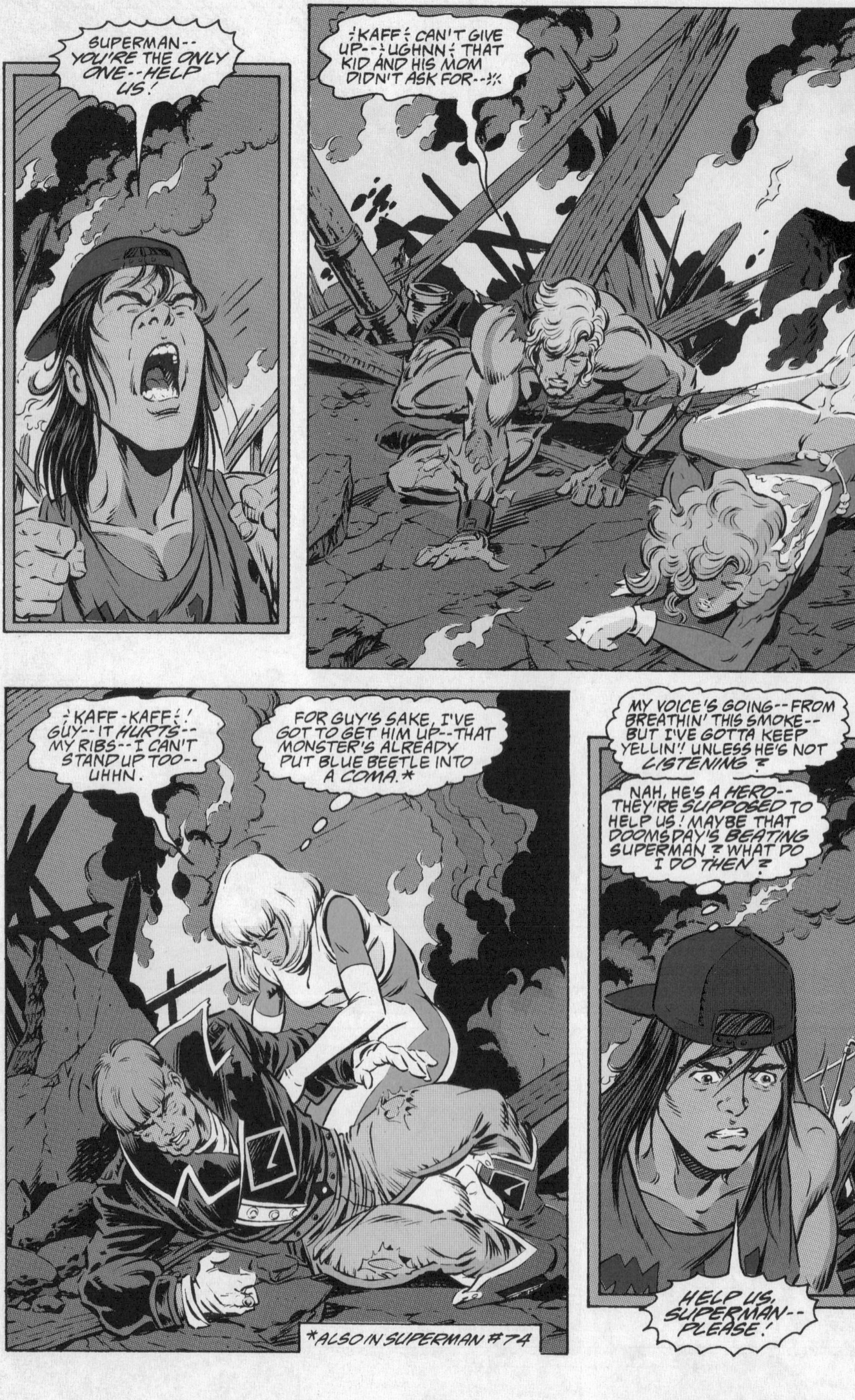
SUPERMAN-- YOU'RE THE ONLY ONE--HELP US!
KAFF CAN'T GIVE UP-- UGHNN THAT KID AND HIS MOM DIDN'T ASK FOR--
KAFF-KAFF! GUY--IT HURTS-- MY RIBS--I CAN'T STAND UP TOO-- UHHN.
FOR GUY'S SAKE, I'VE GOT TO GET HIM UP--THAT MONSTER'S ALREADY PUT BLUE BEETLE INTO A COMA.*
MY VOICE'S GOING--FROM BREATHIN' THIS SMOKE-- BUT I'VE GOTTA KEEP YELLIN'! UNLESS HE'S NOT LISTENING?
NAH, HE'S A HERO-- THEY'RE SUPPOSED TO HELP US! MAYBE THAT DOOMSDAY'S BEATING SUPERMAN? WHAT DO I DO THEN?
HELP US, SUPERMAN-- PLEASE!
*ALSO IN SUPERMAN #74

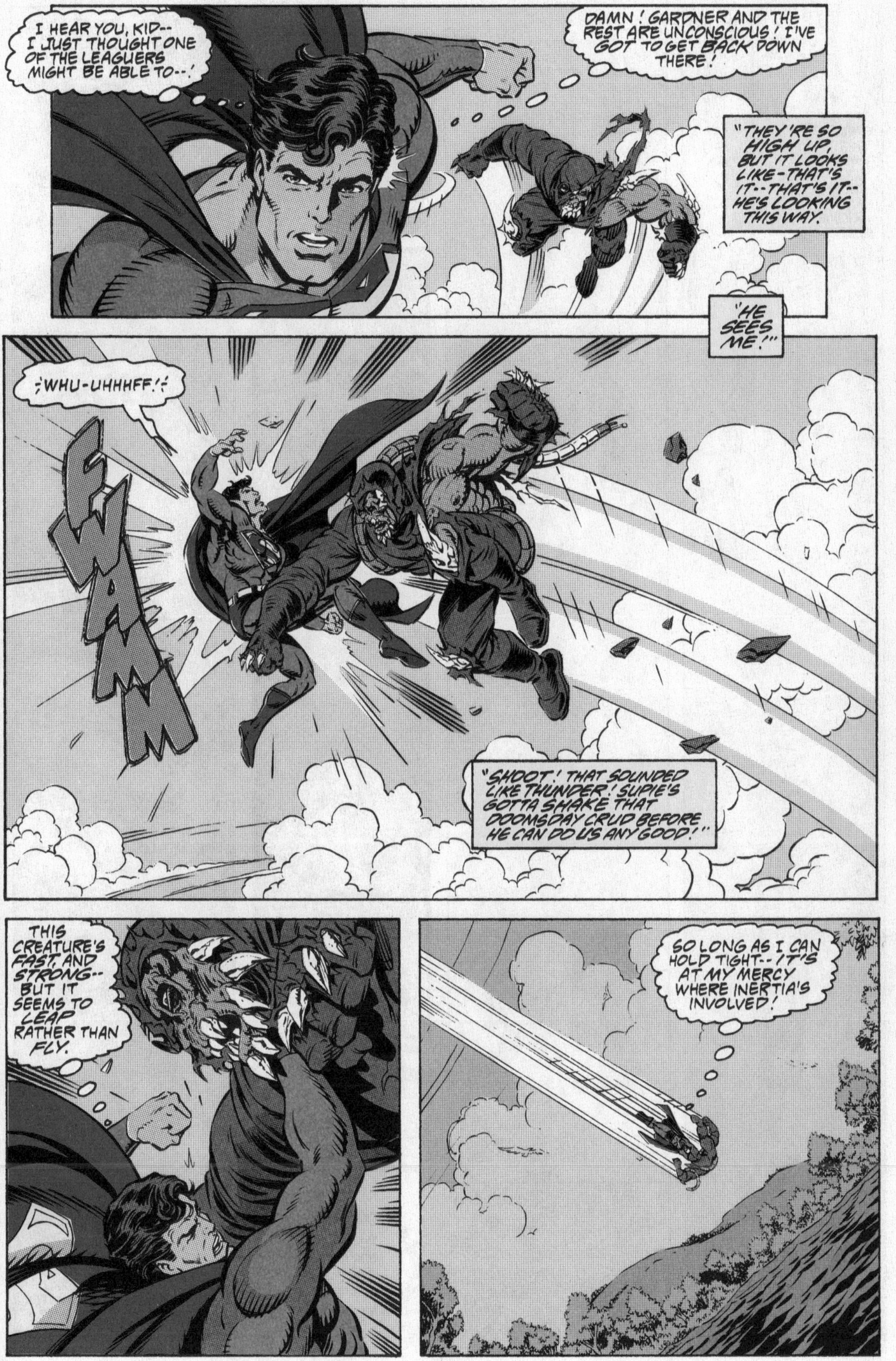
I HEAR YOU, KID-- I JUST THOUGHT ONE OF THE LEAGUERS MIGHT BE ABLE TO--.'
DAMN! GARDNER AND THE REST ARE UNCONSCIOUS! I'VE GOT TO GET BACK DOWN THERE!
"THEY'RE SO HIGH UP, BUT IT LOOKS LIKE--THAT'S IT--THAT'S IT-- HE'S LOOKING THIS WAY.
"HE SEES ME!"
¡WHU-UHHHFF!¡
CWAMM
"SHOOT! THAT SOUNDED LIKE THUNDER! SUPIE'S GOTTA SHAKE THAT DOOMSDAY CRUD BEFORE HE CAN DO US ANY GOOD!"
THIS CREATURE'S FAST, AND STRONG-- BUT IT SEEMS TO LEAP RATHER THAN FLY.
SO LONG AS I CAN HOLD TIGHT--IT'S AT MY MERCY WHERE INERTIA'S INVOLVED!

I'VE GOT TO FORCE THIS *THING* FAR ENOUGH INTO THE LAKE'S SILT...

CHOOM

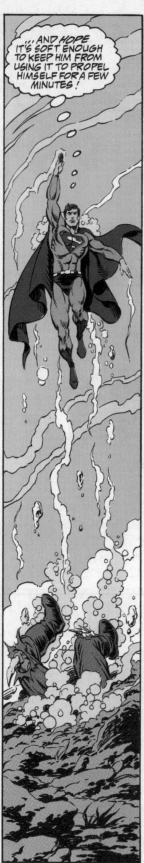

"...AND HOPE IT'S *SOFT* ENOUGH TO KEEP HIM FROM USING IT TO PROPEL HIMSELF FOR A FEW MINUTES!"

"I JUST *PRAY* I'VE STILL GOT TIME TO *HELP* THAT FAMILY!"

KERACK

OH, *MERCY--* DON'T LET THAT BE THE SOUND OF THOSE BEAMS GIVING WAY!

UGHNN! HOPE IS *NOT* LOST...

"...NOT WHILE *BLOODWYND* STILL STANDS!"

I DON'T KNOW *WHERE* YOU CAME FROM, MISTER-- BUT *THANK GOD* YOU'RE HERE!

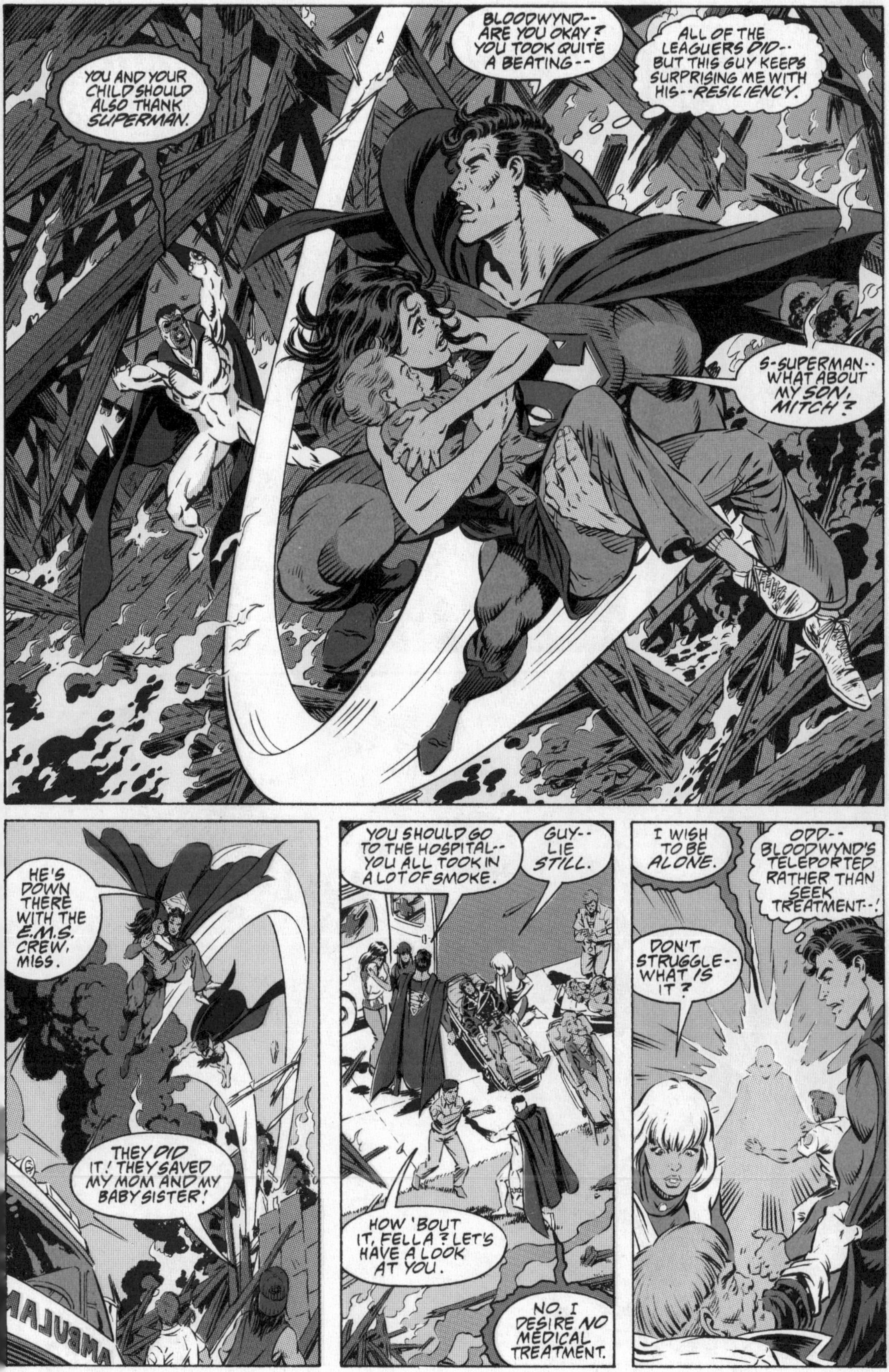
YOU AND YOUR CHILD SHOULD ALSO THANK SUPERMAN.
BLOODWYND-- ARE YOU OKAY? YOU TOOK QUITE A BEATING--
ALL OF THE LEAGUERS DID-- BUT THIS GUY KEEPS SURPRISING ME WITH HIS--RESILIENCY.
S-SUPERMAN-- WHAT ABOUT MY SON, MITCH?
HE'S DOWN THERE WITH THE E.M.S. CREW, MISS.
THEY DID IT! THEY SAVED MY MOM AND MY BABY SISTER!
YOU SHOULD GO TO THE HOSPITAL-- YOU ALL TOOK IN A LOT OF SMOKE.
GUY-- LIE STILL.
HOW 'BOUT IT, FELLA? LET'S HAVE A LOOK AT YOU.
NO. I DESIRE NO MEDICAL TREATMENT.
I WISH TO BE ALONE.
ODD-- BLOODWYND'S TELEPORTED RATHER THAN SEEK TREATMENT--!
DON'T STRUGGLE-- WHAT IS IT?

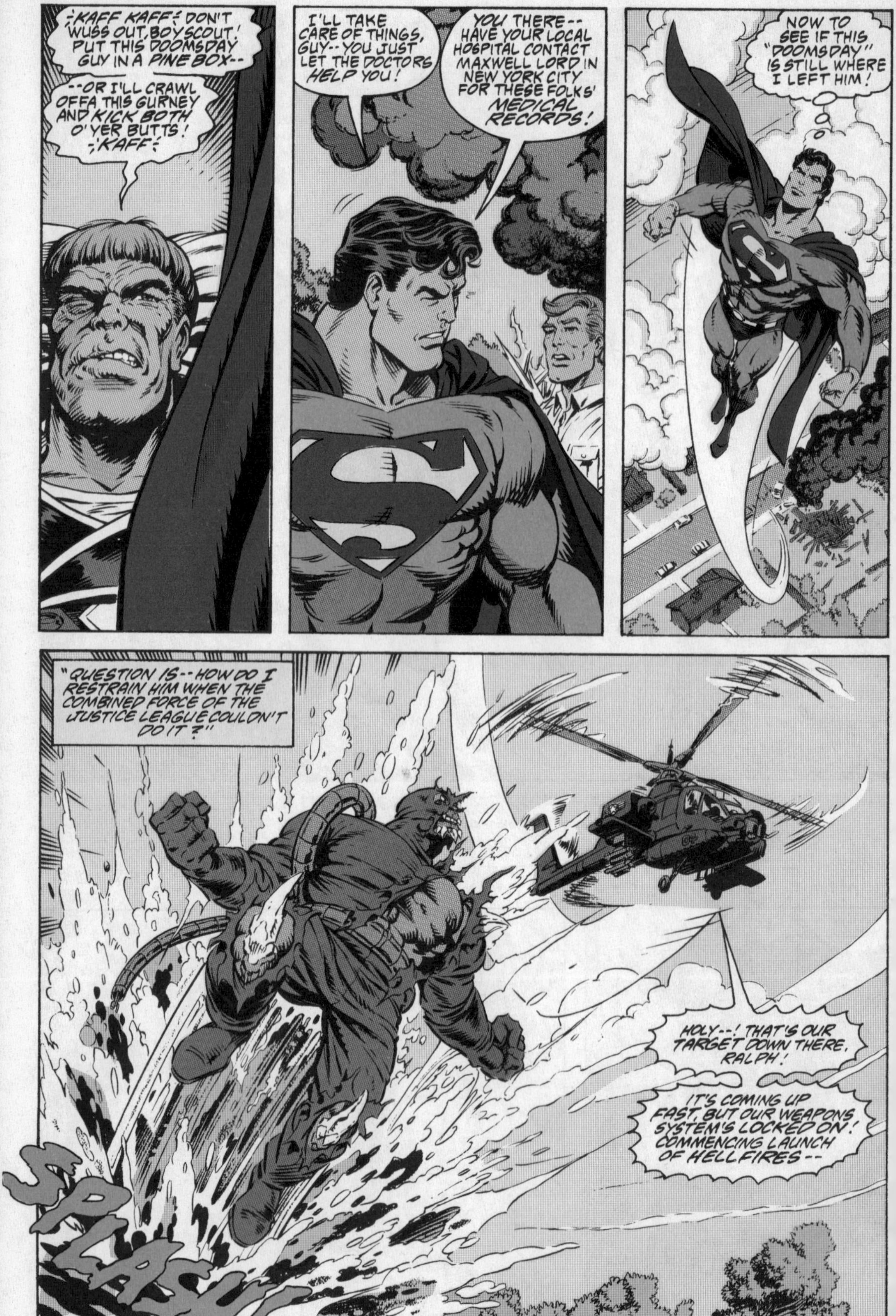

-KAFF KAFF- DON'T WUSS OUT, BOY SCOUT! PUT THIS DOOMSDAY GUY IN A PINE BOX--
--OR I'LL CRAWL OFFA THIS GURNEY AND KICK BOTH O' YER BUTTS! -KAFF-
I'LL TAKE CARE OF THINGS, GUY--YOU JUST LET THE DOCTORS HELP YOU!
YOU THERE--HAVE YOUR LOCAL HOSPITAL CONTACT MAXWELL LORD IN NEW YORK CITY FOR THESE FOLKS' MEDICAL RECORDS!
NOW TO SEE IF THIS "DOOMSDAY" IS STILL WHERE I LEFT HIM!
"QUESTION IS--HOW DO I RESTRAIN HIM WHEN THE COMBINED FORCE OF THE JUSTICE LEAGUE COULDN'T DO IT?"
HOLY--! THAT'S OUR TARGET DOWN THERE, RALPH!
IT'S COMING UP FAST, BUT OUR WEAPONS SYSTEM'S LOCKED ON! COMMENCING LAUNCH OF HELLFIRES--
SPLASH!

SOMETHING TORE UP A STRETCH OF PROPERTY OUT ON ROUTE 110, RUSTY!

KIRBY COUNTY POLICE

LOWELL SAID A BUNCH OF FOLK--INCLUDING SOME OF THE *JUSTICE LEAGUE* --ARE BEING RUSHED TO THE HOSPITAL!

SAY, YOU *HEAR* THAT? KIND OF A *CARTOON SOUND* A *BOMB* MAKES JUST BEFORE IT--

SHOULD I CRANK UP THE *CIVIL DEFENSE SIREN*, CHIEF? MAYBE WE SHOULD GET EVERYONE INTO THEIR BASEMENTS--

CRA-SH!

MOTHER OF *PEARL*!

KIRBY COUNTY POLICE STATION

UH, CHIEF-- THINK I'M *GONNA* NEED A *BIGGER GUN*!

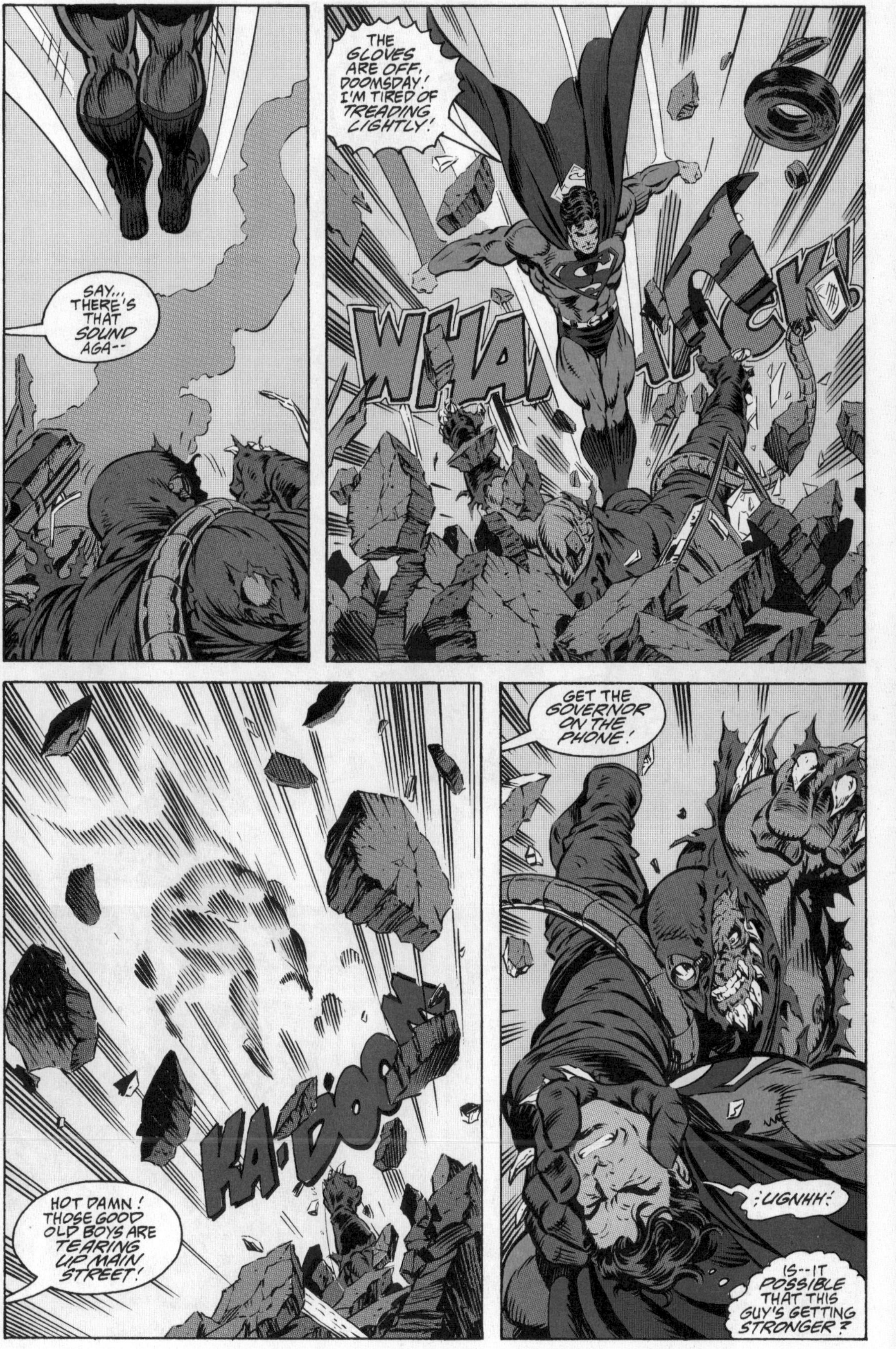
SAY... THERE'S THAT SOUND AGA--
THE GLOVES ARE OFF, DOOMSDAY! I'M TIRED OF TREADING LIGHTLY!
WHAMMMMMACK!
HOT DAMN! THOSE GOOD OLD BOYS ARE TEARING UP MAIN STREET!
KA-DOOOM
GET THE GOVERNOR ON THE PHONE!
UGNHH
IS--IT POSSIBLE THAT THIS GUY'S GETTING STRONGER?

LOOK, MR. VICE-LIEUTENANT GOVERNOR--I'M TELLING YOU THIS IS GOING TO BE MORE THAN "JUST" A LOCAL EMERGENCY...

...IF'N YOU DON'T GET THE BLASTED NATIONAL GUARD HERE A.S.A.P.!

SKAAASH

MOTHER O' MERCY! YOU HEAR THAT, YOU TIN-HORN BUREAUCRAT?

THIS IS BLUE LEADER-- TARGET SIGHTED AND WE'RE READY FOR A RUN. OVER.

THWACK

BLUE LEADER--APPROACH WITH EXTREME CAUTION-- WE'VE ALREADY LOST ONE CHOPPER TO THIS THING! OVER.

POK POK

POK

WE HEAR YA, CONTROL. OVER AND OUT.

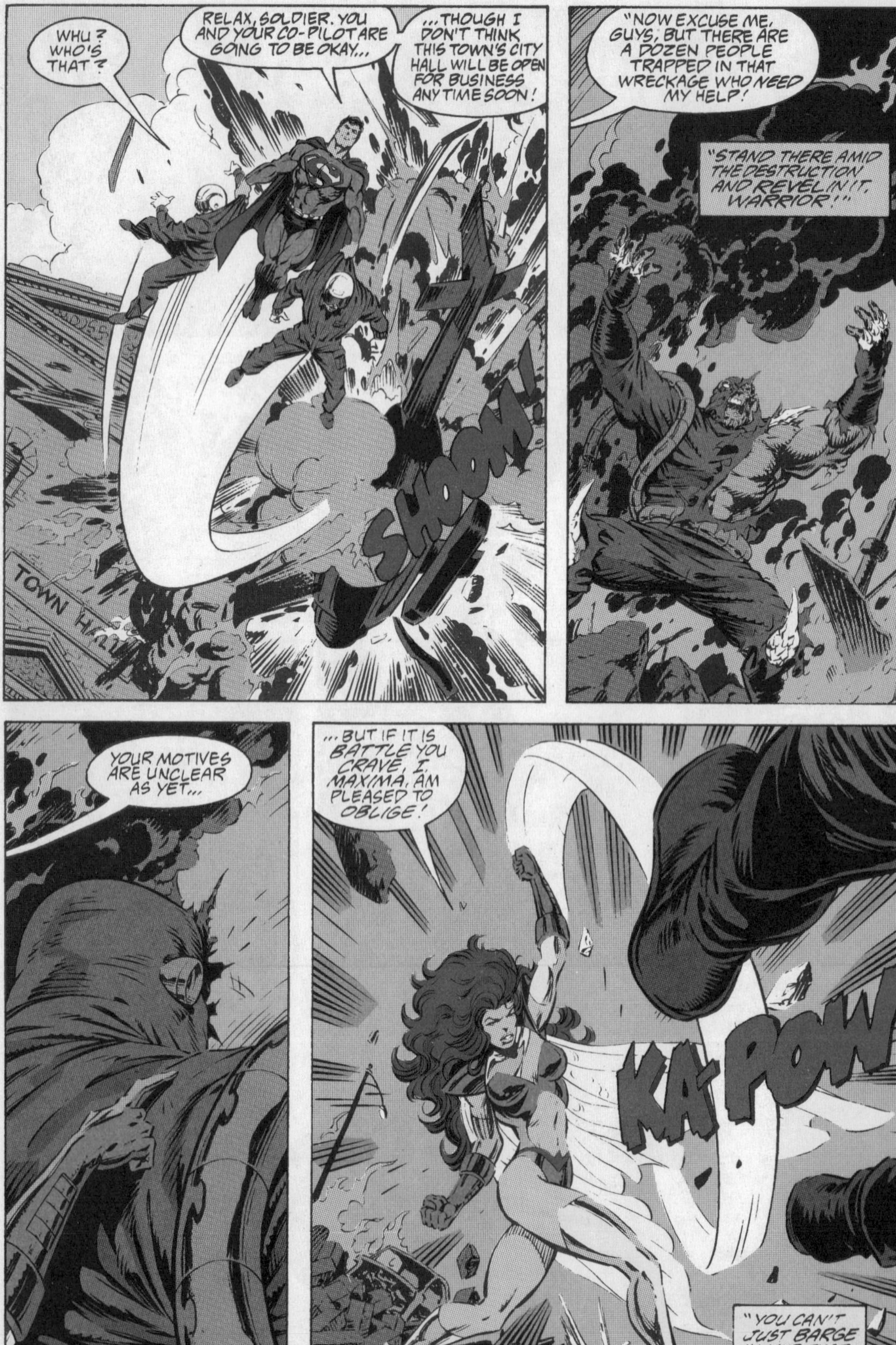

WHU? WHO'S THAT?
RELAX, SOLDIER. YOU AND YOUR CO-PILOT ARE GOING TO BE OKAY...
...THOUGH I DON'T THINK THIS TOWN'S CITY HALL WILL BE OPEN FOR BUSINESS ANY TIME SOON!
SHOOM!
TOWN HALL
"NOW EXCUSE ME, GUYS, BUT THERE ARE A DOZEN PEOPLE TRAPPED IN THAT WRECKAGE WHO NEED MY HELP!"
"STAND THERE AMID THE DESTRUCTION AND REVEL IN IT, WARRIOR!"
YOUR MOTIVES ARE UNCLEAR AS YET...
...BUT IF IT IS BATTLE YOU CRAVE, I, MAXIMA, AM PLEASED TO OBLIGE!
KA-POW
"YOU CAN'T JUST BARGE IN LIKE THAT, LADY!"

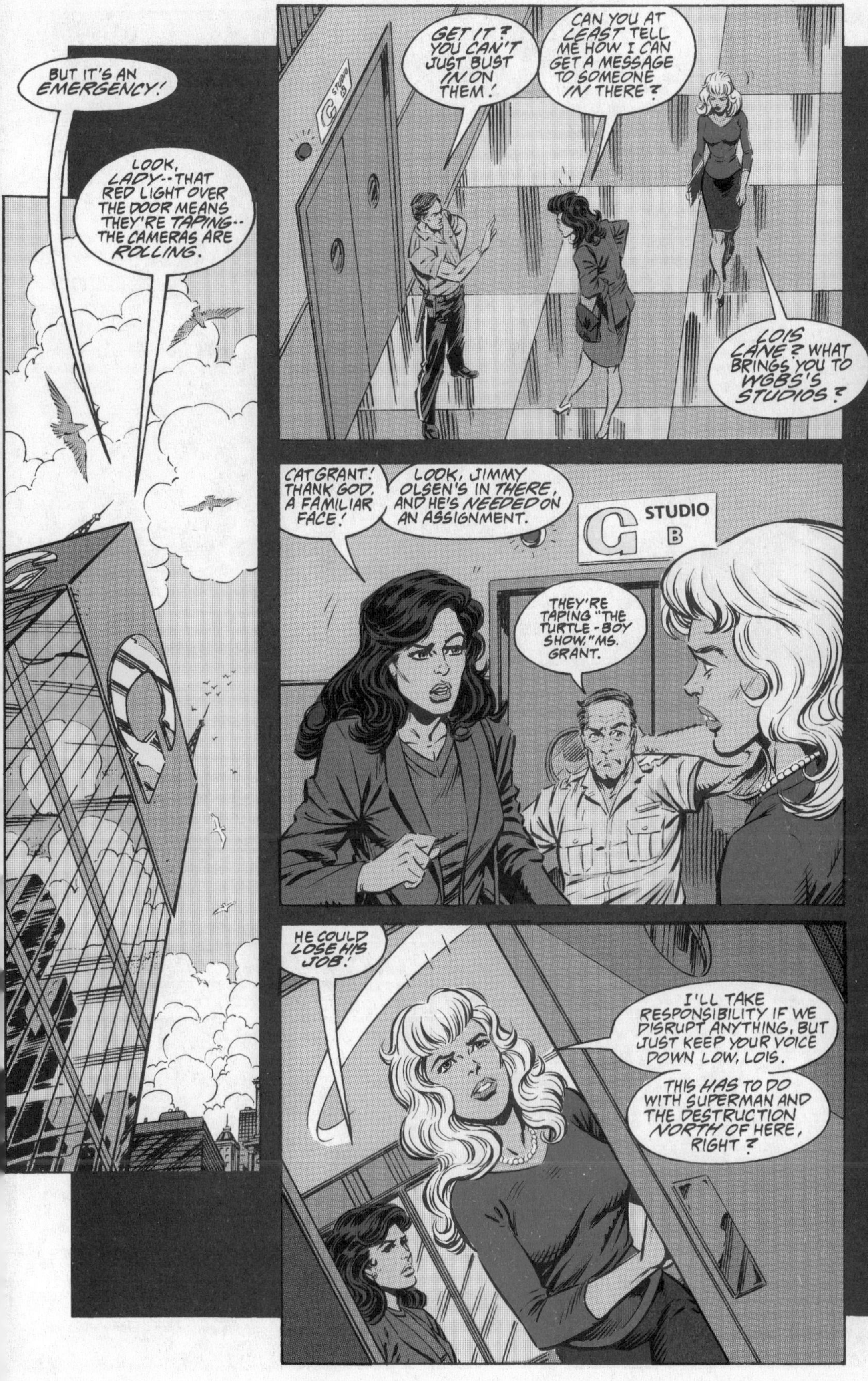

BUT IT'S AN EMERGENCY!
LOOK, LADY--THAT RED LIGHT OVER THE DOOR MEANS THEY'RE TAPING--THE CAMERAS ARE ROLLING.
GET IT? YOU CAN'T JUST BUST IN ON THEM!
CAN YOU AT LEAST TELL ME HOW I CAN GET A MESSAGE TO SOMEONE IN THERE?
LOIS LANE? WHAT BRINGS YOU TO WGBS'S STUDIOS?
CAT GRANT! THANK GOD. A FAMILIAR FACE!
LOOK, JIMMY OLSEN'S IN THERE, AND HE'S NEEDED ON AN ASSIGNMENT.
STUDIO B
THEY'RE TAPING "THE TURTLE-BOY SHOW," MS. GRANT.
HE COULD LOSE HIS JOB!
I'LL TAKE RESPONSIBILITY IF WE DISRUPT ANYTHING, BUT JUST KEEP YOUR VOICE DOWN LOW, LOIS.
THIS HAS TO DO WITH SUPERMAN AND THE DESTRUCTION NORTH OF HERE, RIGHT?

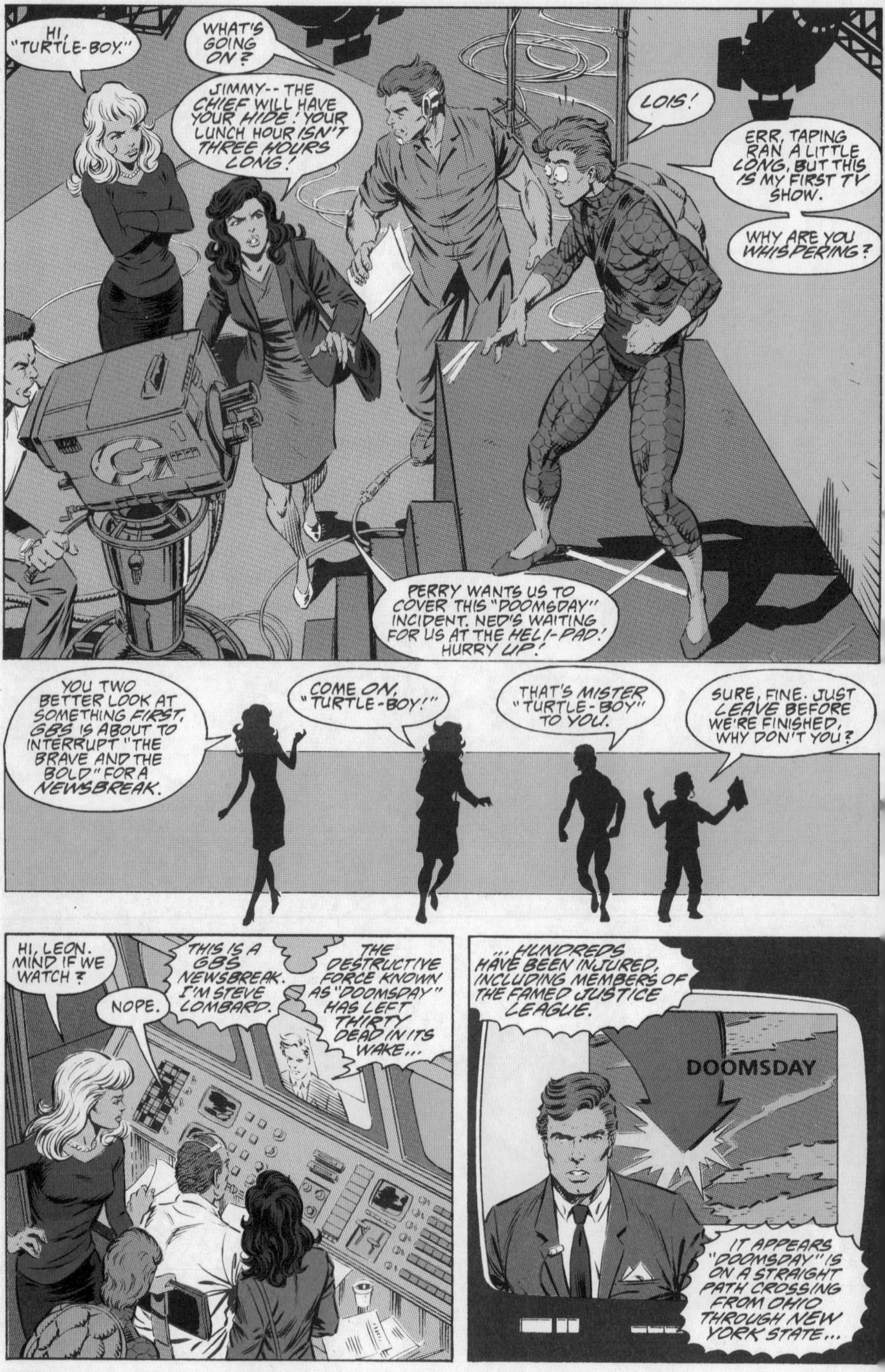
HI, "TURTLE-BOY."
WHAT'S GOING ON?
JIMMY-- THE CHIEF WILL HAVE YOUR HIDE! YOUR LUNCH HOUR ISN'T THREE HOURS LONG!
LOIS!
ERR, TAPING RAN A LITTLE LONG, BUT THIS IS MY FIRST TV SHOW.
WHY ARE YOU WHISPERING?
PERRY WANTS US TO COVER THIS "DOOMSDAY" INCIDENT. NED'S WAITING FOR US AT THE HELI-PAD! HURRY UP!
YOU TWO BETTER LOOK AT SOMETHING FIRST. GBS IS ABOUT TO INTERRUPT "THE BRAVE AND THE BOLD" FOR A NEWSBREAK.
COME ON, "TURTLE-BOY!"
THAT'S MISTER "TURTLE-BOY" TO YOU.
SURE, FINE. JUST LEAVE BEFORE WE'RE FINISHED, WHY DON'T YOU?
HI, LEON. MIND IF WE WATCH?
NOPE.
THIS IS A GBS NEWSBREAK. I'M STEVE LOMBARD.
THE DESTRUCTIVE FORCE KNOWN AS "DOOMSDAY" HAS LEFT THIRTY DEAD IN ITS WAKE...
...HUNDREDS HAVE BEEN INJURED, INCLUDING MEMBERS OF THE FAMED JUSTICE LEAGUE.
DOOMSDAY
IT APPEARS "DOOMSDAY" IS ON A STRAIGHT PATH CROSSING FROM OHIO THROUGH NEW YORK STATE...

"...SOME THEORIZE THAT THE CREATURE IS ON A COURSE STRAIGHT TO--OR THROUGH-- METROPOLIS.

WE NOW RETURN YOU TO "THE BRAVE AND THE BOLD," ALREADY IN PROGRESS.

BLOODY--!

LEX, I SHOULD GO-- MAYBE I CAN LEND A HAND.

THERE'S GOT TO BE A MILLION THINGS I COULD--

DOOMSDAY

LISTEN, LOVE--YOU CAN'T JUST UP AND RUN OFF LIKE YOU DID DURING THAT SATANUS BUSINESS. *

I NEED MY SUPERGIRL HERE WITH ME...

AS SEEN IN ACTION #680

"...WE NEED A CONTINGENCY PLAN IN CASE THIS MENACE MAKES HIS WAY TO METROPOLIS."

FOOD SUPERMARKET

BY THE HOUSE OF ALMERAC--YOU STILL STAND, EH?

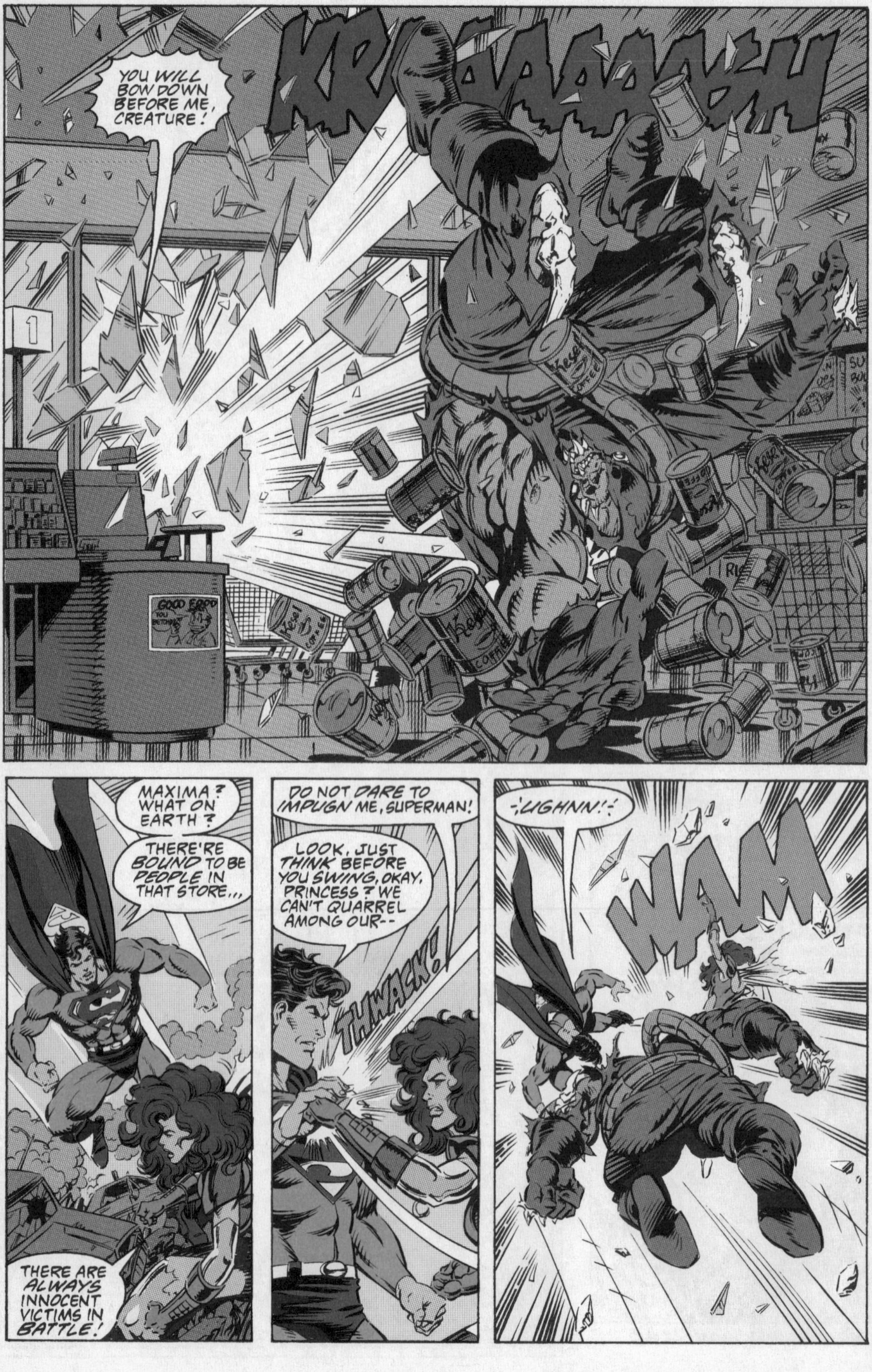
YOU WILL BOW DOWN BEFORE ME, CREATURE!
KRAAAAASH
MAXIMA? WHAT ON EARTH?
THERE'RE BOUND TO BE PEOPLE IN THAT STORE...
THERE ARE ALWAYS INNOCENT VICTIMS IN BATTLE!
DO NOT DARE TO IMPUGN ME, SUPERMAN!
LOOK, JUST THINK BEFORE YOU SWING, OKAY, PRINCESS? WE CAN'T QUARREL AMONG OUR--
THWACK!
UGHNN!
WAM

93

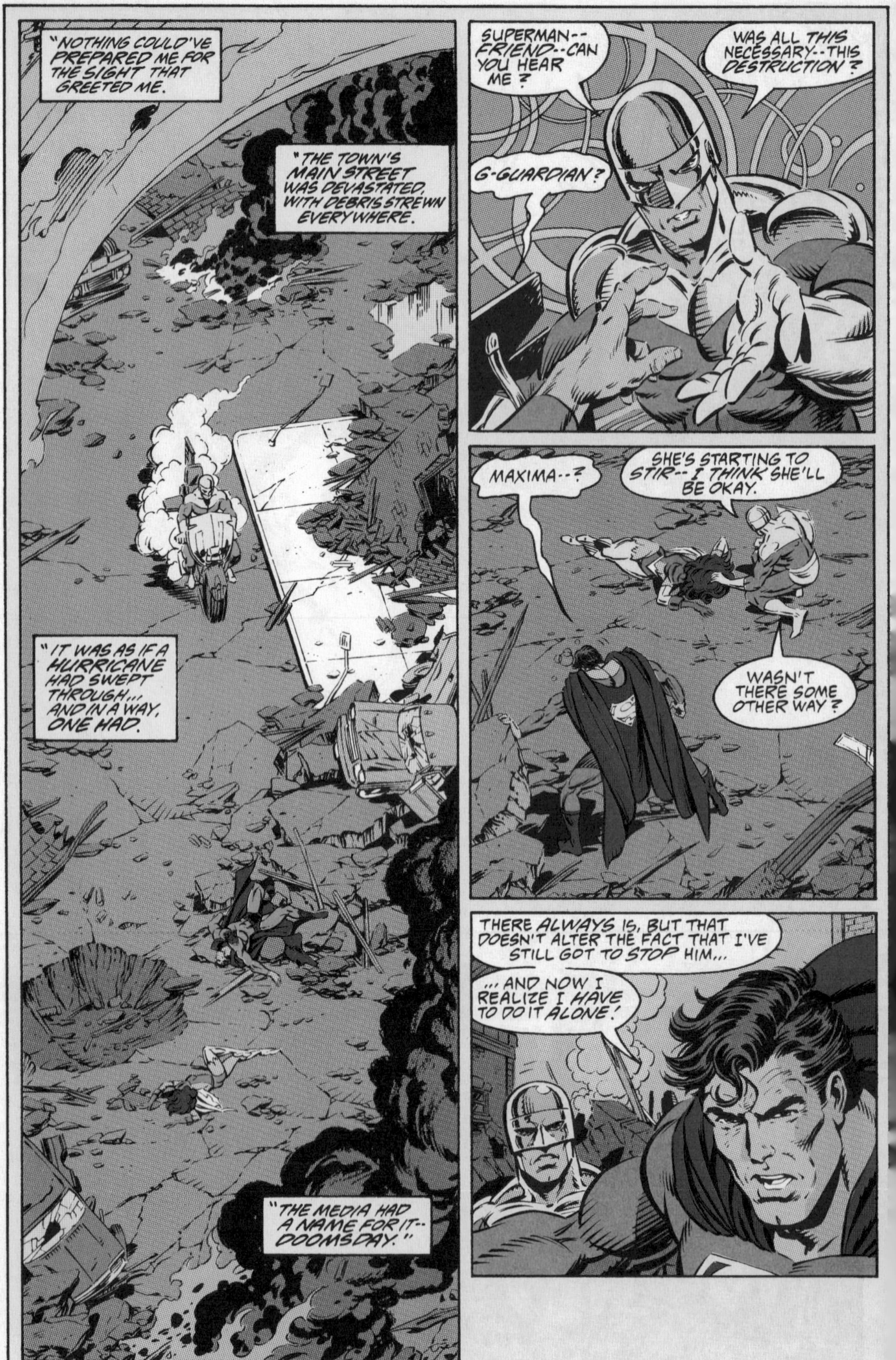
"NOTHING COULD'VE PREPARED ME FOR THE SIGHT THAT GREETED ME.
"THE TOWN'S MAIN STREET WAS DEVASTATED, WITH DEBRIS STREWN EVERYWHERE.
"IT WAS AS IF A HURRICANE HAD SWEPT THROUGH... AND IN A WAY, ONE HAD.
"THE MEDIA HAD A NAME FOR IT-- DOOMSDAY."
SUPERMAN-- FRIEND--CAN YOU HEAR ME ?
G-GUARDIAN ?
WAS ALL THIS NECESSARY--THIS DESTRUCTION ?
MAXIMA--?
SHE'S STARTING TO STIR-- I THINK SHE'LL BE OKAY.
WASN'T THERE SOME OTHER WAY ?
THERE ALWAYS IS, BUT THAT DOESN'T ALTER THE FACT THAT I'VE STILL GOT TO STOP HIM...
...AND NOW I REALIZE I HAVE TO DO IT ALONE!

...DOOMSDAY IS NEAR!

A BATTLE THAT HAS RAGED ACROSS HALF THE NATION SINCE MIDDAY, HAS LEFT SEVERAL MEMBERS OF JUSTICE LEAGUE AMERICA SERIOUSLY INJURED.

THE BLUE BEETLE IS REPORTED TO BE COMATOSE, AND BOOSTER GOLD SERIOUSLY INJURED FOLLOWING... ONE MOMENT!

SPECIAL REPORT

THIS JUST HANDED ME... THE VILLAGE OF GRIFFITH IN UPSTATE KIRBY COUNTY WAS ROCKED BY AN EXPLOSION MOMENTS AGO, AS SUPERMAN AND MAXIMA FOUGHT TO STOP THE CREATURE-- DUBBED DOOMSDAY--

CAMCORDER FOOTAGE

--WHOSE RAMPAGE HAS BROKEN THE JLA AND LEFT A TRAIL OF DEATH AND DESTRUCTION BEHIND HIM. DESPITE THEIR EFFORTS, HOWEVER, THE CREATURE IS REPORTEDLY STILL ON THE LOOSE.

CIVIL DEFENSE UNITS IN CITIES ALL ALONG THE EASTERN SEABOARD ARE ON ALERT, AS AUTHORITIES TRY TO DETERMINE IF ...

DOOMSDAY... MUST STOP DOOMSDAY...

PLEASE, MAXIMA... TAKE IT SLOW AND EASY. YOU'VE SUFFERED A PRETTY SERIOUS CONCUSSION.

SORRY I DIDN'T GET HERE SOONER, SUPERMAN.

I DOUBT THAT YOU COULD HAVE HELPED US AVOID THIS, GUARDIAN.

WE'VE NEVER FACED ANYTHING QUITE LIKE THIS BEFORE.

ROGER STERN • JACKSON GUICE & DENIS RODIER
WRITER   ARTISTS

BILL   GLENN   JENNIFER   MIKE
OAKLEY • WHITMORE •   FRANK •   CARLIN
LETTERER   COLORIST   ASSISTANT   EDITOR

SUPERMAN created by JERRY SIEGEL & JOE SHUSTER

95

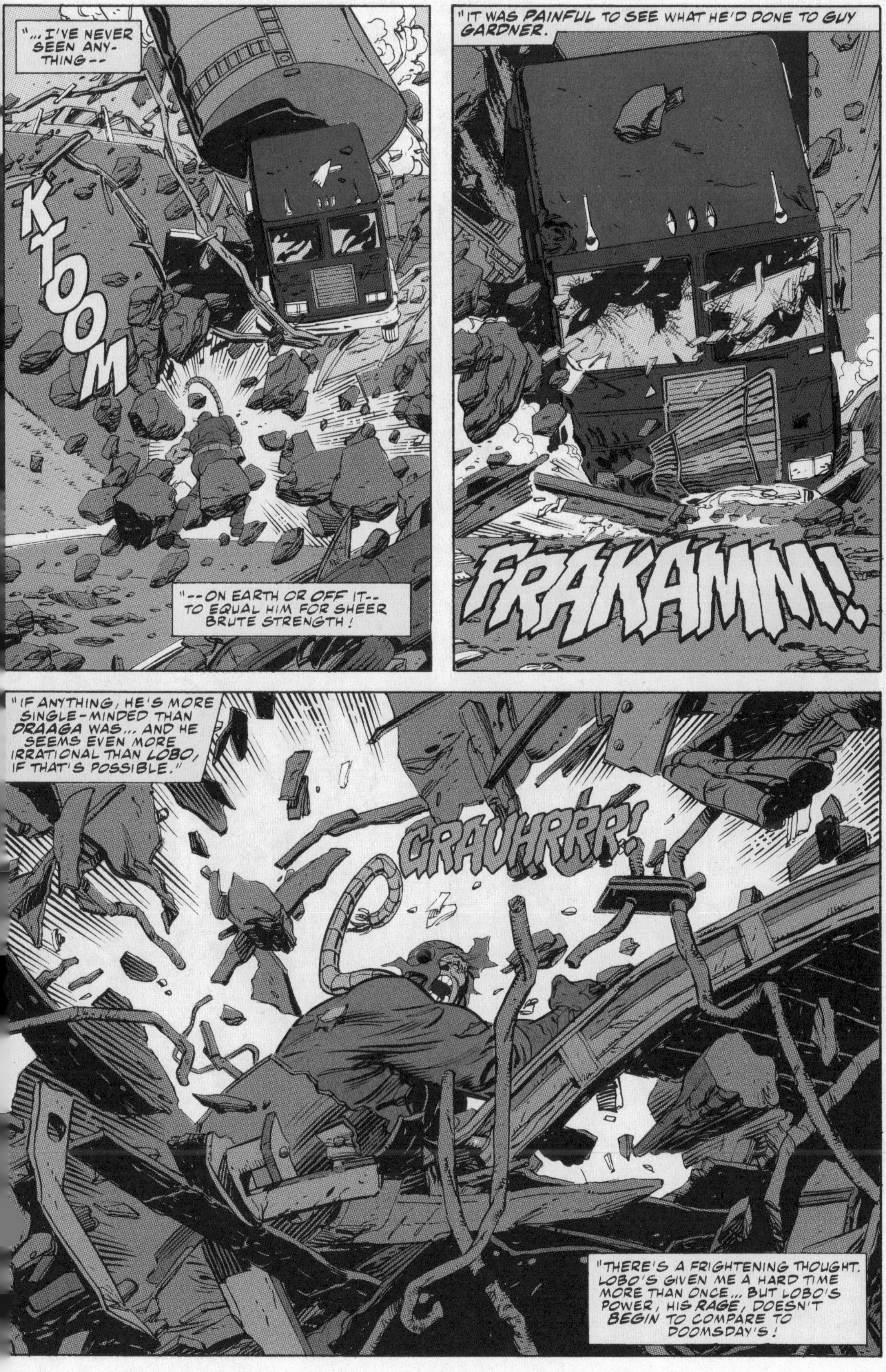
"... I'VE NEVER SEEN ANYTHING--
KTOOM
"--ON EARTH OR OFF IT--TO EQUAL HIM FOR SHEER BRUTE STRENGTH!
"IT WAS PAINFUL TO SEE WHAT HE'D DONE TO GUY GARDNER.
FRAKAMM!
"IF ANYTHING, HE'S MORE SINGLE-MINDED THAN DRAAGA WAS... AND HE SEEMS EVEN MORE IRRATIONAL THAN LOBO, IF THAT'S POSSIBLE."
GRAUHRRR!
"THERE'S A FRIGHTENING THOUGHT. LOBO'S GIVEN ME A HARD TIME MORE THAN ONCE... BUT LOBO'S POWER, HIS RAGE, DOESN'T BEGIN TO COMPARE TO DOOMSDAY'S!

"THERE'S NO DISCERNIBLE PATTERN TO HIS MOVEMENTS--"

MY GOD, THE OVERPASS HAS COLLAPSED!

WHAT'S THAT COMING OUT--?

NO! CAN'T STOP IN TIME! I'M GONNA HIT--

HRAURR!

--HIM! HUH? HE...?

WHAT DID--? HOW DID HE--?

OMIGOD... I DON'T BELIEVE THIS!

I'M.... FLYING?

"-- HE JUST SEEMS TO WANDER FROM PLACE TO PLACE, ATTACKING WHATEVER CATCHES HIS EYE."

RAURR?

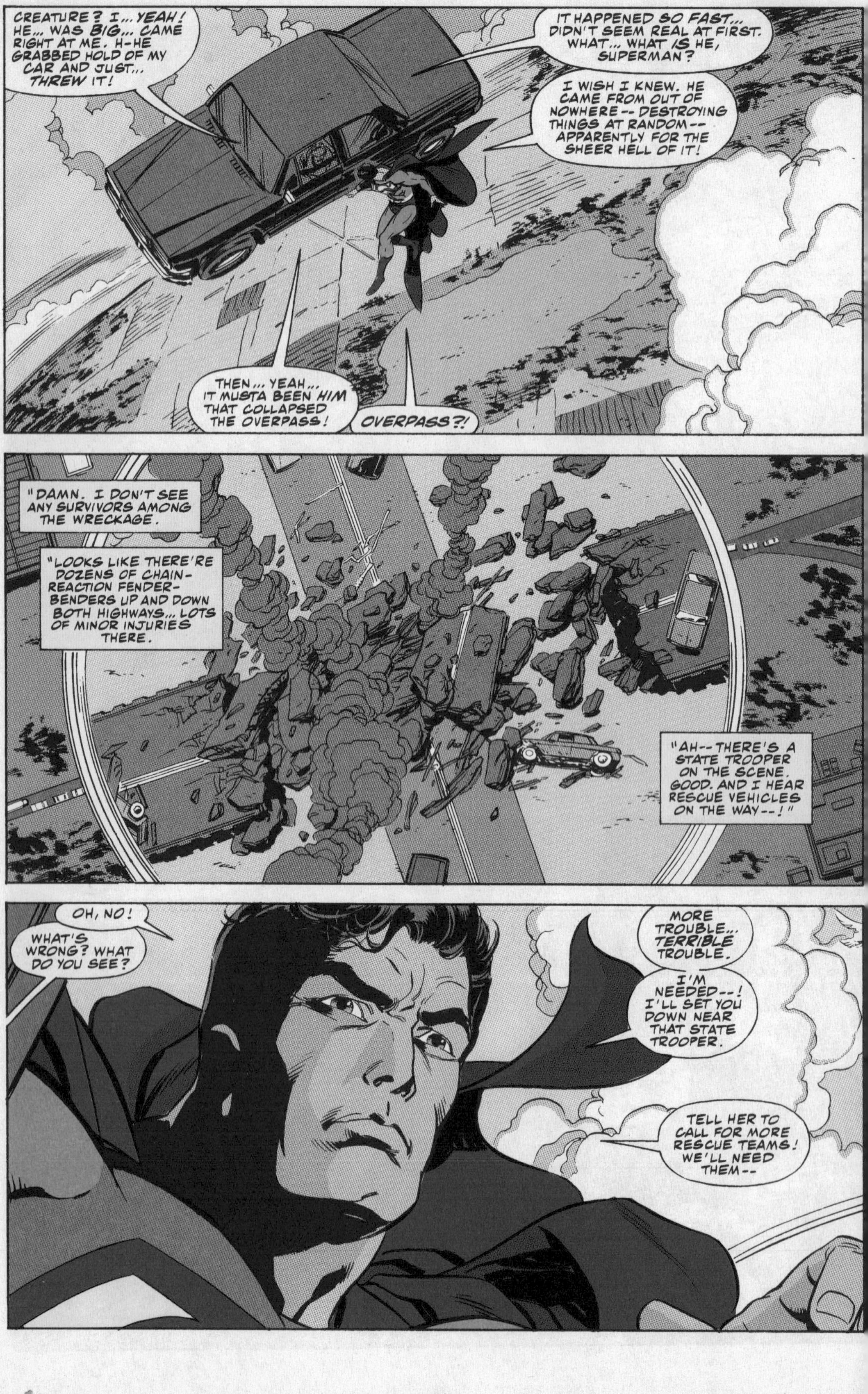

CREATURE? I... YEAH! HE... WAS BIG... CAME RIGHT AT ME. H-HE GRABBED HOLD OF MY CAR AND JUST... THREW IT!
IT HAPPENED SO FAST... DIDN'T SEEM REAL AT FIRST. WHAT... WHAT IS HE, SUPERMAN?
I WISH I KNEW. HE CAME FROM OUT OF NOWHERE -- DESTROYING THINGS AT RANDOM -- APPARENTLY FOR THE SHEER HELL OF IT!
THEN... YEAH... IT MUSTA BEEN HIM THAT COLLAPSED THE OVERPASS!
OVERPASS?!
"DAMN. I DON'T SEE ANY SURVIVORS AMONG THE WRECKAGE.
"LOOKS LIKE THERE'RE DOZENS OF CHAIN-REACTION FENDER-BENDERS UP AND DOWN BOTH HIGHWAYS... LOTS OF MINOR INJURIES THERE.
"AH -- THERE'S A STATE TROOPER ON THE SCENE. GOOD. AND I HEAR RESCUE VEHICLES ON THE WAY -- !"
OH, NO!
WHAT'S WRONG? WHAT DO YOU SEE?
MORE TROUBLE... TERRIBLE TROUBLE.
I'M NEEDED -- ! I'LL SET YOU DOWN NEAR THAT STATE TROOPER.
TELL HER TO CALL FOR MORE RESCUE TEAMS! WE'LL NEED THEM --

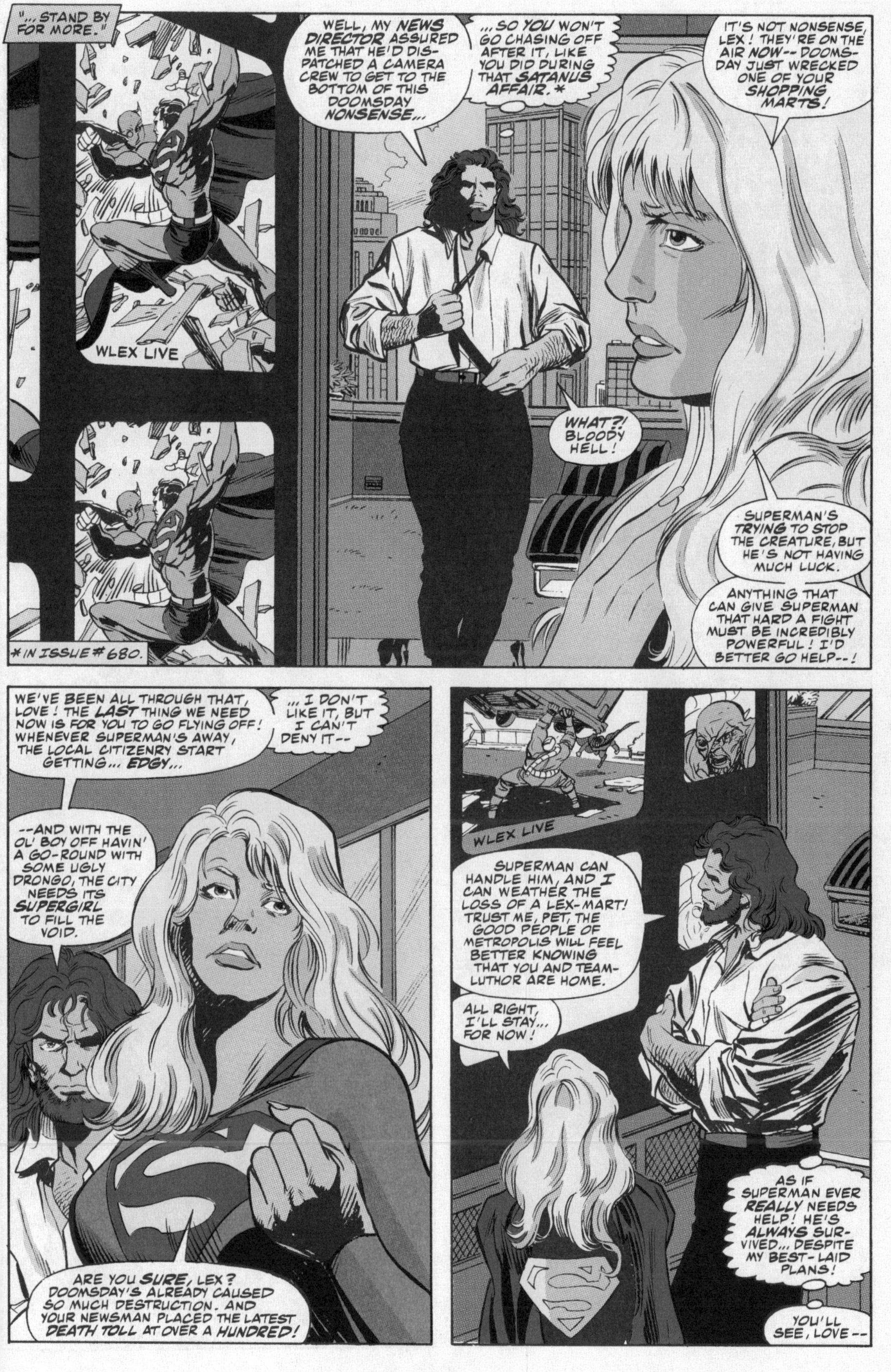
"... STAND BY FOR MORE."
WELL, MY NEWS DIRECTOR ASSURED ME THAT HE'D DISPATCHED A CAMERA CREW TO GET TO THE BOTTOM OF THIS DOOMSDAY NONSENSE...
...SO YOU WON'T GO CHASING OFF AFTER IT, LIKE YOU DID DURING THAT SATANUS AFFAIR.*
IT'S NOT NONSENSE, LEX! THEY'RE ON THE AIR NOW-- DOOMSDAY JUST WRECKED ONE OF YOUR SHOPPING MARTS!
WLEX LIVE
WHAT?! BLOODY HELL!
SUPERMAN'S TRYING TO STOP THE CREATURE, BUT HE'S NOT HAVING MUCH LUCK.
ANYTHING THAT CAN GIVE SUPERMAN THAT HARD A FIGHT MUST BE INCREDIBLY POWERFUL! I'D BETTER GO HELP--!
*IN ISSUE #680.
WE'VE BEEN ALL THROUGH THAT, LOVE! THE LAST THING WE NEED NOW IS FOR YOU TO GO FLYING OFF! WHENEVER SUPERMAN'S AWAY, THE LOCAL CITIZENRY START GETTING... EDGY...
...I DON'T LIKE IT, BUT I CAN'T DENY IT--
--AND WITH THE OL' BOY OFF HAVIN' A GO-ROUND WITH SOME UGLY DRONGO, THE CITY NEEDS ITS SUPERGIRL TO FILL THE VOID.
ARE YOU SURE, LEX? DOOMSDAY'S ALREADY CAUSED SO MUCH DESTRUCTION. AND YOUR NEWSMAN PLACED THE LATEST DEATH TOLL AT OVER A HUNDRED!
WLEX LIVE
SUPERMAN CAN HANDLE HIM, AND I CAN WEATHER THE LOSS OF A LEX-MART! TRUST ME, PET, THE GOOD PEOPLE OF METROPOLIS WILL FEEL BETTER KNOWING THAT YOU AND TEAM-LUTHOR ARE HOME.
ALL RIGHT, I'LL STAY... FOR NOW!
AS IF SUPERMAN EVER REALLY NEEDS HELP! HE'S ALWAYS SURVIVED... DESPITE MY BEST-LAID PLANS!
YOU'LL SEE, LOVE--

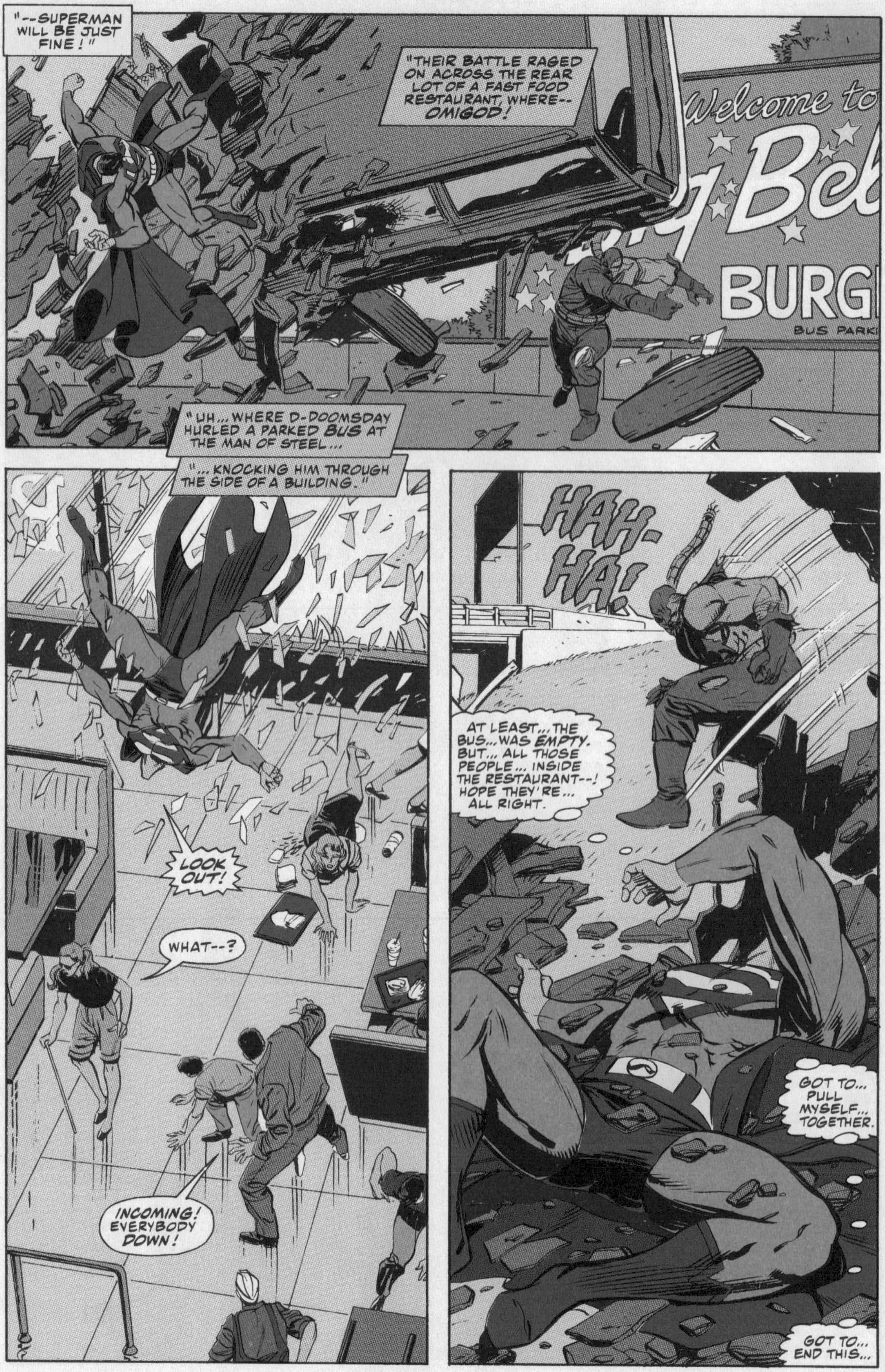
"--SUPERMAN WILL BE JUST FINE!"
"THEIR BATTLE RAGED ON ACROSS THE REAR LOT OF A FAST FOOD RESTAURANT, WHERE-- OMIGOD!
Welcome to
BURG
BUS PARK
"UH... WHERE D-DOOMSDAY HURLED A PARKED BUS AT THE MAN OF STEEL...
"...KNOCKING HIM THROUGH THE SIDE OF A BUILDING."
LOOK OUT!
WHAT--?
INCOMING! EVERYBODY DOWN!
HAH-HA!
AT LEAST... THE BUS... WAS EMPTY. BUT... ALL THOSE PEOPLE... INSIDE THE RESTAURANT--! HOPE THEY'RE... ALL RIGHT.
GOT TO... PULL MYSELF... TOGETHER.
GOT TO... END THIS...

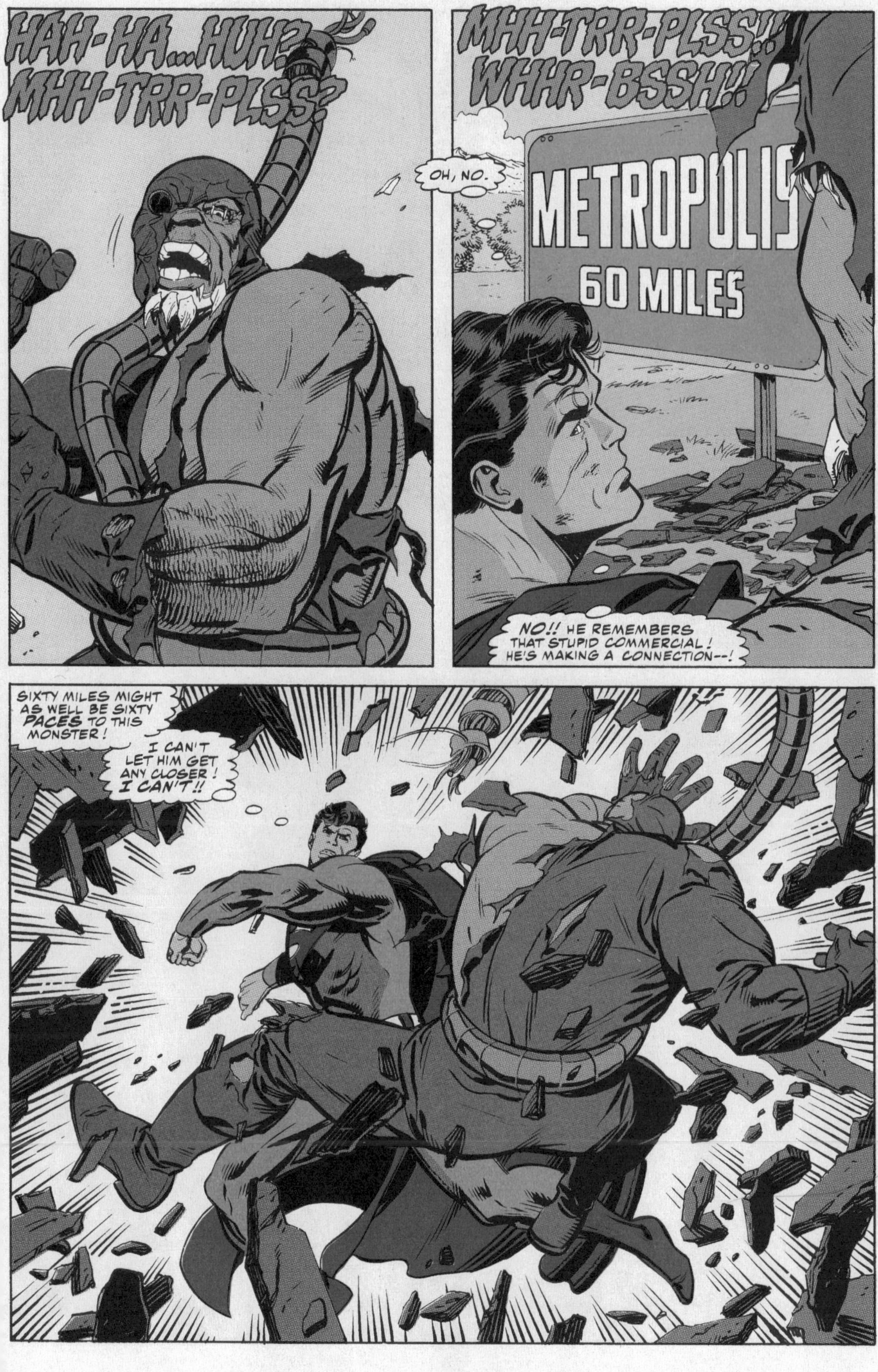
HAH-HA...HUH? MHH-TRR-PLSS?
MHH-TRR-PLSS!! WHHR-BSSH!!
OH, NO.
METROPOLIS
60 MILES
NO!! HE REMEMBERS THAT STUPID COMMERCIAL! HE'S MAKING A CONNECTION--!
SIXTY MILES MIGHT AS WELL BE SIXTY PACES TO THIS MONSTER!
I CAN'T LET HIM GET ANY CLOSER! I CAN'T!!

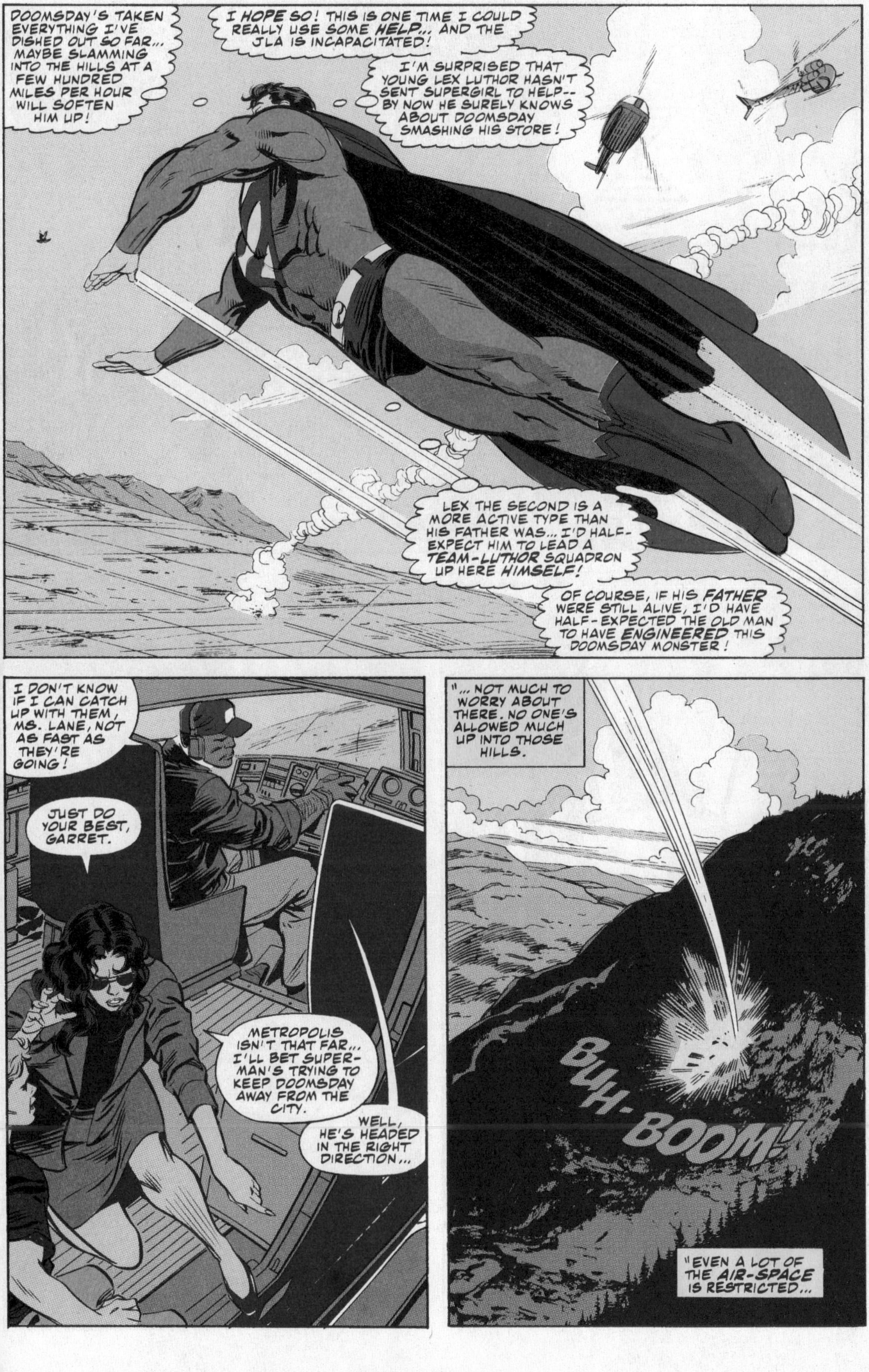
DOOMSDAY'S TAKEN EVERYTHING I'VE DISHED OUT SO FAR... MAYBE SLAMMING INTO THE HILLS AT A FEW HUNDRED MILES PER HOUR WILL SOFTEN HIM UP!
I HOPE SO! THIS IS ONE TIME I COULD REALLY USE SOME HELP... AND THE JLA IS INCAPACITATED!
I'M SURPRISED THAT YOUNG LEX LUTHOR HASN'T SENT SUPERGIRL TO HELP-- BY NOW HE SURELY KNOWS ABOUT DOOMSDAY SMASHING HIS STORE!
LEX THE SECOND IS A MORE ACTIVE TYPE THAN HIS FATHER WAS... I'D HALF-EXPECT HIM TO LEAD A TEAM-LUTHOR SQUADRON UP HERE HIMSELF!
OF COURSE, IF HIS FATHER WERE STILL ALIVE, I'D HAVE HALF-EXPECTED THE OLD MAN TO HAVE ENGINEERED THIS DOOMSDAY MONSTER!
I DON'T KNOW IF I CAN CATCH UP WITH THEM, MS. LANE, NOT AS FAST AS THEY'RE GOING!
JUST DO YOUR BEST, GARRET.
METROPOLIS ISN'T THAT FAR... I'LL BET SUPER-MAN'S TRYING TO KEEP DOOMSDAY AWAY FROM THE CITY.
WELL, HE'S HEADED IN THE RIGHT DIRECTION...
"... NOT MUCH TO WORRY ABOUT THERE. NO ONE'S ALLOWED MUCH UP INTO THOSE HILLS.
BUH-BOOM!
"EVEN A LOT OF THE AIR-SPACE IS RESTRICTED...

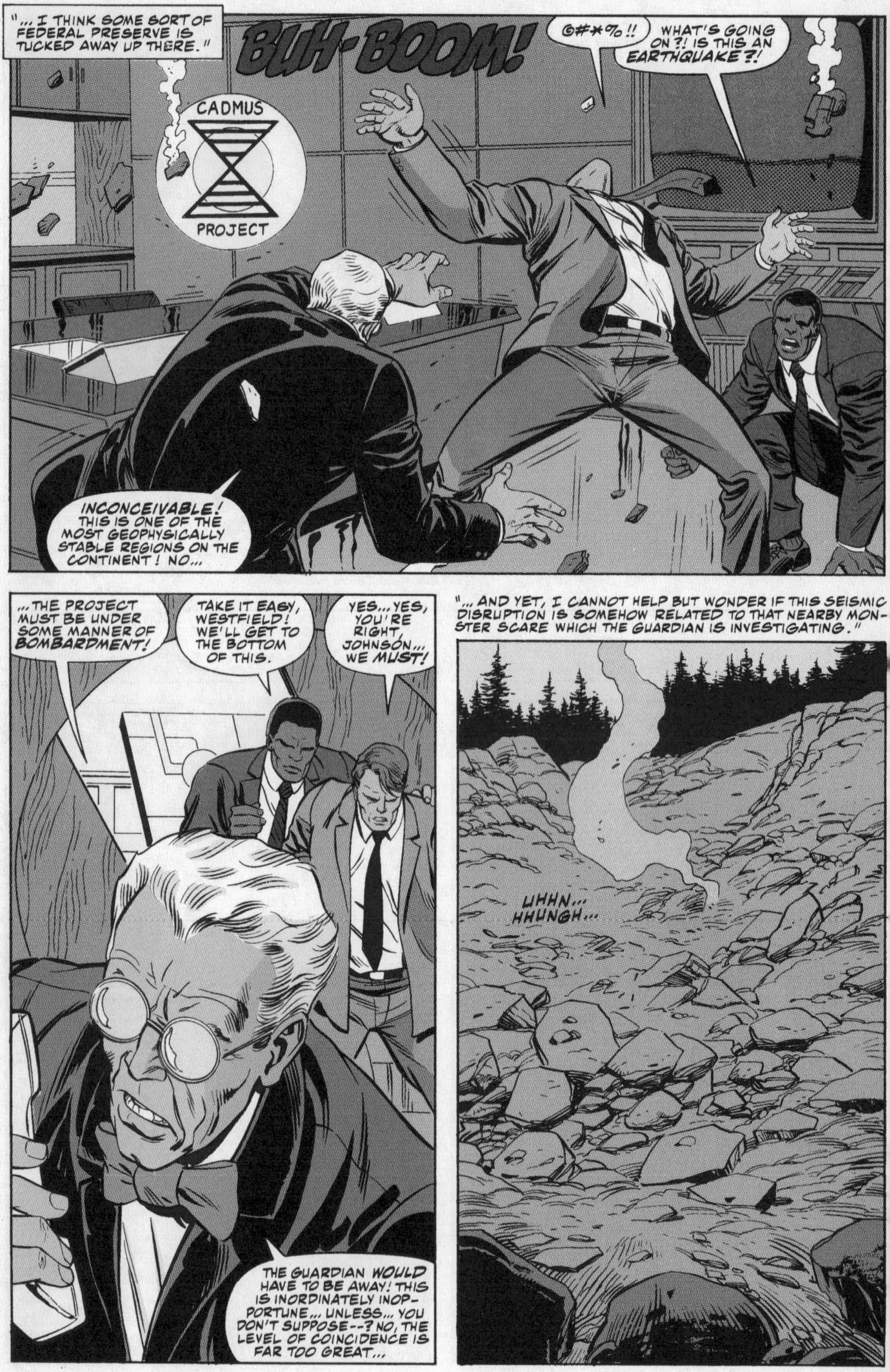
"... I THINK SOME SORT OF FEDERAL PRESERVE IS TUCKED AWAY UP THERE."
BUH-BOOM!
CADMUS
PROJECT
©#*%!!
WHAT'S GOING ON?! IS THIS AN EARTHQUAKE?!
INCONCEIVABLE! THIS IS ONE OF THE MOST GEOPHYSICALLY STABLE REGIONS ON THE CONTINENT! NO...
...THE PROJECT MUST BE UNDER SOME MANNER OF BOMBARDMENT!
TAKE IT EASY, WESTFIELD! WE'LL GET TO THE BOTTOM OF THIS.
YES... YES, YOU'RE RIGHT, JOHNSON... WE MUST!
THE GUARDIAN WOULD HAVE TO BE AWAY! THIS IS INORDINATELY INOP-PORTUNE... UNLESS... YOU DON'T SUPPOSE--? NO, THE LEVEL OF COINCIDENCE IS FAR TOO GREAT...
"... AND YET, I CANNOT HELP BUT WONDER IF THIS SEISMIC DISRUPTION IS SOMEHOW RELATED TO THAT NEARBY MON-STER SCARE WHICH THE GUARDIAN IS INVESTIGATING."
UHHN... HHUNGH...

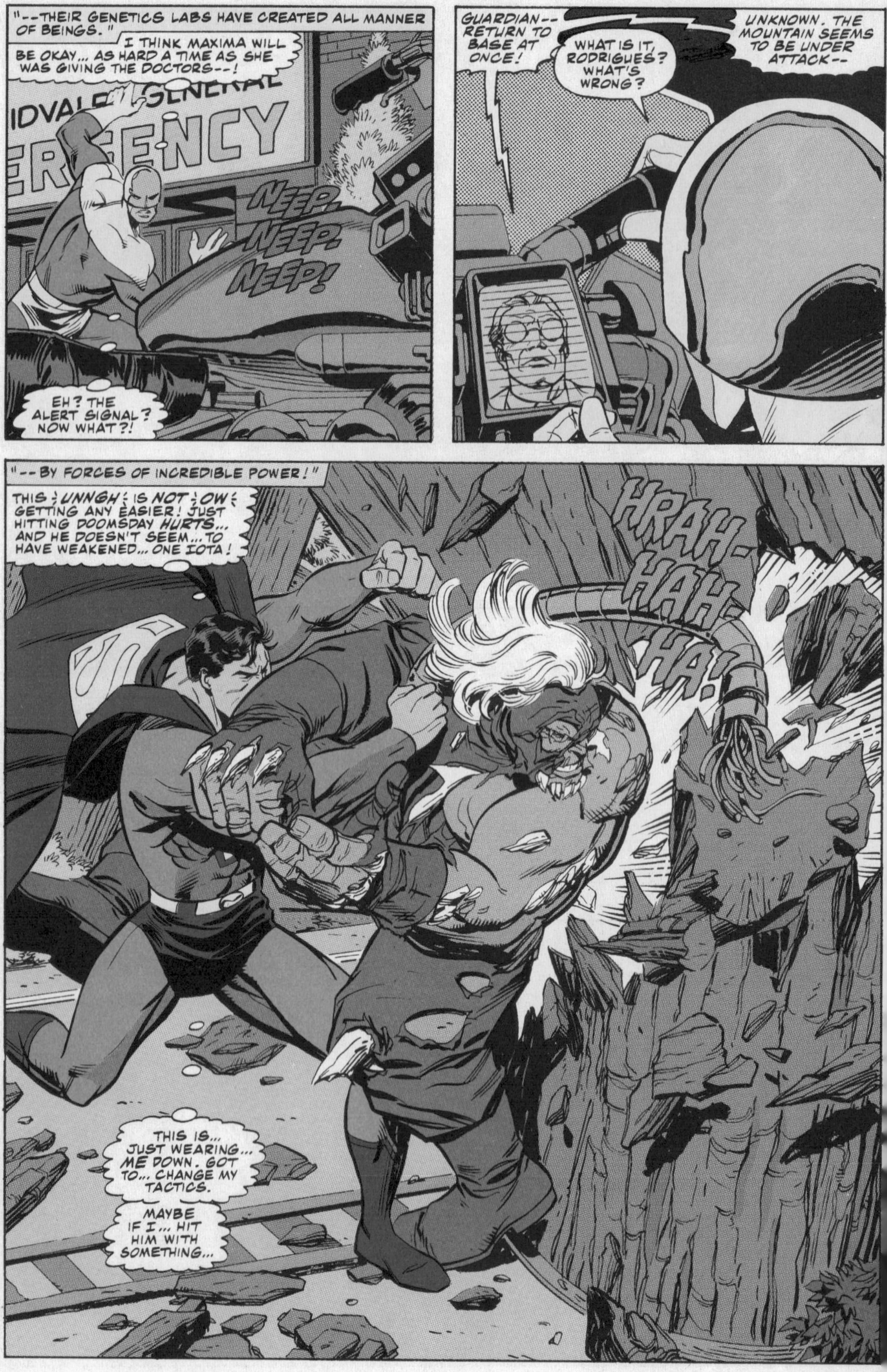
"--THEIR GENETICS LABS HAVE CREATED ALL MANNER OF BEINGS."
I THINK MAXIMA WILL BE OKAY... AS HARD A TIME AS SHE WAS GIVING THE DOCTORS--!
NEEP. NEEP. NEEP!
EH? THE ALERT SIGNAL? NOW WHAT?!
GUARDIAN-- RETURN TO BASE AT ONCE!
WHAT IS IT, RODRIGUES? WHAT'S WRONG?
UNKNOWN. THE MOUNTAIN SEEMS TO BE UNDER ATTACK--
"--BY FORCES OF INCREDIBLE POWER!"
THIS UNNGH IS NOT OW GETTING ANY EASIER! JUST HITTING DOOMSDAY HURTS... AND HE DOESN'T SEEM... TO HAVE WEAKENED... ONE IOTA!
HRAH-HAH-HA!
THIS IS... JUST WEARING... ME DOWN. GOT TO... CHANGE MY TACTICS.
MAYBE IF I... HIT HIM WITH SOMETHING...

113

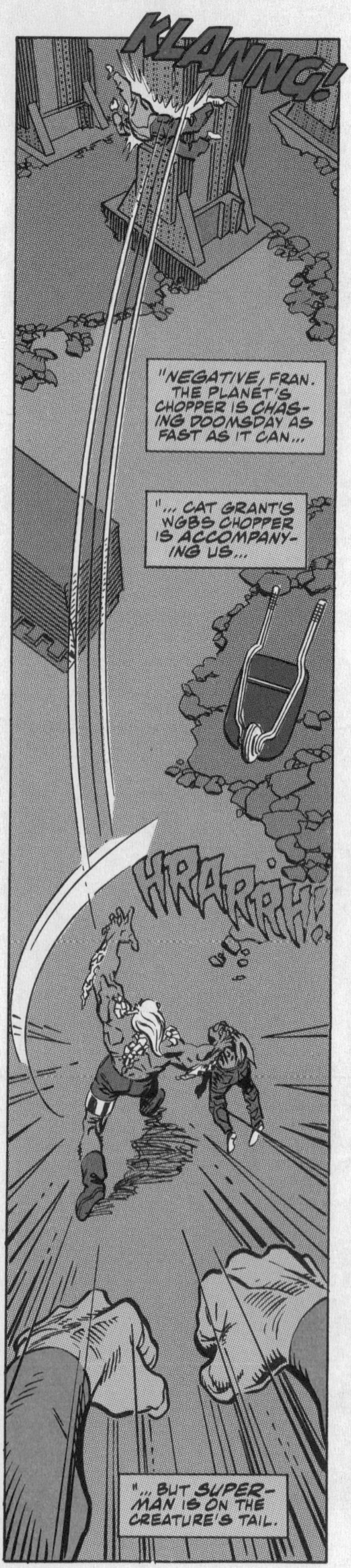
KLANNG!
"NEGATIVE, FRAN. THE PLANET'S CHOPPER IS CHASING DOOMSDAY AS FAST AS IT CAN...
"...CAT GRANT'S WGBS CHOPPER IS ACCOMPANYING US...
HRARRH!
"...BUT SUPERMAN IS ON THE CREATURE'S TAIL.

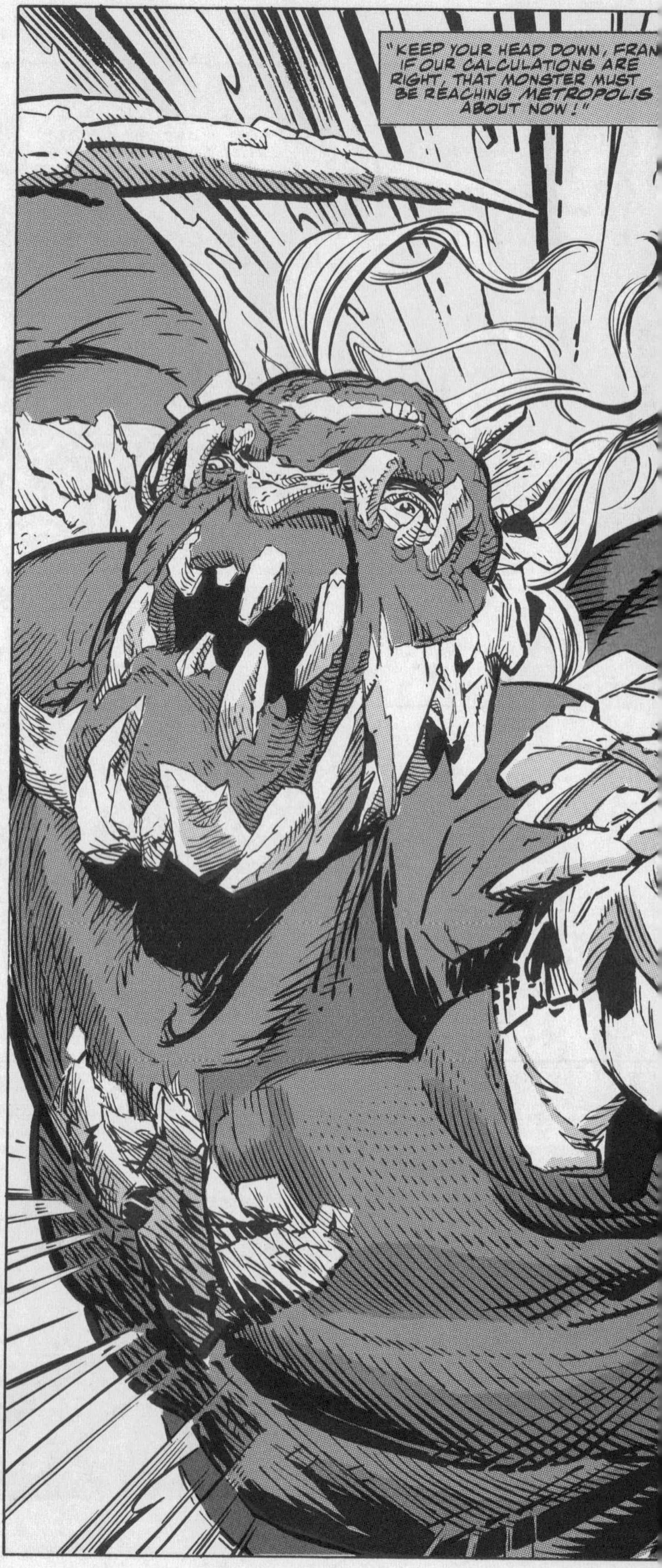
"KEEP YOUR HEAD DOWN, FRAN IF OUR CALCULATIONS ARE RIGHT, THAT MONSTER MUST BE REACHING METROPOLIS ABOUT NOW!"

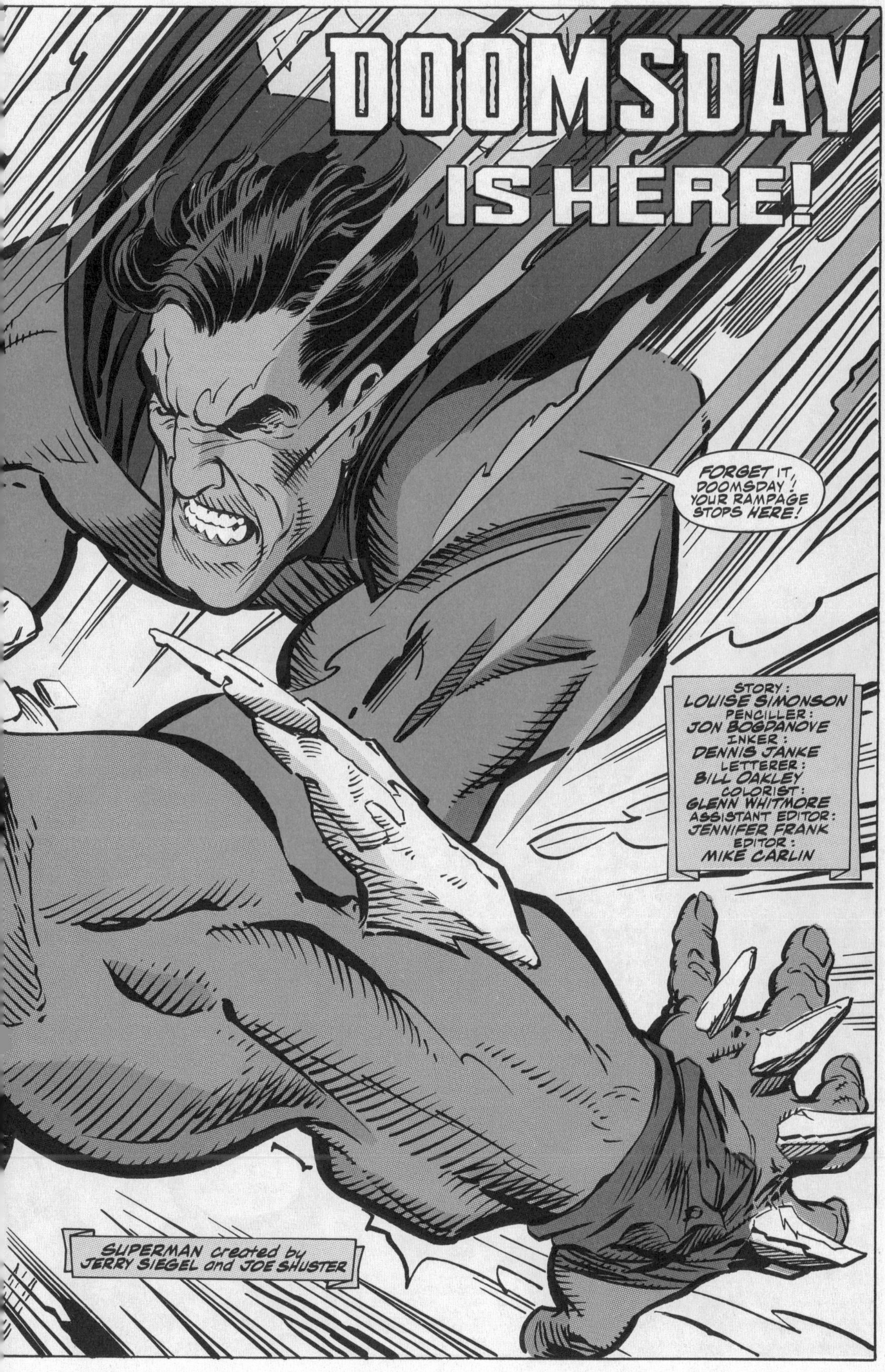

"--HE'S GOTTA BE OKAY!"

GUARDIAN, ARE YOU ALL RIGHT?

DUBBILEX! WHAT... HAPPENED?

DOOMS-DAY SMASHED HABITAT! YOU WERE FELLED BY THE RUBBLE.

AND SUPER-MAN...?

EVEN NOW HE BATTLES THE CREATURE.

I'M AFRAID DOOMSDAY IS TOO BIG FOR SUPERMAN TO HANDLE ALONE.

DOOMSDAY MAY BE ONE OF OURS, GUARDIAN, A D.N.ALIEN... A CADMUS-DABNEY DONOVAN CREATION.

TRY TO MIND-READ THE CREATURE, DUB. FIND OUT. I JUST PRAY THAT CADMUS ISN'T RESPONSIBLE--

"--FOR THE DAMAGE THAT MONSTER'S CAUSED!"

WHACK

CREATURE'S AS AGILE... AS IT IS STRONG! TWISTED AWAY ...COULDN'T HOLD HIM...

KICKED ME... CAN'T BREATHE...

THERE IS NOTHING IN HIS MIND BUT ANGER--

121

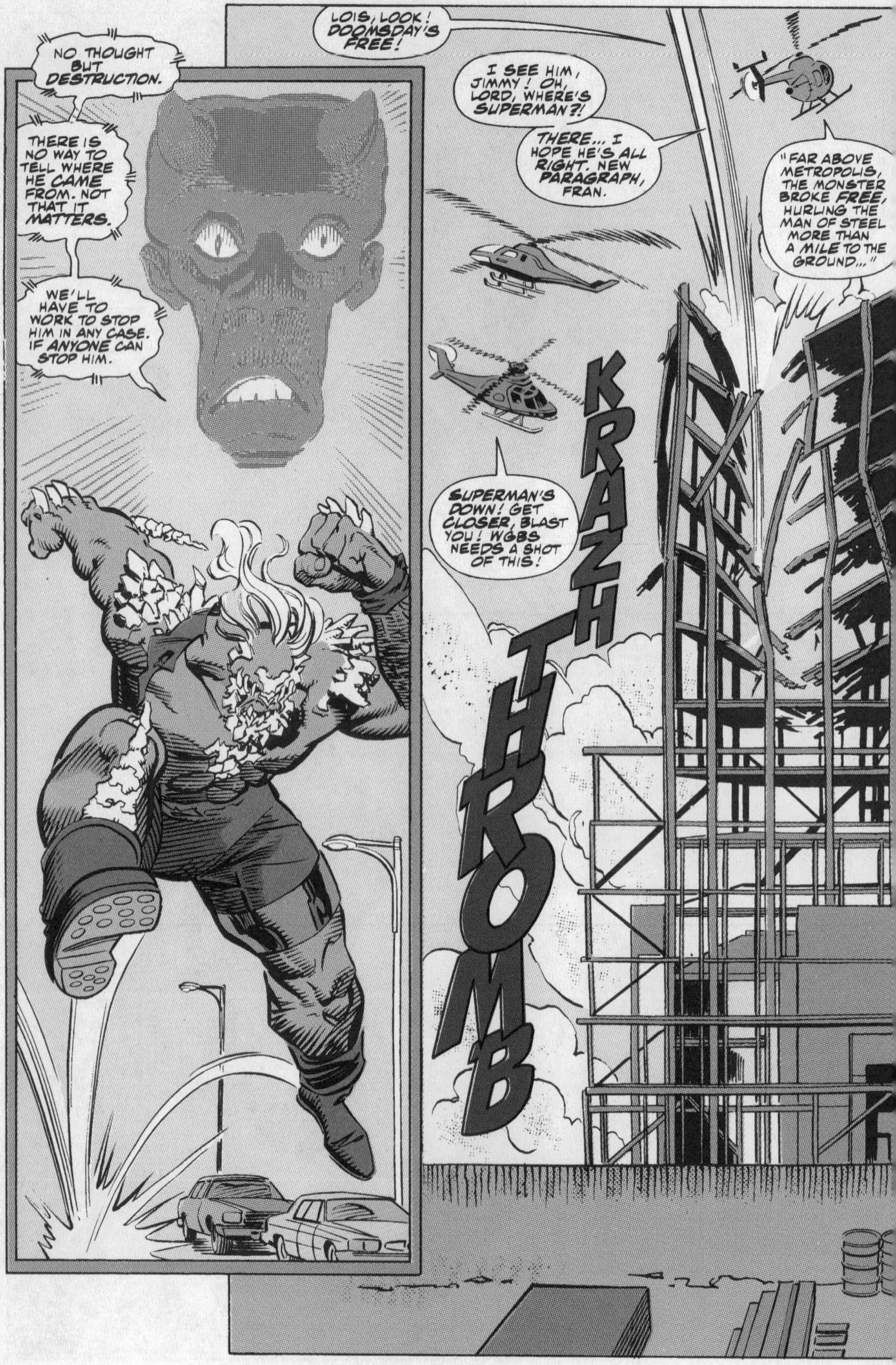
NO THOUGHT BUT DESTRUCTION.
THERE IS NO WAY TO TELL WHERE HE CAME FROM. NOT THAT IT MATTERS.
WE'LL HAVE TO WORK TO STOP HIM IN ANY CASE. IF ANYONE CAN STOP HIM.
LOIS, LOOK! DOOMSDAY'S FREE!
I SEE HIM, JIMMY! OH, LORD, WHERE'S SUPERMAN?!
THERE... I HOPE HE'S ALL RIGHT. NEW PARAGRAPH, FRAN.
"FAR ABOVE METROPOLIS, THE MONSTER BROKE FREE, HURLING THE MAN OF STEEL MORE THAN A MILE TO THE GROUND..."
SUPERMAN'S DOWN! GET CLOSER, BLAST YOU! WGBS NEEDS A SHOT OF THIS!
KRAZH
THROMB

123

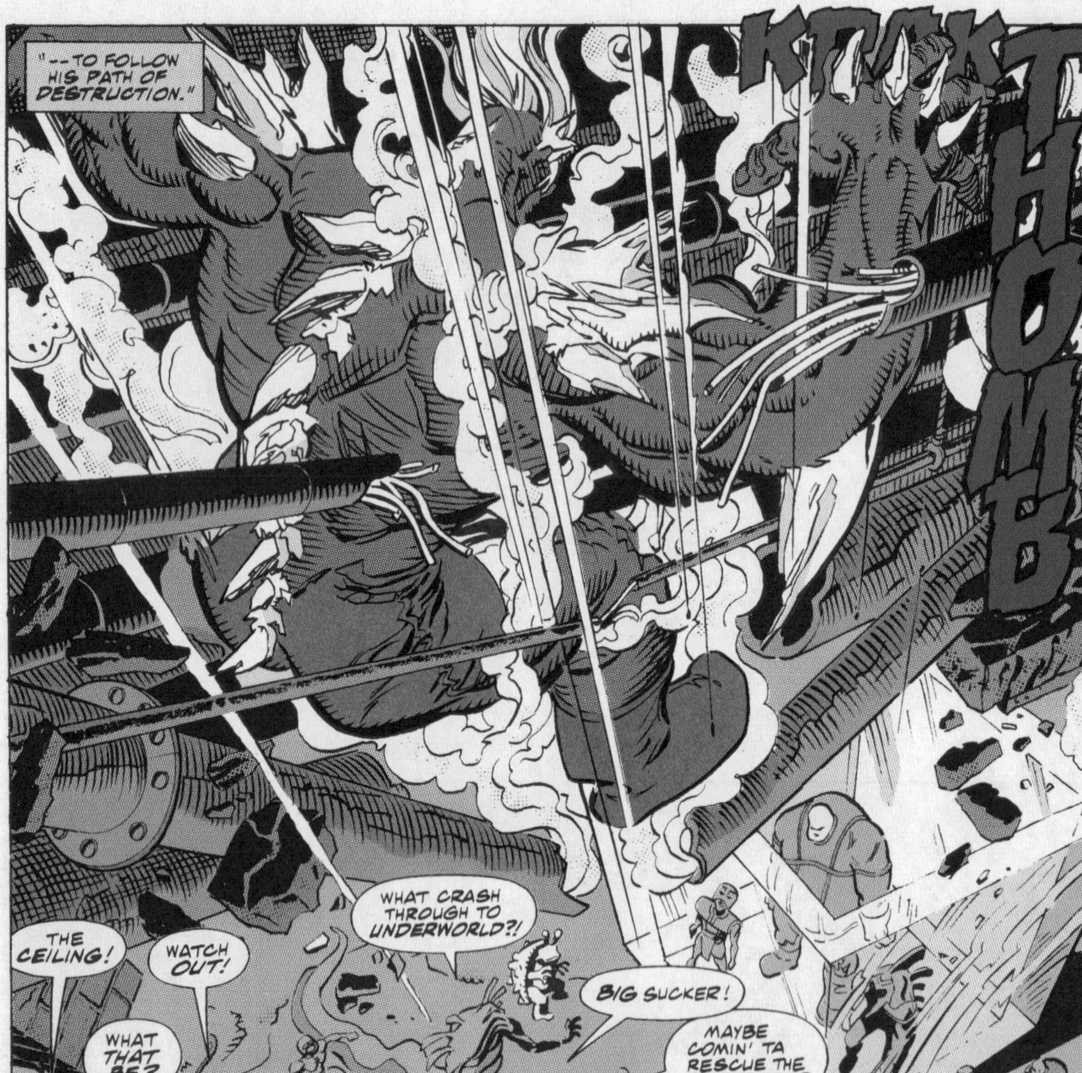
"--TO FOLLOW HIS PATH OF DESTRUCTION."
KRAKT
THOMB
THE CEILING!
WATCH OUT!
WHAT THAT BE?
WHAT CRASH THROUGH TO UNDERWORLD?!
BIG SUCKER!
MAYBE COMIN' TA RESCUE THE PRISONERS?
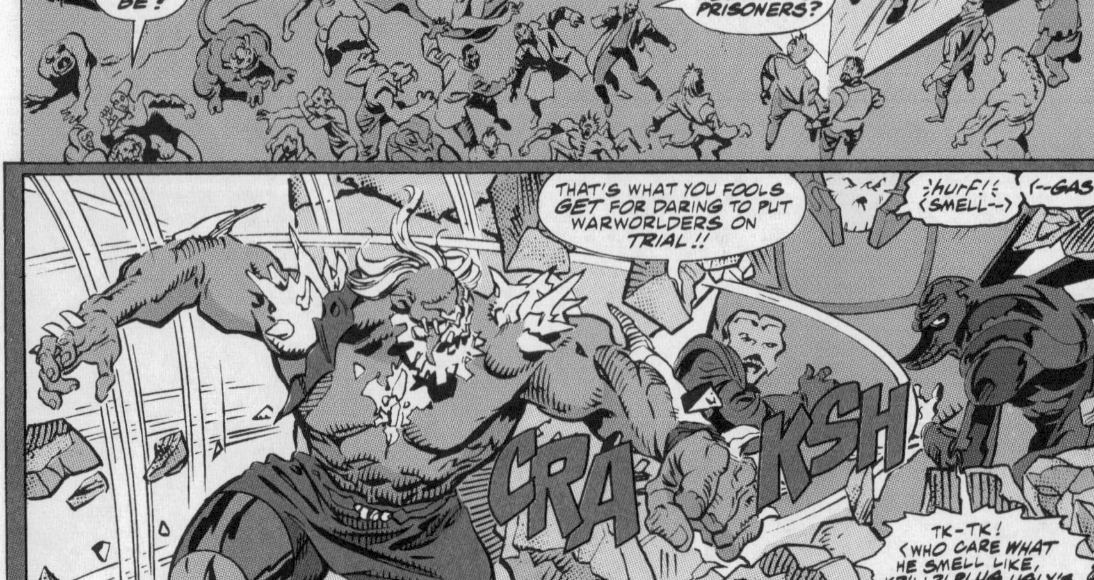
THAT'S WHAT YOU FOOLS GET FOR DARING TO PUT WARWORLDERS ON TRIAL!!
:huff! : (SMELL--)
(--GAS?)
CRA
KSH
TK-TK! (WHO CARE WHAT HE SMELL LIKE, KR'LI?! PLUG UGLY'S OUR TICKET TO FREEDOM!) TK-TK!

126

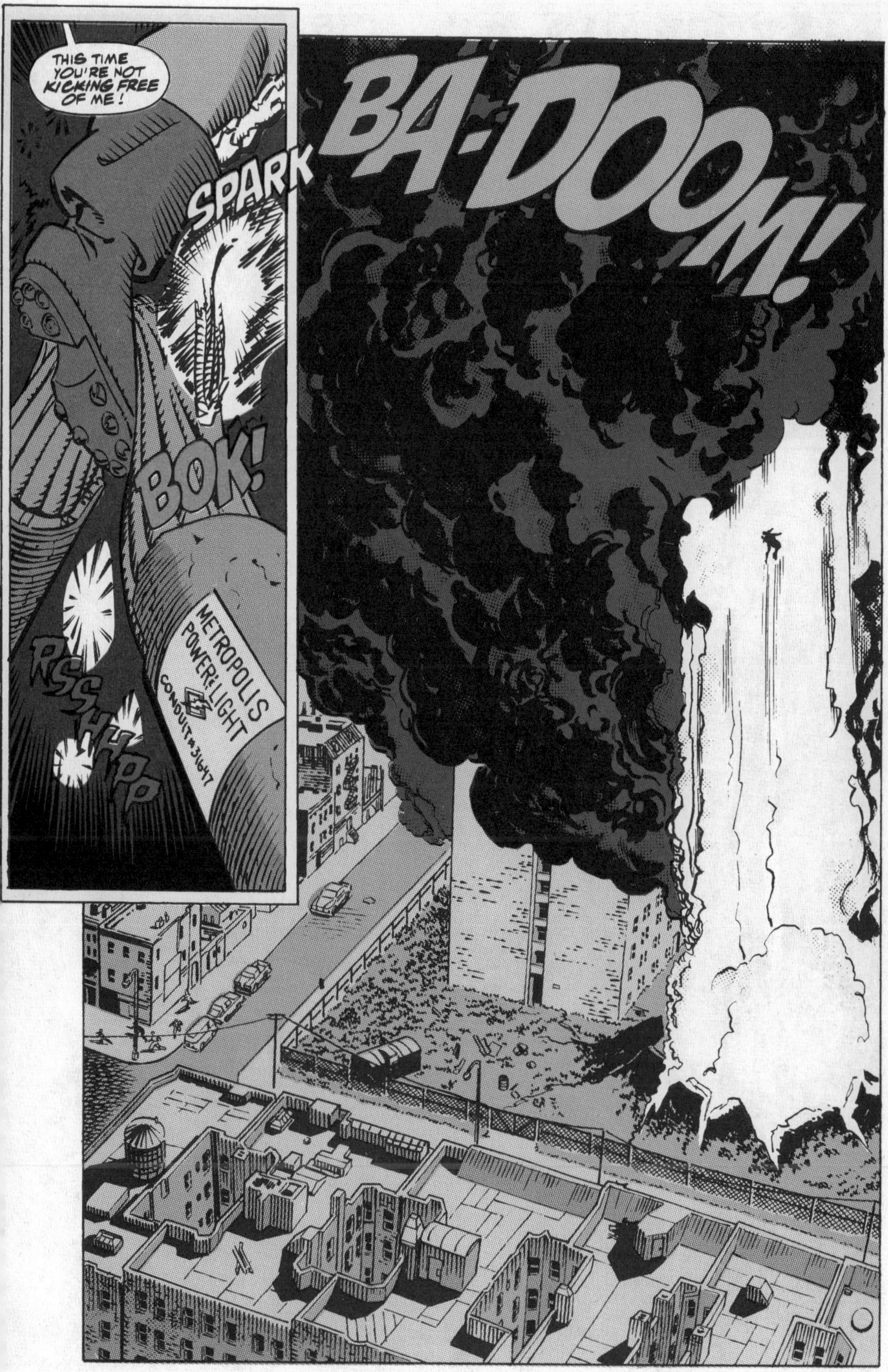
THIS TIME YOU'RE NOT KICKING FREE OF ME!
SPARK
BA-DOOM!
BOK!
RSSHHPP
METROPOLIS POWER & LIGHT
CONDUIT #31647

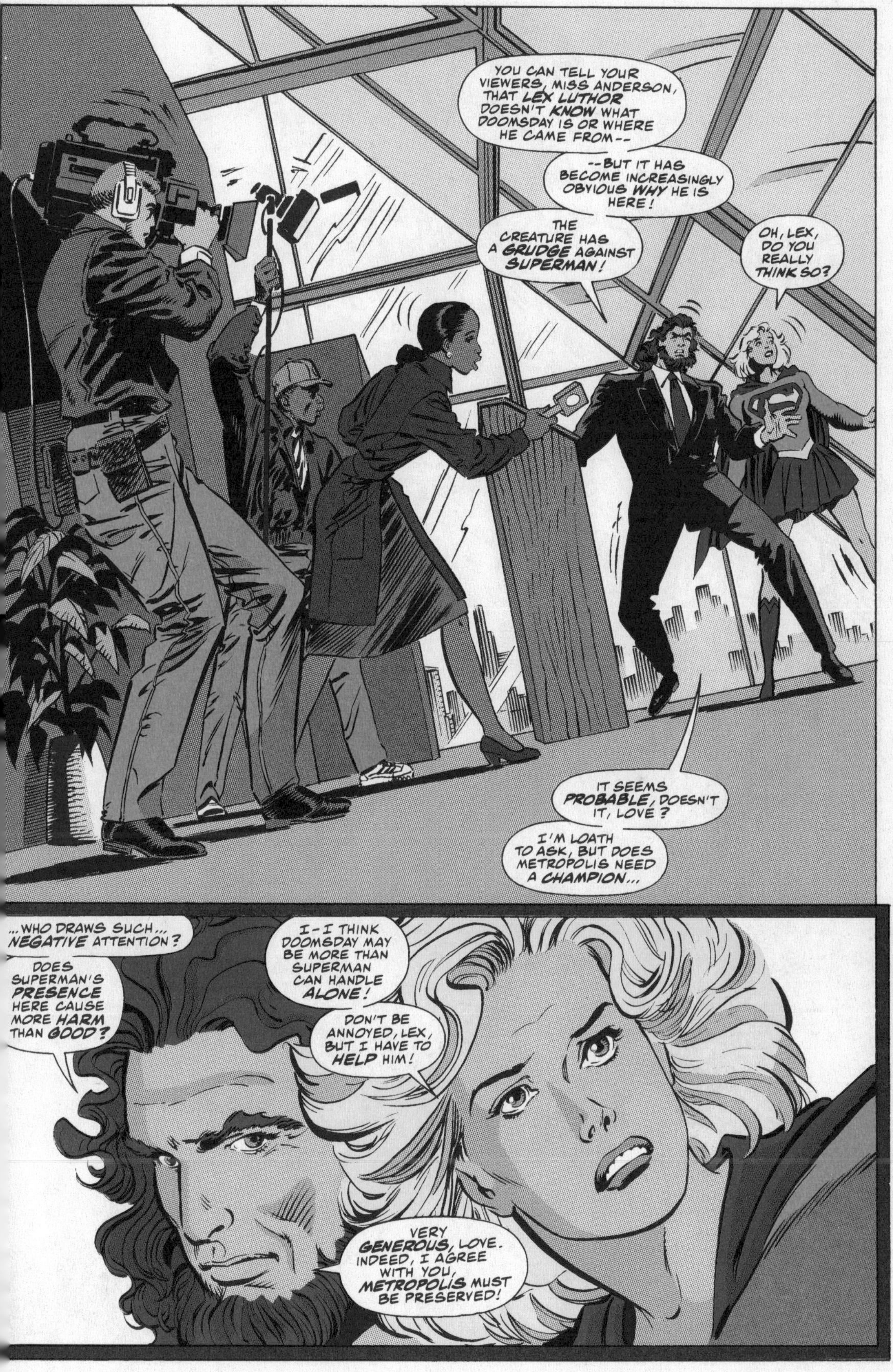
YOU CAN TELL YOUR VIEWERS, MISS ANDERSON, THAT LEX LUTHOR DOESN'T KNOW WHAT DOOMSDAY IS OR WHERE HE CAME FROM--
--BUT IT HAS BECOME INCREASINGLY OBVIOUS WHY HE IS HERE!
THE CREATURE HAS A GRUDGE AGAINST SUPERMAN!
OH, LEX, DO YOU REALLY THINK SO?
IT SEEMS PROBABLE, DOESN'T IT, LOVE?
I'M LOATH TO ASK, BUT DOES METROPOLIS NEED A CHAMPION...
...WHO DRAWS SUCH... NEGATIVE ATTENTION?
DOES SUPERMAN'S PRESENCE HERE CAUSE MORE HARM THAN GOOD?
I-I THINK DOOMSDAY MAY BE MORE THAN SUPERMAN CAN HANDLE ALONE!
DON'T BE ANNOYED, LEX, BUT I HAVE TO HELP HIM!
VERY GENEROUS, LOVE. INDEED, I AGREE WITH YOU, METROPOLIS MUST BE PRESERVED!

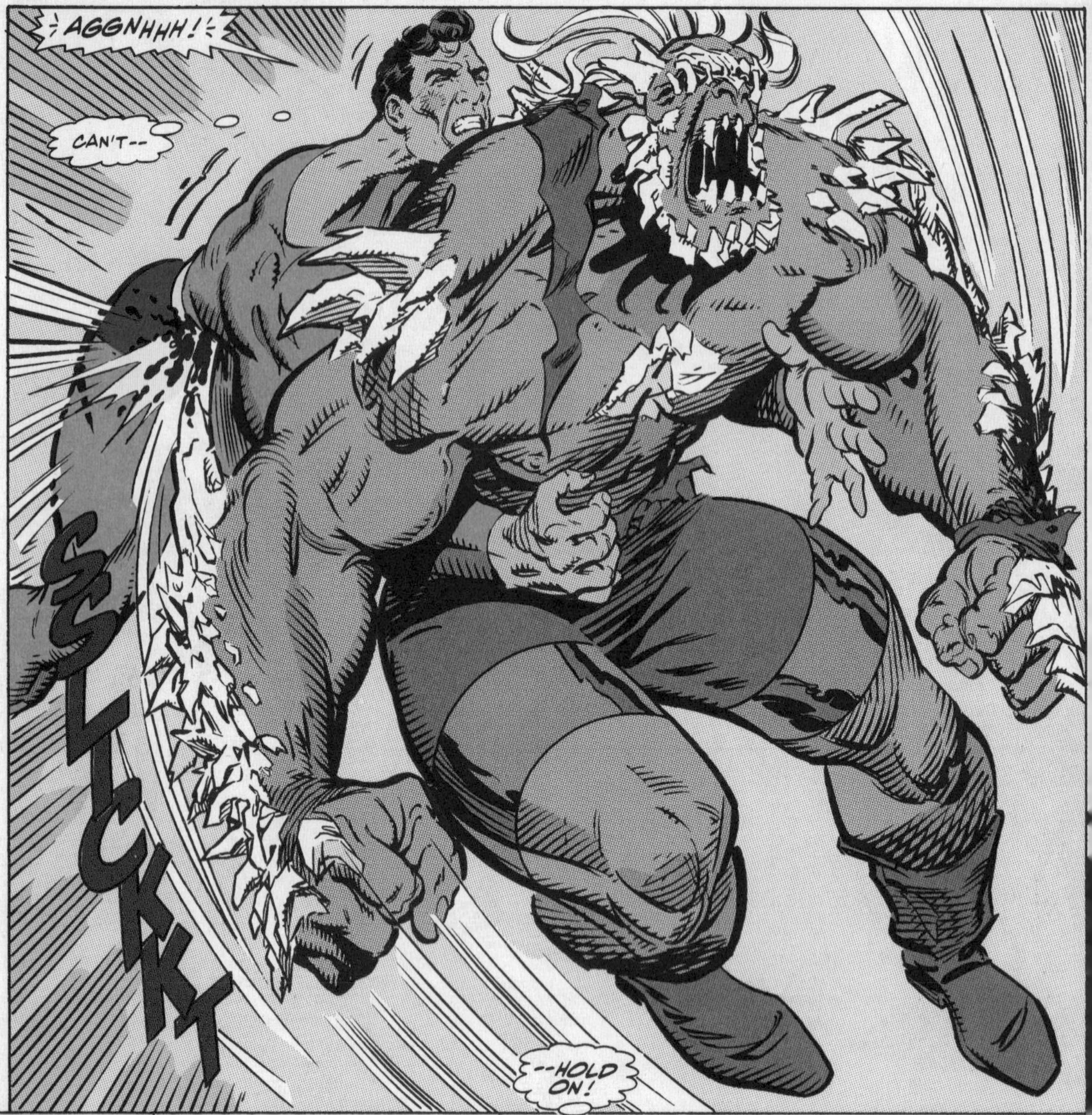
AGGNHHH!
CAN'T--
SSLICKKT
--HOLD ON!

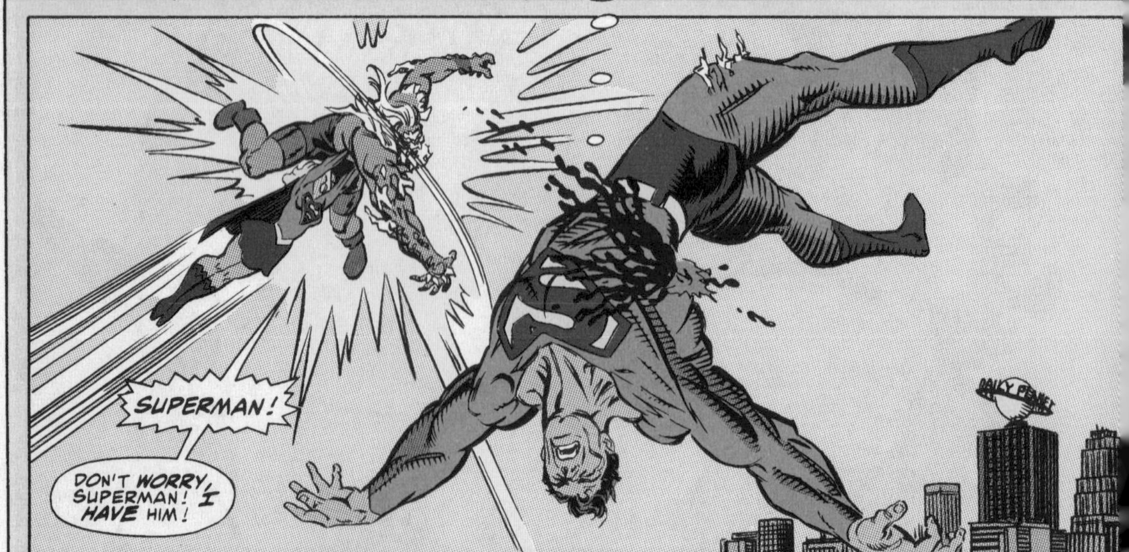
SUPERMAN!
DON'T WORRY, SUPERMAN! I HAVE HIM!

MY LORD IN HEAVEN! HE'S THROWN OFF *SUPERMAN!*

WHAT-- WHAT *IS* THAT CREATURE?

I SUS- PECT IT'S A *DOOMSDAY WEAPON,* MILDRED...

...LEFT BEHIND BY WARWORLD TO *DECI- MATE* THE EARTH IN CASE THEIR SWARM *FAILED!*

WE FINALLY GOT DIS *LASER CANNON* SHOVED UP ON DA ROOF O' YOUR LAB, PER- FESSER HAM...

...SO LET'S *USE* IT!!

AS SOON AS *SUPERGIRL* GETS OUT OF THE WAY, BIBBO!

YOU AND MILDRED KEEP YOUR *FORCE BELTS* BUCKLED TIGHT!

WHEN THE CREATURE FEELS THE *BLAST,* HE'S GOING TO BE *ANGRY!*

NEVER SEEN A CREATURE THIS *POWERFUL.* MUST BE SOME--

BLASH

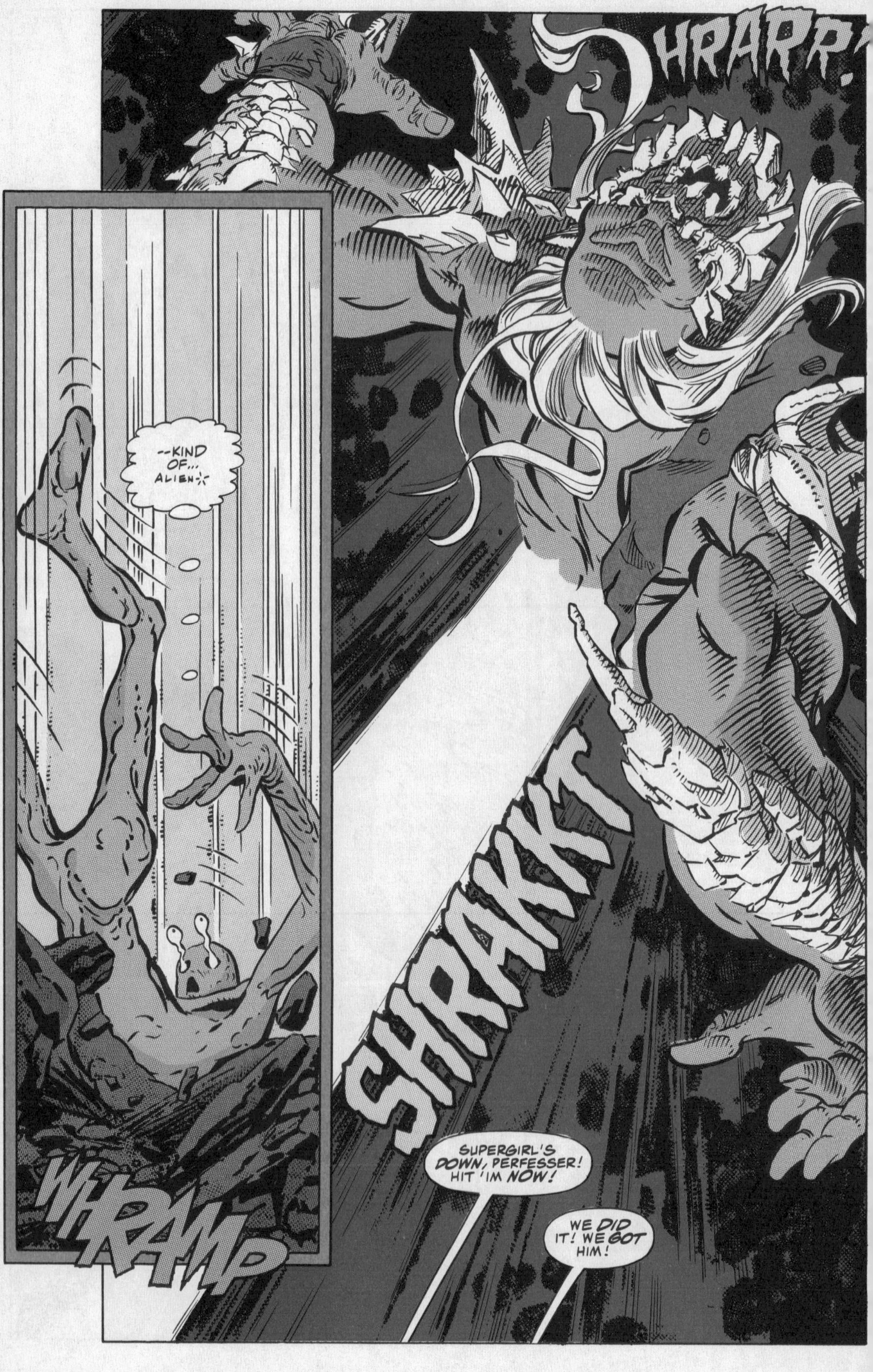
HRARR!
--KIND OF... ALIEN--
WHRAM
SHRAKKT
SUPERGIRL'S DOWN, PERFESSER! HIT 'IM NOW!
WE DID IT! WE GOT HIM!

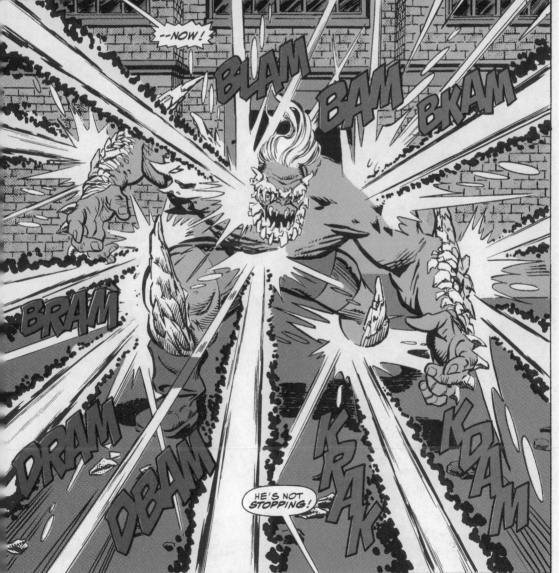

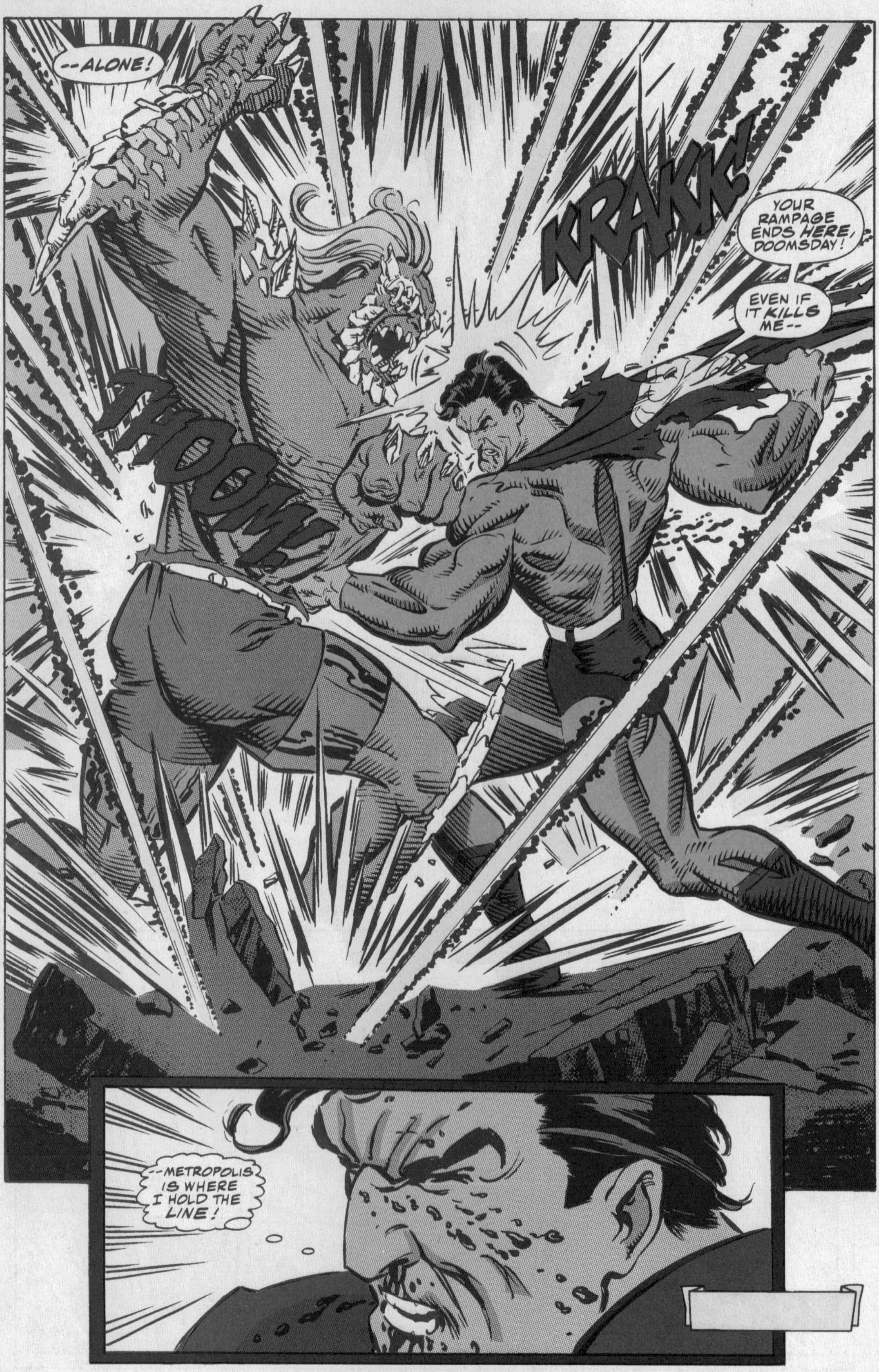
--ALONE!
KRAKK!
YOUR RAMPAGE ENDS HERE, DOOMSDAY!
EVEN IF IT KILLS ME--
THOOM!
--METROPOLIS IS WHERE I HOLD THE LINE!

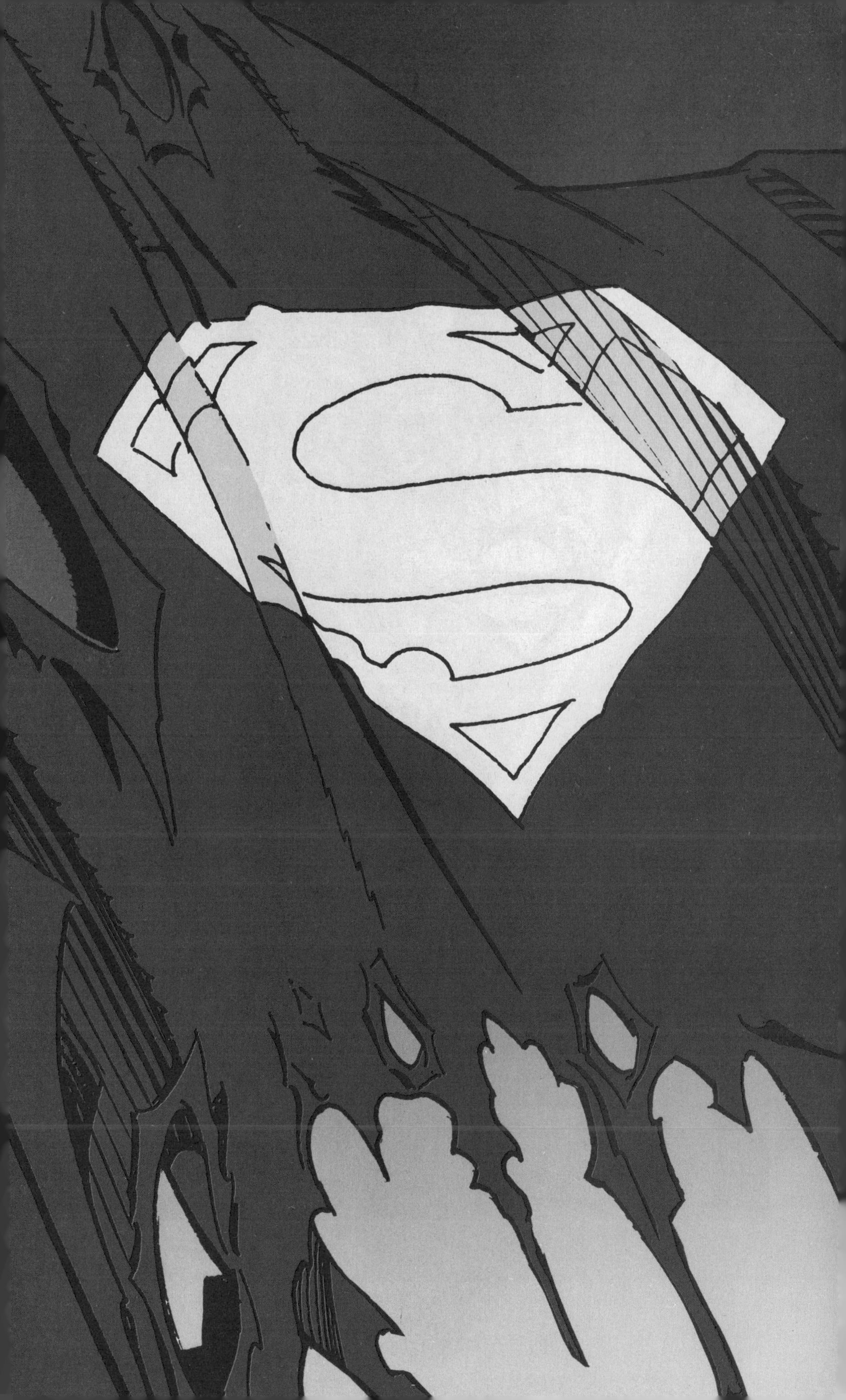

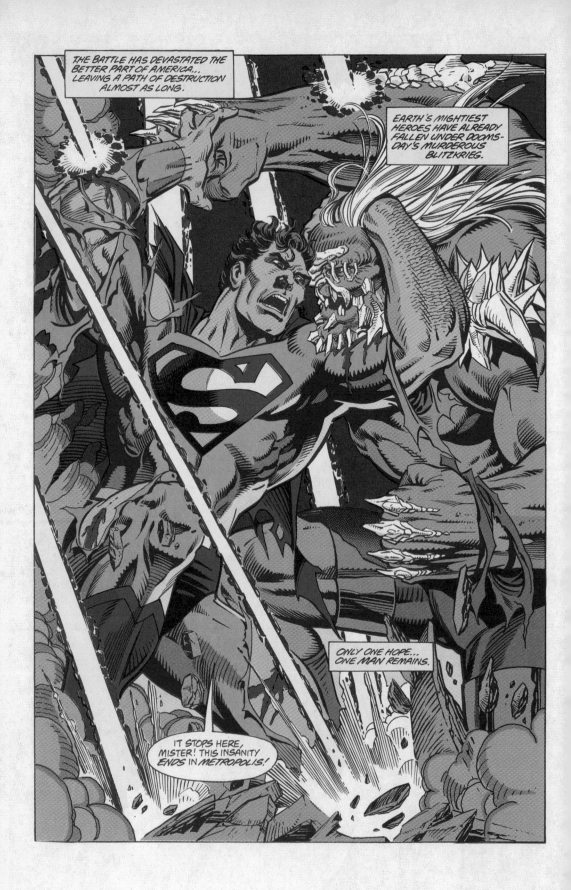

141

DOOMSDAY!

DAN JURGENS / BRETT BREEDING
Words & Pictures / Finished Art

JOHN COSTANZA / GLENN WHITMORE
Letters / Colors

JENNIFER FRANK / MIKE CARLIN
Assistant / Editor

SUPERMAN created by
JERRY SIEGEL & JOE SHUSTER

HAVE TO MOVE FASTER-- MATCH DOOMSDAY'S SPEED... OR I'M *DONE!*

HAH!

143

144

145

149

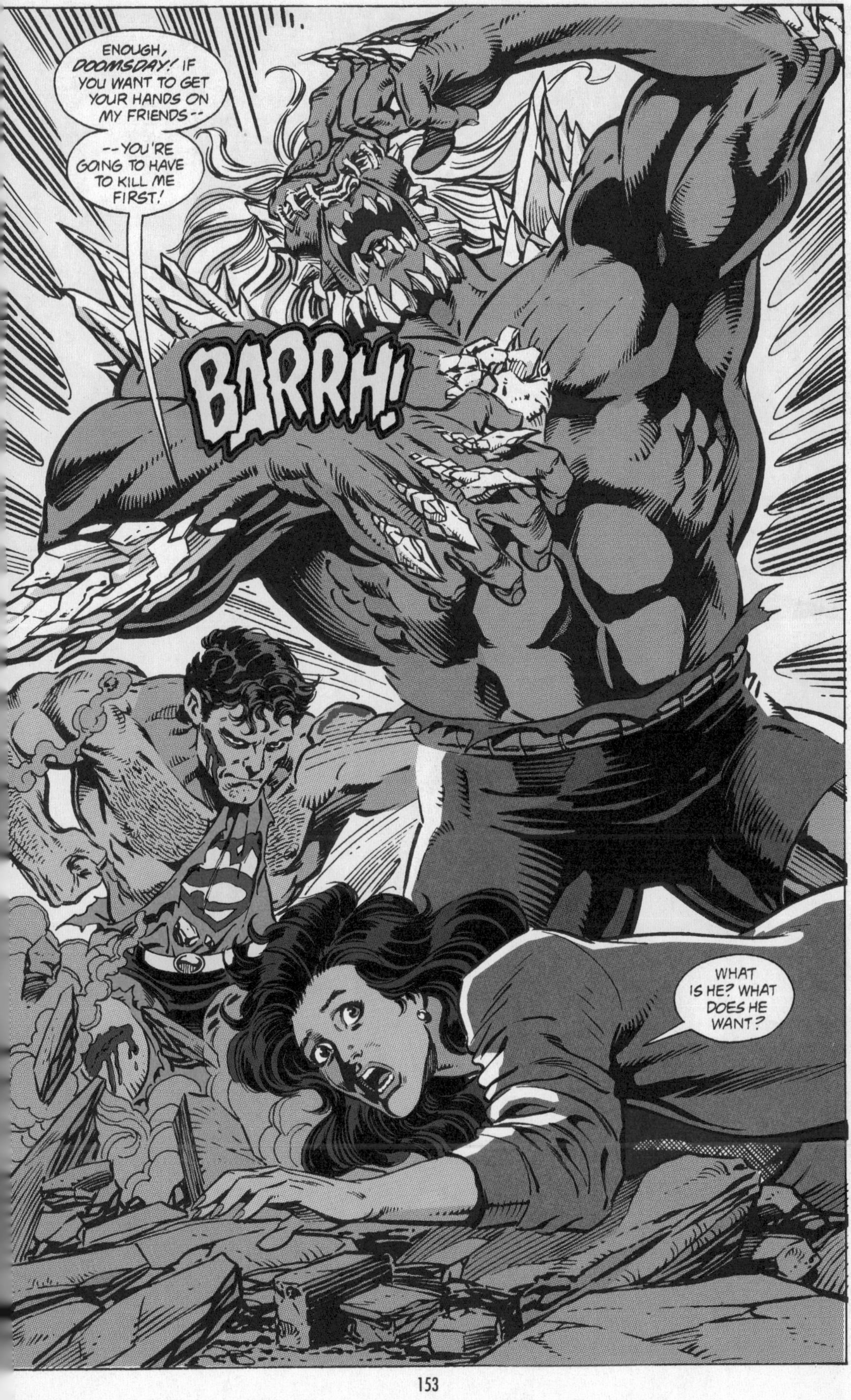

ENOUGH, DOOMSDAY!! IF YOU WANT TO GET YOUR HANDS ON MY FRIENDS--
--YOU'RE GOING TO HAVE TO KILL ME FIRST!
BARRH!
WHAT IS HE? WHAT DOES HE WANT?

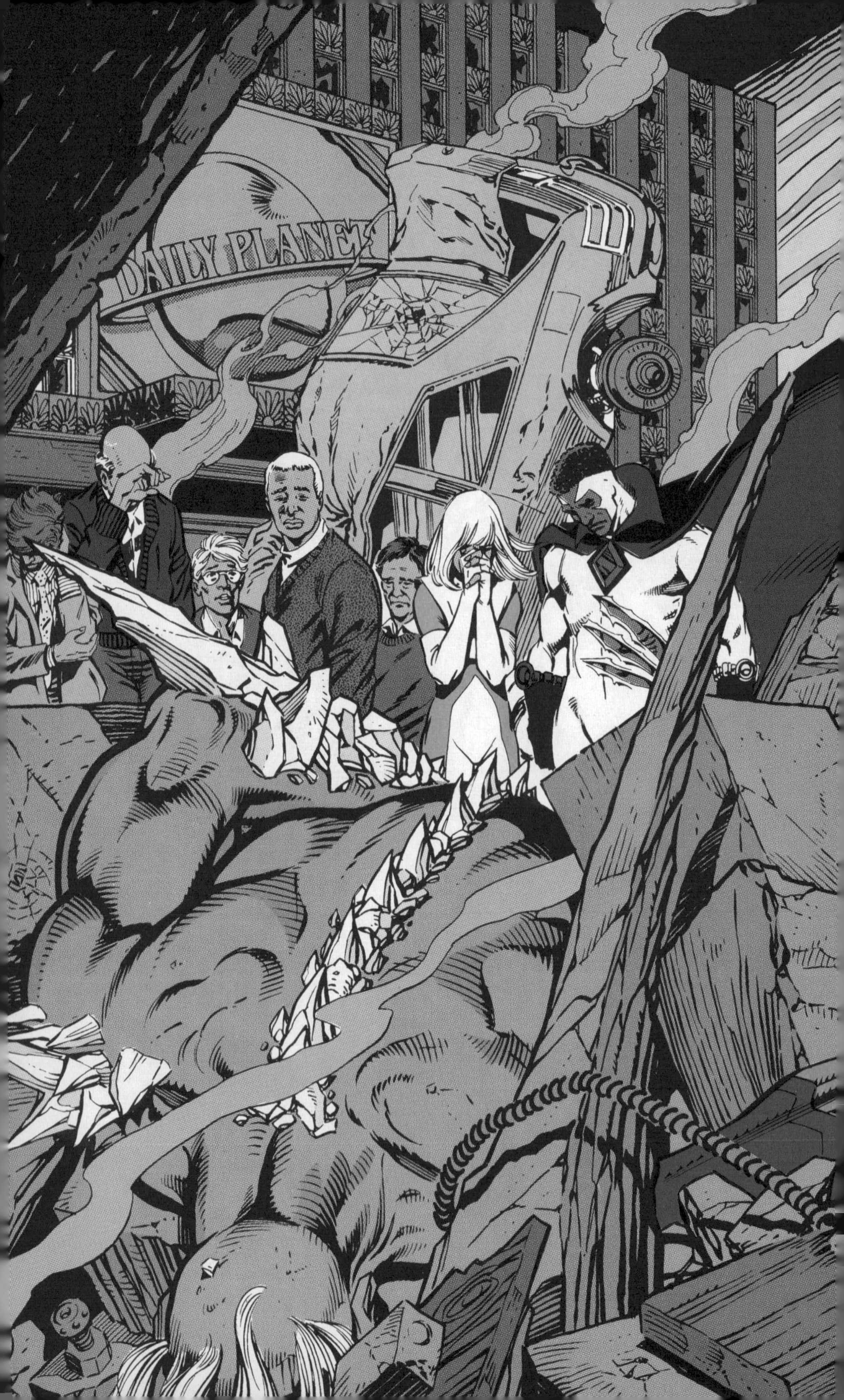
DAILY PLANET

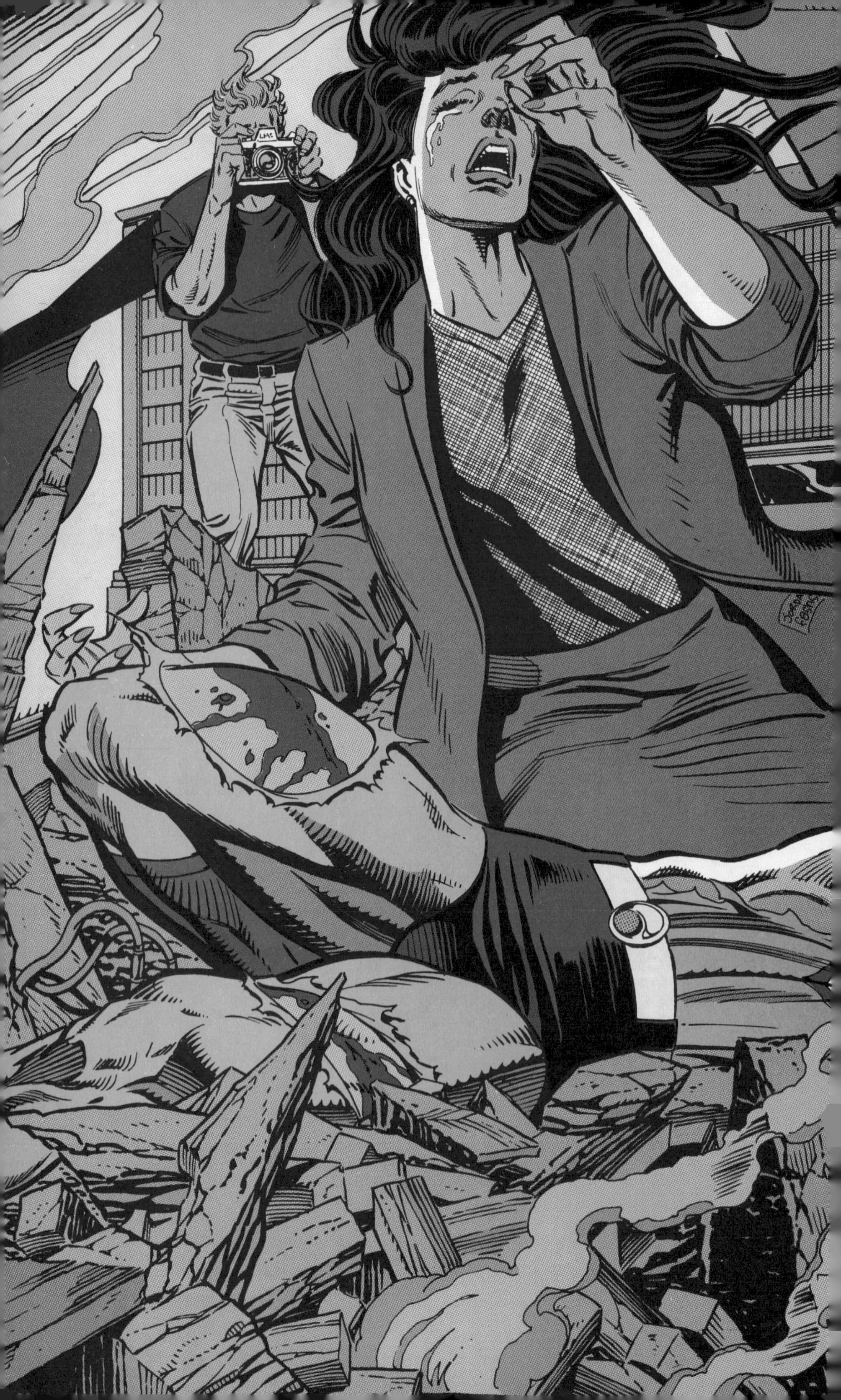

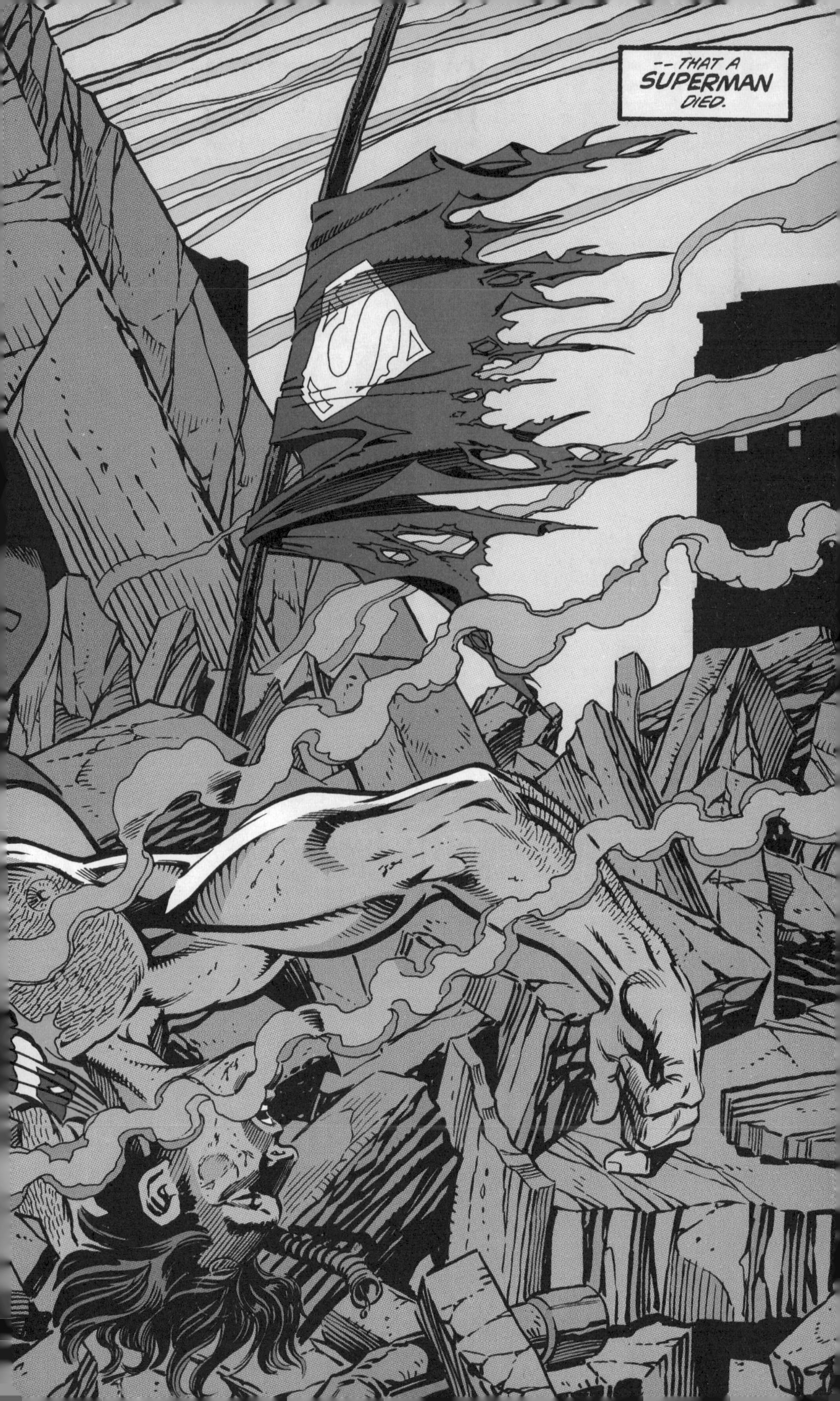
-- THAT A SUPERMAN DIED.

SUPERMAN

[redacted]

READ MORE OF THE MAN OF STEEL'S ADVENTURES IN THESE COLLECTIONS FROM DC COMICS:

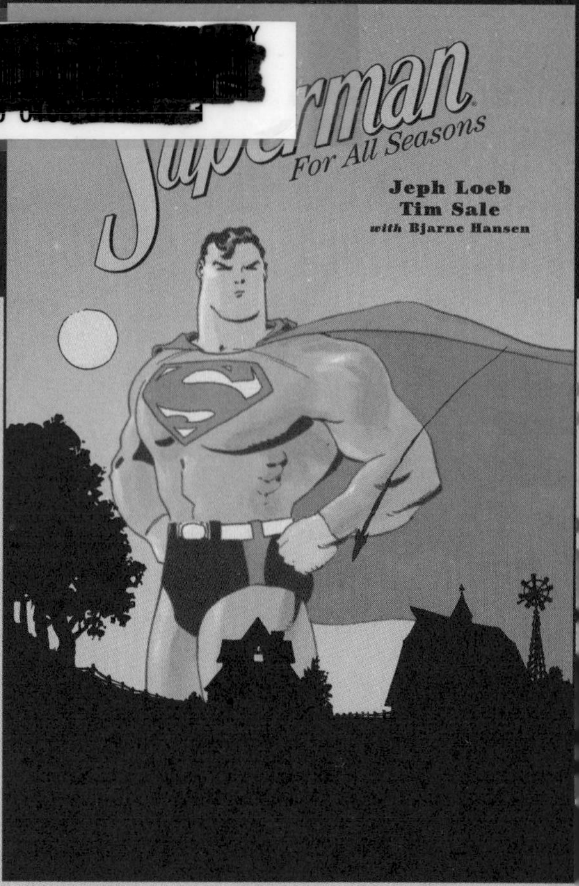

Superman
For All Seasons
Jeph Loeb
Tim Sale
with Bjarne Hansen

SUPERMAN FOR ALL SEASONS

A tale of Superman's earliest adventures told on a mythic scale by the award-winning creative team of **Jeph Loeb** and **Tim Sale**, with spectacular colors by **Bjarne Hansen**.

SUPERMAN: SECRET IDENTITY

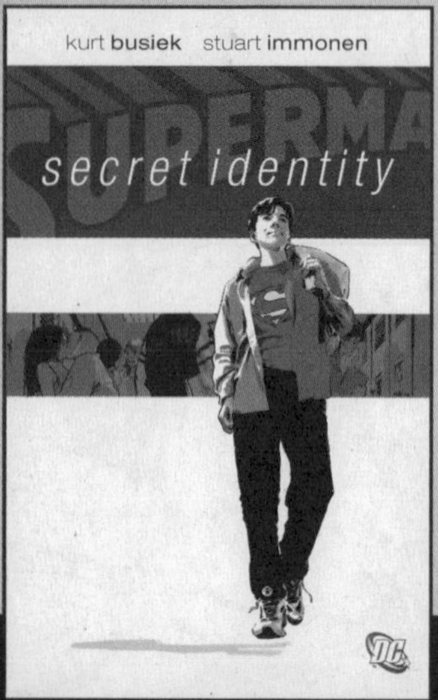

kurt busiek stuart immonen
Superman
secret identity

KURT BUSIEK
STUART IMMONEN

SUPERMAN: THE MAN OF STEEL

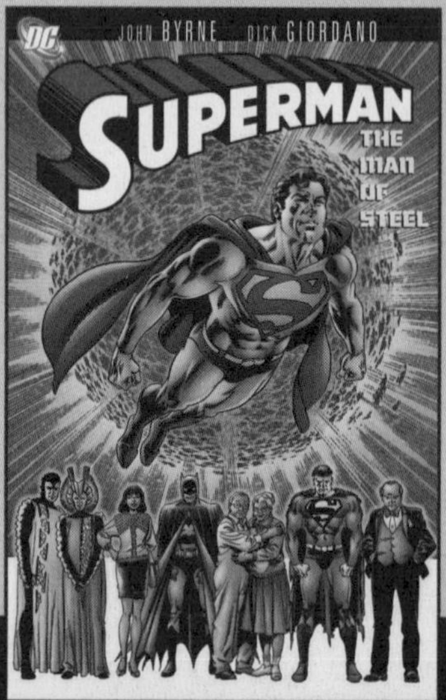

JOHN BYRNE DICK GIORDANO
SUPERMAN
THE MAN OF STEEL

JOHN BYRNE
DICK GIORDANO

SUPERMAN: UNCONVENTIONAL WARFARE

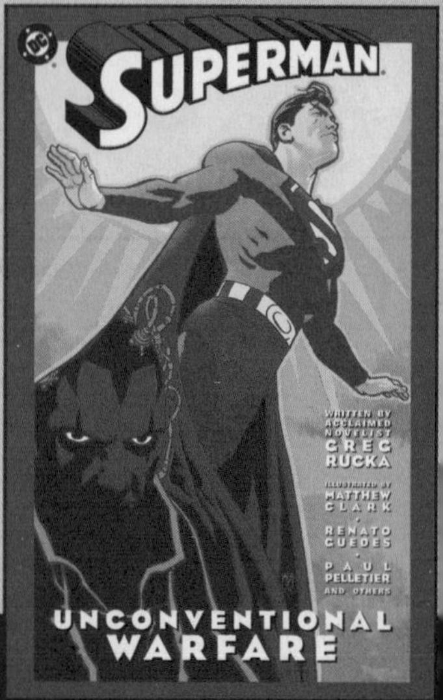

SUPERMAN
WRITTEN BY ACCLAIMED NOVELIST GREG RUCKA
ILLUSTRATED BY MATTHEW CLARK
RENATO GUEDES
PAUL PELLETIER AND OTHERS
UNCONVENTIONAL WARFARE

GREG RUCKA
MATTHEW CLARK
VARIOUS

SEARCH THE GRAPHIC NOVELS SECTION OF

www.DCCOMICS.com

FOR ART AND INFORMATION ON ALL OF OUR BOOKS!